D1498182

Saul Bellow

Garland Reference Library of the Humanities (Vol. 59)

Photograph © 1976 Jill Krementz

Saul Bellow
His Works and His Critics
An Annotated International Bibliography

Marianne Nault

Garland Publishing, Inc., New York & London

1977

19761

Library of Congress Cataloging in Publication Data

Nault, Marianne.
   Saul Bellow.

   (Garland reference library of the humanities ; v. 59)
   Includes index.
   1. Bellow, Saul--Bibliography.
Z8087.8.N33 [PS3503.E4488]   016.813'5'2   76-24738
ISBN 0-8240-9939-7

Printed in the United States of America

To Bill and Sandra

Contents

Frontispiece (Photograph supplied by the Alison Press, Secker and Warburg, Ltd., courtesy of Ms. Barley Alison)

vii

Acknowledgments

It is not possible to compile a bibliography such as this without the assistance of a number of people and institutions. First of all, I am most indebted to the unlimited kindness and generosity of my mother, who has provided both moral and financial support throughout the past four years of study in Europe. I am also grateful for the encouragement of two benevolent uncles who came to my assistance in several hours of need.

It is a pleasure to thank Mr. Saul Bellow, who extended an invitation to visit with him in the spring of 1975. Not only did he graciously give of his time to discuss his work and my research on a number of occasions, but he also granted me permission to examine the extensive collection of manuscripts housed in the Regenstein Library at the University of Chicago. I should also like to take this opportunity to thank his secretary, Mrs. Esther Corbin, who accorded both a great deal of warmth and hospitality to me personally, and also paved the way for additional meetings with her elusive boss.

During my research visit to the University of Chicago, the staff of the Special Collections Department in the Regenstein Library offered daily assistance, notably in their efficiency and friendliness. I should like to thank the entire staff, particularly Alice Eysenbach, who has continued to help me in my research on this side of the Atlantic, as well as the curator, Mr. Robert Rosenthal, who has allowed me to include a copy of a holograph draft of *The Adventures of Augie March* as an introduction to the manuscript section.

I should like to acknowledge and thank a number of friends in foreign lands who have provided extensive lists of references, and, in many cases, copies of the Bellow criticism as well. Special thanks go to Mme. Christine de Montauzon at the University of Geneva, Switzerland, for the French entries; Ulrich Immig in Mainz, Germany; Sheela Thakar-Bhide in India; Professor Akihiro Yamada for assistance with the Japanese items; and particularly Djordjina Radivojević in Belgrade for a number of

ACKNOWLEDGMENTS

interesting articles, including an unusual Bellow interview with Yugoslavian journalists.

I also wish to thank those closer to home who assisted in this project. Professor Howell Daniels of the Institute of United States Studies in London has been most helpful, as were Joan Otto at the University of London and Judie Newman at Clare College, Cambridge. Current American critical works were provided by Joan Damm at Stanford University, Susan Washburn at the University of Oregon, and Wendy Ripp at the University of Chicago, all of whom have my undying gratitude and friendship.

Several members of the English Department at the University of Birmingham have given invaluable assistance in a number of ways. Dr. Brian Harding, my thesis supervisor, has offered both encouragement and advice throughout the past three years, as did Dr. Park Honan and Professor David Lodge. Mr. T. R. Davis, our resident bibliographer, provided crucial information and suggestions at the very outset of the project. I also owe a great deal to Dr. Goronwy Tudor-Jones, an interdisciplinary physicist-cum-poet, who helped compile the initial bibliography and unselfishly contributed in various ways too numerous to mention. I should also like to express my gratitude to Professor T. J. B. Spencer for his interest in my work, as well as for providing a room at the top of the beautiful Shakespeare Institute in which to work, despite the non-Shakespearean nature of my research.

I should also like to acknowledge the assistance of a number of people in the publishing world. First of all, I am indebted to Ms. Carol Irelan of Garland Publishing, Inc., for her interest, which in turn made this book possible. Mr. Bellow's English and American publishers were most co-operative in providing current bio-graphical information about the writer, who is continually con-tributing to his impressive body of work. I would like to extend special thanks to Mrs. Elizabeth Sifton of Viking Press in New York, Harriet Wasserman of Russel and Volkening in New York, and Barley Alison of the Alison Press, Secker and Warburg, in London.

I was particularly pleased with the favorable response to my requests for information from Bellow scholars in the States. Professor Sanford Pinsker promptly provided me with a current listing of his works, as well as a copy of the unpublished typescript of a relatively unknown Bellow lecture (see entry 98). Current

ACKNOWLEDGMENTS

copies of criticism on Bellow were supplied by Professor Eusebio Rodrigues of Georgetown University, for which I am most grateful. Former professors of mine have also extended encouragement and enthusiasm in my recent undertaking, as well as in my postgraduate work over the years. I should therefore like to thank Professor John Blair and Professor Gregory Polletta of the University of Geneva, Switzerland, and Professor John Vickery of the University of California.

Additional assistance was voluntarily offered by Professor A. P. D. Thompson, Executive Dean of the University of Birmingham. Professor Thompson was sufficiently impressed with the scope of my research when I applied for a travel grant that he personally located monies which enabled me to travel to the States for research purposes. To Professor Thompson and the executors of the Kathleen Elliott Scholarship Fund, I am most appreciative.

The efficiency and diligence of my typists should not go unrecognized. I should therefore like to mention Mrs. Woolridge, Melanie Bradnack, and particularly Mandy Stephens for their services.

I am most deeply indebted to my research assistant and dearest friend, Pedja Jovanović, who has helped to make the entire project a publishable reality. Not only has he done a great deal of the collating of foreign articles, corrected spellings and notations in the foreign entries, and proofread the final draft, but he has also supplied an unlimited amount of encouragement and whole-hearted support.

Preface

It is remarkable that no extensive bibliography on Saul Bellow has yet appeared, especially since he has long been associated with key movements in modern American literature. During the years of research in Bellow's work, I have been aware of the need for a detailed and accurate listing of his writings and the plethora of critical commentary that surrounds them. This need has also been echoed by other scholars and students, both in their published utterances and in their private expressions of encouragement to persevere in the task at hand.

Saul Bellow is now receiving the kind of world-wide recognition given only to great writers. He has attained a prominent place in the American literary tradition with the publication of his latest novel, *Humboldt's Gift,* for which he was awarded the Pulitzer Prize; most recently his total literary achievements have merited the much-coveted Nobel Prize for Literature. This bibliography reflects the international response to Bellow throughout the years and, it is hoped, will enhance it by the presentation of a complete listing of his ever-extending *oeuvre* and criticism. Arduous as the undertaking has sometimes been, I am certain that others, students and critics alike, will welcome this research tool when they witness the sheer bulk of data already available and increasing each month. The imposition of order on the chaotic proliferation of primary and secondary sources is needed, and this I have attempted to do.

Turning to the individual sections of the bibliography, I feel the necessity to make certain observations to assist the reader. The first portion includes a comprehensive listing of Bellow's published works, up to the point at which this typescript was completed. As this book goes to press, Saul Bellow is at the height of his powers, producing works which will render a book of this nature obsolete at the date of publication. Given such limitations, however, I have made every effort to compile as complete a collection of his writings as possible.

The second section provides a descriptive catalogue of Bellow

PREFACE

material, accessible to the scholar with the author's permission. As a result of a research trip to the States, I was able to examine an extensive collection of Bellow's published and unpublished writings, a complete set of working materials and holographs for several major novels, plays, short stories, and critical essays. My main purpose for including the lengthy portion on the manuscripts is to alert the Bellow scholar to the existence of the wealth of material housed at the University of Chicago's Regenstein Library and at the Humanities Research Center at the University of Texas, Austin. The numerous drafts, corrected galley proofs, and fragments of familiar and unknown fiction by Bellow should afford insights into the techniques and concerns of this most conscientious and deliberate writer.

In addition to the foreign editions of Bellow's works collected in the Regenstein Library and noted in the second portion of the bibliography, a more extensive list of translations is presented in the third section. I have received details of various works from friends and contacts in a number of countries, along with a wide range of foreign critical commentary. Representative items written in a variety of languages have been included in the seventh part of the book, but no systematic attempt has been made to locate them all.

A sampling of American and British reviews of Bellow's fiction has been provided in the fourth section; capsule summaries of those that were particularly notable have been included in the critical annotations.

Exhaustiveness has been the ideal in the compilation of the secondary criticism for this bibliography. A concerted effort has been made to locate all of the articles and books written in English on Bellow's works during the last three decades. Some of the items in the sixth section are admittedly minor efforts, but others represent major contributions to our understanding not only of Bellow but of contemporary American literature as well. Although my critical biases and preferences may be revealed at times, the annotations of the criticism are not designed to be evaluative. I have restricted my comments to American and British writings since the foreign material ranges beyond my linguistic capabilities.

I have deliberately omitted the use of abbreviations for journals and newspapers throughout the text because the inclusion of

PREFACE

foreign criticism would have involved an unduly long and impractical key of abbreviations. Whenever necessary, a parenthetical reference to the country in which the journal was published has been inserted.

A complete checklist of American and British doctoral dissertations on Bellow, along with related writers and topics, has been provided in the eighth section. The reader, however, is encouraged to consult the *Dissertation Abstracts International* for the most recent American entries, as well as for any inadvertent omissions.

Finally, I should be grateful for any comments, additions, or suggestions from Bellow scholars with regard to this bibliography and to a possible revised edition.

M.N.
Shakespeare Institute
University of Birmingham
Great Britain

Chronology

1915   Born on June 10 in Lachine, a suburb of Montreal in the province of Quebec, Canada, to parents Abraham and Liza Bellows, who had emigrated from St. Petersburg, Russia, in 1913. Saul is the youngest of four children.

1924   Bellow family moves to Chicago, Illinois.

1933   Graduates from Tuley High School (on the northwest side of Chicago).

1935   Transfers to Northwestern University, Chicago.

1937   Graduates from Northwestern with honors in anthropology and sociology.
Marries Anita Goshkin; son Gregory is born of this marriage.

1938   Awarded Scholarship at University of Wisconsin; begins postgraduate research for Master's thesis in anthropology, but abandons research in favor of writing.

1938-42   Teaches at the Pestalozzi—Froebal Teacher's College. Writes biographical studies on writers for WPA Writers Project.

1941   Publishes first short story, "Two Morning Monologues," in *Partisan Review*.

1943-46   On the editorial board of the Encyclopaedia Britannica; works on the Index (Synopticon) of the Great Books Series.
A brief service in the Merchant Marines.

1944   Publishes first novel, *Dangling Man*, with Vanguard Press.

CHRONOLOGY

1946-48   Teaches at the University of Minnesota in Minne-apolis.

1947   Publishes *The Victim.*

1948-49   Awarded Guggenheim Fellowship and National Institute of Arts and Letters Award; travels throughout Europe.

1952-53   Creative Writing Fellowship at Princeton University.

1953   Publishes *The Adventures of Augie March.*

1954   Wins the National Book Award for *The Adventures of Augie March.*

1955-56   Awarded second Guggenheim Fellowship.

1956   Marries Alexandra Tschacbasov; second son Adam is born of this marriage. Publishes *Seize the Day.*

1958-60   Receives two-year Ford Foundation grant.

1959   Publishes *Henderson the Rain King.*

1960-62   Edits the literary journal *The Noble Savage*, along with Keith Botsford and Aaron Asher. Five editions published.

1960   The Friends of Literature Award and the Certificate of Distinguished Service to Literature for *Henderson the Rain King.*

1961   Marries Susan Alexandra Glassman; son Daniel is born of this marriage. Teaches at University of Puerto Rico.

1962   Receives Honorary D.Litt. from Northwestern University.

1963   Edits *Great Jewish Short Stories* and writes introduction to the collection. D.Litt. from Bard College.

1964   Publishes *Herzog*, which wins him the National Book Award for second time; also receives the James L. Dow Award.

1965   Publishes *The Last Analysis*; production of play on

and off Broadway for a short run.

1966   Becomes professor at the University of Chicago and fellow of the Committee on Social Thought. Currently acts as Chairman of the Committee.

Three one-act plays collectively entitled *Under the Weather* are produced on Broadway and in London.

1967   Off-Broadway production of *Seize the Day*, a dramatization of the novella of the same name, adapted by Bellow and Mary Otis.

1968   Publishes *Mosby's Memoirs and Other Stories*. Receives the B'nai B'rith Jewish Heritage Award. Awarded the Croix de Chevalier des Arts et Lettres by the French Government.

Becomes war correspondent for *Newsday* during the Six-Day War in Israel; correspondence then published by Bill Moyers. *Herzog* receives the Prix Littéraire International.

1970   Publishes *Mr. Sammler's Planet*. Receives the National Book Award for the third time. Awarded the Formentor Prize in New York. Awarded honorary doctorates by New York University, Harvard University, and Yale University. Becomes a Fellow of the American Academy of Arts and Sciences.

1975   Marries Alexandra Ionescu Tulcea. Publishes *Humboldt's Gift*.

1976   Wins the Pulitzer Prize for Literature for *Humboldt's Gift*.

Travels throughout Europe and Israel on a lecture tour with his wife, a professor of theoretical mathematics at Northwestern University.

Publishes *To Jerusalem and Back: A Personal Account*.

Receives Nobel Prize for Literature.

The Published Works of Saul
Bellow: Major Works; Short
Fiction; Essays, Reviews,
Tributes, and Miscellaneous
Articles

I. Major Works

1. Dangling Man (Vanguard, New York, 1944; John Lehmann, London, 1946).

2. The Victim (Vanguard, New York, 1947; John Lehmann, London, 1948).

3. The Adventures of Augie March (Viking, New York, 1953; Weidenfeld and Nicolson, London, 1954).

4. Seize the Day (Viking, New York, 1956; Weidenfeld and Nicolson, London, 1957).

5. Henderson the Rain King (Viking, New York, 1959; Weidenfeld and Nicolson, London, 1959).

6. Herzog (Viking, New York, 1964; Weidenfeld and Nicolson, London, 1965).

7. The Last Analysis (Viking, New York, 1965; Weidenfeld and Nicolson, London, 1966).

8. Mosby's Memoirs and Other Stories (Viking, New York, 1968; Weidenfeld and Nicolson, London, 1969).

9. Mr. Sammler's Planet (Viking, New York, 1970; Weidenfeld and Nicolson, London, 1970).

10. Humboldt's Gift (Viking, New York, 1975; Secker and Warburg, London, 1975).

11. To Jerusalem and Back; A Personal Account (Viking, New York, 1976; Secker and Warburg, London, 1976).

II. Short Fiction

12. "Address by Gooley MacDowell to the Hasbeens Club of Chicago", Hudson Review, 4 (Summer, 1951), 222-27. Reprinted in Nelson Algren's Book of Lonesome Monsters ed. N. Algren, (New York, 1962), 147-53. Also collected in The Writer's Signature: Idea in Story and Essay, eds. E.G. Hemley and J. Matthews, (Illinios, 1972).

13. "By the Rock Wall", Harper's Bazaar, 85 (April 1951), 135-205, 207-8, 214-16. Similar scenes and details reappear in The Adventures of Augie March.

14. "Coblins, The", Sewanee Review, 59 (Autumn 1951), 653-53. A slightly revised version appears as Chapter 2 of Augie March.

15. "Dora", Harper's Bazaar, 83 (November 1949), 118, 188-90, 198-99. Bellow's first and only attempt at first-person feminine persona.

16. "Eagle, The", Harper's Bazaar, 87 (February 1953), 126-27, 196, 203-06. An early draft of Chapters 15-16 of Augie March.

17. "Einhorns, The", Partisan Review, 18 (November - December 1951), 619-45. Reprinted in Perspectives, U.S.A., 2 (Winter 1953), 101-29. The story appears in Augie March as Chapter 5 with few changes.

18. "Father-to-be, A", New Yorker, 30 (5 February 1955), 26-30. Collected in Seize the Day (New York, 1956). Reprinted in Mosby's Memoirs (New York, 1968; London 1969).

19. "From the Life of Augie March", Partisan Review, 16 (November 1949), 1077-89. A late version of Chapter I of Augie March with minor alterations in the opening paragraphs. Cited as the first chapter of a novel entitled Life Among the Machiavellians.

20. "Gonzago Manuscripts, The", Discovery, 4 ed., V. Bourgaily, (New York, 1956). Reprinted in Seize the Day, (New York 1956). Reprinted in Prize Stories of 1956: The O. Henry Awards, (Garden City, 1956). Reprinted in Mosby's Memoirs (New York 1968: London, 1969).

21. "Henderson the Rain King", Hudson Review, 11 (Spring 1958), 11-28. An early draft of Chapters I-IV of the novel of the same name. Additional portions of the novel appeared under the title of Henderson in Africa" in

Botteghe Oscure, 21, (1958), 187-225, an early version of Chapters X-XIII.

22. "Herzog", Esquire, 56, (July 1961), 116-30. An early draft of the novel of the same name, incorporating several events and characters which were deleted from the finished work. Portions of Chapters 4, 7, 8 and 9 also appeared under the title "Herzog Visits Chicago" in The Saturday Evening Post, 237 (8 August 1964) 44-69. The short story summarizes Herzog's life and includes numerous letters which are condensed drafts of the final versions. A short piece dealing with Herzog's affair with Sono appeared in Location, (Spring 1963).

23. "Humboldt's Gift", Playboy (January 1974), 87-88, 250-60. A section of an early draft of the novel of the same name deals with Citrine's confrontation with the Mafia gangster, Cantabile. An additional portion appeared in Esquire in the December 1974 issue, centering on Citrine's meditations on the past days with the poet Von Humboldt Fleisher. A brief excerpt entitled "On Boredom" appeared in the August 7 issue of The New York Review of Books which was taken directly from the essay Citrine composes while waiting outside the courtroom.

24. "Interval in a Lifeboat", New Yorker, 28 (December 1952), 24-28, 33-39. A relatively early draft of Chapter 25 of Augie March with major differences in the text.

25. "Leaving Yellow House", Esquire, 49 (January 1958; 112-26. Originally entitled "Hattie", see entries 556-57. Reprinted in Mosby's Memoirs, (New York, 1968; London 1969).

26. "Letter to Dr. Edvig", Esquire, 60 (July 1963), 61-62 103-105. An early draft of Chapter 2 of Herzog. For details of similar holograph versions collected in the Bellow Papers, see entries 429-36, 511.

27. "Looking for Mr. Green", Commentary, (March 1951), 251-61 Reprinted in Seize the Day, (New York, 1956). Reprinted in Mosby's Memoirs, (New York, 1968; London, 1969).

28. "Mexican General, The", Partisan Review, 9 (May-June 1942), 178-94. Reprinted in More Stories in the Modern Manner, (New York, 1954). Reprinted in Partisan Reader (New York, 1946), 91-96.

29. "Mintouchian", Hudson Review, 6 (Summer 1953), 239-49 A late draft of Chapter 24 of Augie March with few changes.

30. "Mr. Sammler's Planet", Atlantic Monthly, (November 1969), 95-150; (December 1969) 99-142. A relatively late version of the text, with important alterations in the conclusion of the novel.

31. "Mosby's Memoirs", The New Yorker, (20 July 1968). Reprinted in Mosby's Memoirs and Other Stories (New York, 1968).

32. "Napoleon Street", Commentary, 38 (July 1964), 30-38. A late draft of Chapter 4 of Herzog with minor omissions.

33. "Notes of a Dangling Man", Partisan Review, 10 (September-October 1943), 402-38.

34. "Old System, The", Playboy, (January 1968). Originally entitled "Isaac and Tina". See entry 663.

35. "Scenes from Humanitis - A Farce", Partisan Review, 29 (Summer 1962), 327-49. Portions of an early draft of Last Analysis.

36. "Seize the Day", Partisan Review, 23 (Summer 1956), 295-319, 376-424, 426-28, 431-32. A relatively late draft of the novella of the same name.

37. "Sermon by Dr. Pep, A", Partisan Review, 16 (May-June 1949), 455-62.
    Reprinted in Best American Short Stories, ed. M. Foley, (Boston, 1950).
    Reprinted in The New Partisan Reader: 1945-53, (New York, 1953).
    Reprinted in Fiction of the Fifties, edited by H. Gold, (New York, 1959), 65-74.

38. "Trip to Galena, The", Partisan Review, 17 November-December 1950), 769-94. Cited as a chapter in a novel in progress entitled The Crab and the Butterfly, which was abandoned in favor of Augie March.

39. "Two Morning Monologues", Partisan Review, 8 (May-June 1941), 230-36.
    Reprinted in Partisan Reader (New York, 1946), 91-96.
    Also collected in The American Disinherited: A Profile in Fiction, Ed. Abe C. Ravitz (Encino, California, 1970). Bellow's first published piece of fiction which was to appear in an extensively revised version in 1944 as Dangling Man.

40. <u>Under the Weather</u>: a production of three one-act plays
     which appeared on Broadway and in London in 1966. Two
     of the three plays have been published:
     "Orange Soufflé" appeared in <u>Esquire</u>, 64 (October 1965),
     130-36; also reprinted in <u>Traverse Plays</u>, ed. Jim Haynes
     (London, 1966). Reprinted in <u>Best Short Plays of the
     World Theatre</u> 1968-1973, ed. Stanley Richards,(New York,
     1973).
     "A Wen" was published in <u>Esquire,</u> 53 (January 1965), 72-
     74, 111. Reprinted in <u>Traverse Plays</u>, ed. Jim Haynes
     (London, 1966).
     The third unpublished play "Out from Under" has been
     collected in the <u>Bellow Papers</u> (see entry 658). The three
     plays have appeared in French and Italian translations,
     (see entries 982 and 983), and "Orange Soufflé" has been
     translated into Serbo-Croatian and dramatized on radio in
     Zagreb, Yugoslavia; see entry 1592.

41. "Wrecker, The", <u>New World Writing,</u> 6 (1954), 271-87.
     Reprinted in <u>Seize the Day</u>, (New York, 1956).

42. "Zetland: By a Character Witness" in <u>Modern Occasions</u>,
     ed. Philip Rahv (Port Washington, N.Y., 1974).

III. Essays, Reviews, Tributes and Miscellaneous Articles.

43.   "Arias", Noble Savage, 4, edited by Saul Bellow and Keith
         Botsford, (New York, 1961), 4-5. Although unsigned the
         the short editorial piece includes an anecdote about a
         Russian cousin which reappears in a piece by Bellow
         entitled "Starting Out in Chicago". For details see
         entry 89.

44.   "Beatrice Webb's America", Nation, 197 (7 September 1963),
         116. Review of Beatrice Webb's American Diary, published
         in 1898, ed. David. A. Shannon.

45.   "Broadway and the Book Shop", The National Observer, (5
         October 1964), 103-10.

46.   "Cloister Culture" in Page Two, ed. E.F. Brown (New York,
         1969), 3-8.

47.   "Comment on Form and Despair, A", Location, 1 (Summer
         1964), 10-12. Bellow defends his aesthetic/historic
         stance of an earlier essay on recent American fiction
         (see entry 87) against the challenge of Harold Rosenberg.
         Discusses the tendency of "realism" to denigrate
         conditions of modern life, from Flaubert, Tolstoi, Gide,
         to Camus. Insists that the imagination must be freed
         from the shackles of false pretensions in the name of
         historicity.

48.   "Culture Now: Some Animadversions, Some Laughs",
         Modern Occasions, 1 (Winter 1971), 162-78.
         Bellow decries the recent metamorphosis of literature
         into the profitable business of literary culture,,
         complete with social, political, and psychlogical
         emphases. A review of the wealth of "bad writing" that
         dominates the current literary scene illustrates the far-
         reaching ramifications of the intelligentsia's submission
         to the pressure of today's "amusement society".

49.   "Deep Readers of the World, Beware!", New York Times
         Book Review, (15 February 1959), 1, 34.
         Bellow's caveat against symbol-hunting and political,
         psychological, sociological interpretations of
         literature, all of which is equated with"culture-
         idolatry, sophistication, and snobbery".

50.   "Distractions of a Fiction Writer" in The Living Novel,
         ed. Granville Hicks, (New York, 1957), 1-20.
         Reprinted in New World Writing, (12), (New York 1957),
         299-43. Living in a eschatalogical age, the writer is
         confronted with a proliferation of concerns, demands,

disorder, disharmony which threatens to erode all
sense of order and proportion. All is superfluous,
however, if, as Bellow maintains, "we believe in the
existence of others, then what we write is necessary"
and is effective against distraction.

51. "Dreiser and the Triumph of Art", Commentary, 11 (May
1951), 502-3. A review of F.O. Mathiesson's biography,
Theodore Dreiser. The review is reprinted in The
Stature of Theodore Dreiser: A Critical Survey of the
Man and His Work, eds. Alfred Kazin and Charles Shapiro,
(Bloomington, Indiana, 1955).

52. "Facts that Put Fancy to Flight", New York Times Book
Review, (11 February 1962), 1, 28. Reprinted in
Opinions and Perspectives, ed. Francis Brown, 235-40.
Discusses the American preference for literal facts,
documentation, and accuracy in literature to the
exclusion of imagination and aesthetic truth. The
journalistic novel, the social-historical novel, the
modern novel of sensibility create an art of externals
which Bellow finds reprehensible and uninteresting.

53. "French as Dostoevski Saw Them, The", New Republic,
132 (23 May 1955), 17-30. The essay also appeared as
the foreword to F.M. Dostoevski's Winter Notes on Summer
Impressions, translated by Richard L. Renfield, (New
York, 1957), 9-27. Anecdotes of Bellow's experiences in
Paris during the winter of 1948 expressing his disillusion-
ment with the "City of Man" and the French bourgeois
character in which lies the "betrayal of the greatest
hopes of the modern age".

54. "Gide as a Writer and Autobiographer", New Leader,
(4 June 1951), 24. A review of Andre Gide's The
Counterfeiters.

55. "Hemingway and the Image of Man", Partisan Review,
20 (May-June 1953), 342-45. A review of Philip Young's
Ernest Hemingway.

56. "How I Wrote Augie March's Story", New York Times Book
Review, (31 January 1954), 3, 17. Reminiscenses of the
details surrounding the writing of Bellow's third novel,
emphasizing the tendency to write more incisively about
one's homeland when in a foreign country.

57. "Illinois Journey", Holiday, 22 (September 1959), 62,
102-07. An essay on Bellow's own state, complete with
Faulknerian asides about Southern legends and scandals.
The anecdotal quality of Bellow's description lifts the
article above the travelogue subject matter.

Reprinted in the Times Literary Supplement in a slightly
revised form under the title of "The Sealed Treasure"
(1 July 1960), 414. Also reprinted in The Open Form,
edited by A. Kazin,(New York 1961).

58.   "Interview with Myself, An", New Review, 18 (Volume 2,
        1975), 53-56. Reiterates his views on problems facing
        the modern writer. He bemoans the absence of a literary
        world in which communication among writers is possible.
        Instead the writer is endangered by the academic
        professional device of a plethora of talk or forced
        into isolation.

59.   "Isaac Rosenfeld", Partisan Review, 23 (Fall 1956), 565-
        567. A tribute to a friend and fellow writer. The brief
        piece was revised and extended into a character sketch
        which appeared as the foreward to An Age of Enormity,
        by Isaac Rosenfeld, ed. Theodore Solotaroff, (Cleveland,
        Ohio, 1963), 14-22.

60.   "Israeli Six-Day War, The", Newsday, (12 June 1967, also
        13 June and 16 June 1967). Accounts of the Israeli war
        written in Tel Aviv during his assignment as news corres-
        pondent for Newsday, much of which was fictionalised in
        Mr. Sammler's Planet.. For details of the manuscript
        holdings of the articles, see entries 702-06. Reportage
        from Newsday was also revised and reprinted under the
        title of "Israel Diary" in Jewish Heritage Quarterly,
        10 (Winter 1967-68), 31-43.

61.   "Italian Fiction: Without Hope", New Leader (11 December
        1950), 21-22. A review of The New Italian Writers: An
        Anthology from Botteghe Oscure, ed. Marguerite Caetani.

62.   "Jewish Writer and the English Literary Tradition. The",
        Commentary, 8 (October 1949), 366-67. Part of a
        symposium along with Leslie Fielder and Alfred Kazin which
        was concerned with the topic of the Jew's place in
        English literature.

63.   "John Berryman", a tribute to friend and fellow-writer as
        a foreword to Berryman's novel Recovery, published post-
        humously (London 1973), ix-xiv. Reprinted as "John
        Berryman, Friend" in New York Times Book Review (27 March
        1973).

64.   "Keynote Address before the Inaugueral Session of the
        XXXIV International Congress of Poets, Playwrights,
        Essayists, Editors", (13 June 1966), New York University.
        Published in slightly revised form in The Montreal Star,
        (25 June 1966), 2-3.

65.   "Laughter in the Ghetto", Saturday Review of Literature,
        36 (30 May 1953), 15. A review of Sholom Aleichem's The
        Adventures of Mottel the Cantor's Son which was completed
        in 1916 and now translated by his grandaughter Tamara
        Kohana. The review is also reprinted in Jewish Heritage
        Quarterly, 10 (Winter 1967-68), 20-21.

66.   "Literary Notes on Khruschev", Esquire, (March 1961).
        Reprinted in First Person Singular, ed. Herbert Gold,
        (New York, 1963), 46-54. Reprinted in Esquire
        (October 1973), the fortieth anniversary issue. Also
        appeared in The Plain Style, eds. Robert Hogan and
        Herbert Bogart, (New York, 1967).

67.   "Literature", in The Great Ideas Today, ed. Mortimer
        Adler and Robert M. Hutchins, (Chicago; Encyclopaedia
        Britannica, 1963), 135-79.

68.   "Literature in the Age of Technology", in Technology
        and the Frontiers of Knnowledge, Frank K. Nelson Doubleday
        Lecture Series (New York, 1973), 1-22.
        Originally presented as a lecture to the Smithsonian
        Institute's National Museum of History and Technology
        on 14 November 1972.

69.   "Man Underground", Commentary, (June 1952). A review of
        Ralph Ellison's novel, The Invisible Man. Reprinted in
        Ralph Ellison: A Collection of Critical Essays, ed. John
        Hersey, (New Jersey, 1973).

70.   "Mind Over Chatter", New York Herald Tribune Book Week,
        (4 April 1965), 2-4. A slightly revised version of the
        author's acceptance speech at the National Book Award
        Ceremonies for Herzog. The speech was also reprinted in
        its entirety in the New York Times, 10 March 1965, 42.

71.   "Movies: Adrift on a Sea of Gore", Horizon, 5 (March
        1963), 109-11. A review of "Barabbas".

72.   "Movies: Art of Going it Alone", Horizon, 5 (September,
        1962), 108-16. A review of the films of Morris Engel,
        including "The Little Fugitive", "Lovers and Lollipops",
        and "Weddings and Babies".

73.   "Movies: Bunuel's Unsparing Vision", Horizon, 5(Novem-
        ber 1962), 110-12.

74.   "Movies: The Mass-Produced Insight", Horizon, 5 (January
        1963), 111-13.

75.   "My Man Bummidge", New York Times, 27 September 1964,
        1, 5. The author's own comments upon his play, The Last
        Analysis.

76.   "Next Necessary Thing, The", An unpublished typescript
        cited by Tony Tanner in his _Saul Bellow_ (Edinburgh, 1965),
        116-17. The essay is also collected in the _Bellow papers_;
        for details see entry

77.   "On Jewish Story Telling", _Jewish Heritage Quarterly_,
        7 (Winter 1964-65), 5-9. Reprinted in a condensed
        version in _Jewish Digest_, (April 1966), 63-66.

78.   "Perils of Pleasing the Public, The", _Observer_,
        8 December 1968, 16, 18. Reprinted under the title,
        "The Public and the Writer" in the _Chicago Sun-Times
        Book Week_ (15 September 1968), 1-6.
        Bellow criticizes the modern literary community as a
        university-educated elite without good taste, a public
        which demands that its _literati_ become part of popular
        culture and enter the ring like gladiators. He decries
        the proliferation of current writing which does not
        transmit the inner light of truth and imagination but
        the external neon light borrowed from public events,
        thus contributing to the "culture macadam" and crisis
        chatter which threaten to scald the minds of the contem-
        porary audience.

79.   "Personal Record, A", _New Republic_, (22 February 1954),
        A review of Joyce Cary's _Except the Lord._

80.   "Pleasures and Pains of Playgoing", _Partisan Review_, 21
        (May-June 1954), 312. An informal review of four Broad-
        way plays including T.S. Eliot's _Confidential Clerk_ and
        Jean Paul Sartre's _No Exit._

81.   "Poetry of Yevtushenko, The", _New York Review of Books_,
        (26 September 1963), 1-3. Commentary upon the works
        of the contemporary Russian poet.

82.   "Rabbi's Boy in Edinburgh", _Saturday Review of Literature_
        39 (24 March 1956), 19. A review of David Daiches'
        autobiography _Two Worlds_.

83.   "Riddle of Shakespeare's Sonnets The", _The Griffin_, 11
        (June 1962), 4-8. A review of a book by the same name,
        containing sonnets and essays by R.P. Blackmur, Leslie
        Fiedler, Edward Hubler, Northrop Frye, and Stephen
        Spender.

84.   "Skepticism and the Depth of Life", _The Arts and the
        Public_, edited by J.E. Miller and P.D. Herring (Chicago,
        1967), 13-30. Describes the plight of the writer in
        culture-grasping American society which claims the
        literary artists as its rightful property. Universities
        have joined the profitable cultural business, in an

attempt to bring art-life to the campus and to train
professional writers - but not to think or create. Sees
the atmosphere debilitating to the serious artist and
admits that although it is relatively easy to become a
writer today, perhaps it is harder than ever to be one.

85. "So the World Is Too Much with Us", Critical Inquiry,
Vol 2, No 1, (Autumn 1975).

86. "Solzhenitsyn's Truth", New York Times, 15 January 1974?
36. Comments upon the Russian novelist's craft and
philosophy.

87. "Some Notes on Recent American Fiction", Encounter, 21
(November 1963), 22-29. Reprinted with minor changes
as Recent American Fiction, Washington, The Library of
Congress, 1963; bases on a lecture delivered under the
auspices of the Gertrude Clark Whittal Poetry and
Literary Fund. Reprinted in The American Novel Since
World War II, ed. Marcus Klein (Connecticut 1969).
Bellow scorns his literary contemporaries who have become
part of the embittered, nihilistic age of industralization
and mass culture. It is with an "unearned bitterness" that
the modern writer belittles modern life and thereby
contributes to the "dehumanisation of the arts".

88. "Spanish Letter", Partisan Review, 15 (February 1948),
217-30. Reminiscences of a summer in Madrid.

89. "Starting Out in Chicago", American Scholar, 44 (Winter
1974-75), 71-77. An essay which grew out of an commence-
ment address delivered in the Spring 1974 at Brandeis
University. Includes biographical details of the
author's early days as a writer, along with interesting
anecdotes and familial details not to be found elsewhere.

90. "Swamp of Prosperity, The", Commentary, 28 (July 1959),
77-79. A review Philip Roth's Goodbye, Columbus.

91. "Talk with the Yellow Kid, A", The Reporter, 15 (September,
1956), 41-44. An informal biographical sketch of
Joseph Weil, one of the best known confidence men of his
time, celebrating an era and the city of Chicago.

92. "Thinking Man's Waste Land", Saturday Review of Literature,
48 (3 April 1965) 20. An excerpt from the National
Book Award Acceptance Speech for Herzog; for manuscript
details, see entry 929.

93. Translation of Isaac Bashevis Singer's 'Gimpel the Fool',
Partisan Review, 20. (May-June 1953), 300-13.
Reprinted in Great Jewish Short Stories, (New York, 1963),
along with a critical introduction by Bellow (9-16), who
also edited the collection. The translation is reprinted
in A Treasury of Yiddish Stories, ed. Irving Howe and

11

Eliezer Greenberg (New York, 1954), 401-14. Also in
Isaac Bashevis Singer's Gimpel the Fool and Other Stories
(New York, 1957), 3-21.

94. "Two Faces of a Hostile World", New York Times Book
Review, 61 (26 August 1956), 4-5. A review of "5 a.m."
by Jean Dutourd.

95. "University as Villian, The", The Nation, 185 (16 November 1957), 361-63. Also reprinted in a revised form
under the title, "The Enemy is Academe" in Publishers
Weekly, 190 (18 July 1966), 34. Stresses the autonomy
and inner strength of the writer to discover the
environment which is conducive to his particular
temperament and imagination. Since experience is a
writer's commodity, it is his decision to choose between
heavy security of the ivory tower (which he claims is
not what it used to be) and the anxiety of the gutter.

96. "Uses of Adversity, The", The Reporter, (1 October 1959),
43-45. A review of Oscar Lewis' Five Families, a report
on poverty in Mexico.

97. "Where Do We Go From Here: The Future of Fiction",
Michigan Quarterly Review, 1 (Winter 1962), 27-33.
Reprinted in Saul Bellow and the Critics, ed. I. Malin,
(New York, 1967) Reprinted in To the Young Writer;
Hopwood Lectures, second series, ed. A.L. Bader, (Ann
Arbor, Michigan, 1965). Reprinted The Theory of the
American Novel, ed. G. Perkins (New York, 1970).
Decries the modern novel of ideas, conceived in thought
and a self-indulgent didactic purpose, rather than in the
imagination of the writer. Bellow believes that if
the novel is to recover and flourish, the language,
character, and action of modern fiction which has been
deemed as unfit must be infused with new ideas and beliefs
in humankind, for "there would be no point in continuing"
at all if many writers did not feel and express the existence
of these heretofore unrecognized qualities.

98. "Who's Got the Story: Writing After Joyce". An unpublished
typescript of a lecture delivered at Franklin and
Marshall College, Lancaster, Pennsylvania, on May 1972.
Cited in Sanford Pinster's report, "Saul Bellow in the
Classroom", see entry 1418. (Portions of the lecture
reappear in "Literature in The Age of Technology", see
entry 68.) A survey of the critical diagnoses of the
debilitated modern novel includes a detailed analysis of
Joyce's art of fiction, his conception of the "novel of
process", his unique rendering of modern consciousness
drowned in facts. Bellow sees Joyce as a writer freed from
old assumptions of the novel, but not of romanticism, a
literary problem which remains unsolved for writers before
and after Joyce.

99.   "Word from Writer Directly to Reader, A" in _Fiction of_
       the Fifties, ed. Herbert Gold, (New York, 1959), 20.
       A brief reply to the question concerning the problems
       and demands of writing in the Fifties as opposed to other
       eras. Bellow directs his attention to the assessment of
       human value as a fitting subject for fiction. He
       refects the nihilistic view of mankind, the empty
       ideologies, old historic and aesthetic conceptions of the
       past, and simply asserts, "we are something".

100.   "World-Famous Impossibility", _New York Times_, 6 Decem-
       ber 1970, 1, 12. A straightforward editorial piece
       attacking the "vices" of New York City.

101.   "Writers and the Audience, The', _Perspectives USA_.
       9 (Autumn 1954), 99-102. Introductory portion of a
       symposium on the theme of "The Creative Artist and His
       Audience" with Bellow, Robinson Jeffers, Robert Mother-
       well, and Roger Sessions as participants. Bellow attempts
       to define the multifarious nature of the modern audience
       and the writer's responsibility to himself and his readers.

102.   "Writers as Moralist, The", _Atlantic Monthly_", 211 (March
       1963), 58-62. Defines the current struggle between
       dichotomous nature of American writers as a dispute
       between the "Cleans" and the "Dirties". A survey of past
       and current literature underlines the idelogical
       differences as well as the intellectual, aesthetic, and
       moral similarities which transcend individual concerns
       of the writer as he proceeds to affirm his truth.

103.   "Writing about Presidents", _New York Herald Tribune Book_
       Review, (January 1961), 1-5. Personal and historical
       commentary on recent American presidents.

Manuscript Materials: The
Bellow Papers: University of
Chicago; Bellow Materials:
University of Texas

I had better luck from this time Detroit
on, first a fast lift into Jackson
and then a salesman for a film
company who had to report to
his district office in Chicago and
made good time. He wanted me to
get some orders into this things in the
back seat, sample stills of these
Yakima Canute and other westerns
and of Strongheart the movie-dog.
He was driving a roomy old Chrysler
and when I had gotten his ~~them~~
cards straight and his suit case &
hat on top them, orderly, I went
to sleep on the floor.

As evening come on we were tearing out of Gary and toward South-
Chicago, by the steel furnaces and
there was the city opening its fire
and smudge mouth to me, as the
Bay shined for a homecoming Neapolitan.

Altogether I had it been ~~know four~~
home for something like ten days

As evening came on, we were tearing out of Gary and toward South Chicago and fire and smudge mouth of the city, gorging to me. As the flaming Bay shines for a homecoming Neapolitan, you then again beat your soul like a minnow before the scaly master wagon with the old speed.

I knew I wasn't coming in for peace and easiness, but empty handed, ~~and would have borne~~ to face the housekeeper, probably, who hadn't been paid; and Mama, certain to feel that we weren't steering reliably; to say nothing of Simon, who would have been storing up something for me, and I was prepared to bear hard words and to say a few, for my own part, about the unanswered telegram. But it never came to that. I was in front of super jags

SECTION I.

The most extensive collection of manuscripts, typescripts, galley proofs, correspondence, published and unpublished works, referred to as the Bellow Papers, is held in the Regenstein Library of the University of Chicago. The material has been arranged in four basic series:

Series A: Correspondence

Series B: Manuscripts, galley proofs, reviews, and other material for Bellow's major works.

Series C: Manuscripts and related materials for his short stories, essays and other minor works both published and unpublished.

Series D: Miscellaneous items.

The Bellow papers have been deposited in and donated to the Library at frequent dates since 1963. The papers can be consulted in accordance with the restrictions placed on them by Mr. Bellow, along with his personal permission.

The largest series in the collection is composed of the working material relating to the author's major works arranged chronologically by date of first publication or date of composition. For each work the groups of manuscripts have been arranged in the order in which they were written. An extensive collection of notebooks and holograph fragments is included, followed by early typewritten drafts of the whole work, miscellaneous typescripts, and final typescripts of the entire novel. Following these are galley proofs, clippings and reviews, and lastly, foreign editions of the works.

Series A: Correspondence.

This series is devoted entirely to Bellow's correspondence. It is arranged alphabetically by name of either the individual, or in a few cases, by the institution or society concerned. The bulk of the correspondence dates from about 1960 to the present, although there are a few earlier letters. Thus, there is little in connection with Bellow's first published works such as Dangling Man (1944) and The Victim (1947), except for allusions to these works by readers who write to comment on more recent novels. There is a considerable amount of correspondence from readers of Herzog, and it is interesting to see the variety of reactions which this work evoked. An important point to note is that almost all of the correspondence is incoming; apart from occasional replies by Bellow, the only other record of Bellow's responses is the brief comments sometimes written in pencil on the top of a letter.

As one would expect, many of the letters are from literary
agents and publishers, as well as a great quantity of "fan mail".
A considerable portion of the correspondence related to various
lecture trips to different universities and institutions, and
there is in fact little which does not in some way relate to
Bellow's teaching or writing.

Series B: Major Works.

This, the largest series in the collection, is composed of the
working material relating to the author's major books, arranged
chronologically by date of first publication or writing.

For each work the groups of manuscripts have been arranged more
or less in the order in which they would have been written. That
is to say, notebooks and holograph fragments first, followed by
early typewritten drafts of the whole work, or more usually of
short portions of it, miscellaneous typewritten pages, and final
typewritten proofs, clippings and reviews, and lastly, foreign
language editions of the novel. On the other hand, no attempt
has been made to reconstruct either a precise chronology or the
structural relationship of the material except in fairly obvious
ways. Rather, a detailed description of each item has been
given, collating it whenever possible with the published text.

The holograph fragments for an unpublished novel, Acatla,
written in 1940, represents the first work in this section. As
far as is known, this is the only extant manuscript for this work.
For the second work represented here, Dangling Man (1944), this
collection contains only reviews of the book and no manuscript
material; it is possible there is no extant manuscript.

The manuscript material for The Victim (1947), Bellow's second
published novel, consists of moderately late holograph drafts
of the complete novel, and one foreign edition of the book.

The Adventures of Augie March (1953) established Bellow in the
top rank of American writers, earning him the 1954 National Book
Award for Fiction. For this novel, and similarly for all following
major works except Seize the Day, the Library has what must be
an almost complete set of working material. For The Adventures
of Augie March, this comprises 22 holograph notebooks, typewritten
draft of the complete novel, together with miscellaneous newspaper clippings and two foreign editions of the book. From this
set of manuscript material one can follow through at least a large
part of the revision and development involved in the publishing of
a book.

For Seize the Day (1956) the Regenstein Library's material is
limited to certain American newspaper clippings, and a corrected
multilith copy of the play by the same name, adapted from the
novel and written by Bellow and Mary Otis. The manuscript material,

consisting of a holograph manuscript, and four typewritten drafts for the book Seize the Day, which included several short stories as well as the title novelette, is to be found in the Humanities Research Center of the University of Texas; for details of the Texas holdings, see entries 929-944.

Henderson the Rain King (1959) was Bellow's next major work, and again there is a very full set of working material: 12 notebooks, a few holograph fragments, early typewritten drafts of the complete novel or substantial parts of it, and a large number of miscellaneous typewritten pages which admirably illustrate the amount of rewriting Bellow did befor reaching the final version. Then there is a final typewritten draft, as it was sent to the printers, followed by three sets of galley proofs with different corrections, and finally a number of clippings and three foreign editions of the novel.

The completeness of this material leads to a certain complexity, and this is also true for the material for Bellow's play The Last Analysis (1964 and 1965), which includes notebooks, holograph and typewritten pages, typewritten drafts, galley proofs, and clippings.

The material for the novel Herzog, which finally secured his international reputation, is particularly extensive. There are 27 notebooks followed by a few holograph pages. Next have been placed the typewritten pages, grouped to approximate the final sequence of events in the novel. This was done in an attempt to break down a very large group of manuscripts into an identifiable and usable order; of necessity there is a considerable degree of overlap between the categories. After the final typewritten drafts and galley proofs is a large selection of German clippings and reviews which Bellow's German publishers sent him, and finally foreign editions.

Series C: Minor Works.

Consisting of minor works - short stories, essays, articles, speech drafts, and reviews- this material does not lend itself to the clearcut arrangement of the previous stories. However, the same general procedures have been followed. Publication information is sometimes included, but much of this section relates to unpublished material and to fragmentary portions of unfinished stories and articles.

Series D: Miscellaneous

The final series consists of miscellaneous items which does not fit into the previous series. It has been broken down into three groups:

Firstly, criticisms of Bellow and his work, which does not relate
to any specific novel.

Secondly, miscellaneous items. These take the form of non-
literary material written by Bellow, such as address books and
personal artifacts of his, such as passports, invitations, bank
cheque books, and photographs, etc. Also included are writings
of other persons, usually in the form of reprints, typewritten
copies, or galley proofs, sent to Bellow for his comments and
corrections. This is followed by miscellaneous newspaper clippings
(such as that on New York parking tickets), presumably either
collected by Bellow or sent to him.

Thirdly, there are 12 folders of material by or about Isaac
Rosenfeld, the literary critic, and personal friend of Bellow's
which had been in Bellow's possesion.

Although the guide should be fairly straightforward, there are
certain usages which may need clarification. In the system of
folder identification A:1:1 means Series A, Box I, Folder 1.

When there is a number of notebooks relating to a specific work,
each has been assigned a number to help in identification, and
not to signify any degree of importance or order. For each notebook, as for each group of holograph or typewritten pages in one
folder, the total number of leaves is given, whether they are
written on or blank. Throughout the description, the page numbers
are taken from the manuscript and are therfore Bellow's and the
number of leaves is the actual count, as in B:21:2 pp. 142-157
(16 l.) In some cases in the notebooks, there are extra loose
leaves inserted, as in B:16:9, 7 l. with 1 loose xerox l. and 1
loose holograph l., meaning that the notebook itself has 7 leaves
and there is one extra xerox leaf inserted and one extra holograph leaf inserted, totalling 9 leaves. Also in connection with
the number of leaves, the phrase in parentheses (various versions)
means that there is more than one version of a particular page;
for example B:14:20 means that there are several versions of page
40, and no attempt has been made to establish separate drafts from
these different versions; the total number of leaves is therefore
provided.

Quotation marks have been used wherever the working is taken
directly from the manuscript, and is therefore Bellow's own.
(Bellow's page numbers have not been put in quotation marks.)
For the chapter numbering, for which quotation marks have also not
been used, an attempt has frequently been made to collate the
manuscript drafts with the published version. For example,
"B:16:17 - Chapter V contains a long section which is an early
version of Chaper VII in the final version", means that Chapter
V is Bellow's numbering taken from the draft itself and Chapter
VII is the numbering in the printed version of the novel.

Generally clippings and reviews are not enumerated, although
this is not true for the German reviews of Herzog, and in a few
other instances where it seemed particularly worthwhile to do so,
as in the case of Dangling Man.

A detailed listing of the contents of the individual folders
follows.

SERIES A:

104. A:1:1   Uncatalogued correspondence. Of particular
               interest are the letters from John Berryman,
               Lionel Trilling, Keith Botsford, Herb Gold, as
               well as various negotiations from a New York
               theatrical agency to dramatize Henderson the Rain
               King, Seize the Day, and The Victim for television
               and films.

SERIES B: MAJOR WORKS.

ACATLA: unpublished work written in 1940.

105. B:1:1   Acatla. Holograph fragments. Yellow paper,
               unlined, in a folder marked "Acatla 1940".
               67 1. Consists of:
               (Untitled). pp. 19-72 (54 1.)
               "Chapter III" pp. 73-78 (6 1.)
               "Earl Huner" pp. 95, 96, 100, 102, 103, 106,
               106, (7 1.)

DANGLING MAN: novel; published in 1944 by Vanguard Press. The
only material in the collection for the work is listed below;
apparently there is no extant manuscript for the first published
novel.

106. B:1:2   Clipping from The Day Jewish Journal, October
               23, 1960.

Review of <u>Dangling Man</u> in Weidenfield and
Nicolson booklist for Spring and Summer,
1961, p. 28.

THE VICTIM: novel; published in 1947 by Vanguard Press.
This is the only version of the manuscript in the collection and
would appear to be a moderately late draft with few corrections.
The chapter numbering is that of the final version.   The
manuscript is entirely holograph. 23 1. Consists of:

107.   B:1:3   Chapter I.   White paper, unlined, pp. 1-33
                 (33 1.)

108.   B:1:4   Chapter II.   White paper, unlined, pp. 34-49
                 (16 1.)

109.   B:1:5   Chapter III.   White and Yellow paper, unlined,
                 pp. 1, 50, 51 (also numbered 34), 52a-52q, 53-
                 56 (25 1.)

110.   B:1:6   Chapter IV. Yellow paper, unlined. pp. 50,
                 58-74 (18 1.)

111.   B:1:7   Chapter V. Yellow paper, unlined. pp. 75-94
                 (20 1.)

112.   B:1:8   Chapter VI. Yellow paper, unlined. pp. 95-113
                 (19 1.)

113.   B:1:9   Chapter VII. Yellow paper, unlined. pp. 114-139
                 (26 1.)

114.   B:1:10   Chapter VIII.   Yellow paper, unlined. pp. 140-
                 158 (19 1.)

115.   B:1:11   Chapter IX. Yellow paper, unlined. pp. 159-
                 183.

116.   B:1:12   Chapter X. Yellow paper, unlined. pp. 184-199 (16 l.)

117.   B:1:13   Chapter XI. Yellow paper, unlined. pp. 200-222 (23 l.)

Foreign Language Editions.

118.   B:1:14   <u>Offeret</u>. Oslo: H. Aschehoug, 1967. 1 copy.

THE ADVENTURES OF AUGIE MARCH: novel; published in 1953 by the Viking Press. The following 22 notebooks are drafts of The Adventures of Augie March. With the exception of noticeable verbal changes and alterations in the order of events, the drafts are similar to the published version of the novel. The notebooks have been arranged according to the sequence of chapters in the final novel, and each has been assigned a number.

119.   B:1:15   Notebook 1. "Augie 3 & 4". Holograph. Orange notebook. 69 l. with 1 torn l. Back of notebook includes Chapters I and II. Chapter II is similar to the conclusion of Chapter I in the final version. The front of the notebook is entitled "Augie 3 & 4" and is similar to the final versions of Chapters II and IV, except for the Sant Claus sequence in Chapter III which, in the final version, is in Chapter IV.

120.   B:1:16   Notebook 2. "Augie March 2 & 3". Holograph. Light green notebook. 48 l. Similar to Chapters II and III in the final version. Chapter II is called "Various Jobs". Chapter III is not a complete draft, and ends with Augie's failure at the newspaper stand job.

121.   B:1:17   Notebook 3. (Untitled), with quotation from Voltaire's Correspondence on the front cover. Holograph. Light brown notebook. 38 l. with 1 torn l. "Cahier D" on back cover.

122.   B:1:18   Notebook 4. (Untitled). Holograph. Green Omega notebook. 139 l. At front of notebook is an "Address by Garley Macdowell to the Has-beens Club of Chicago". Back of notebook contains drafts of Chapters VII, VIII, and IX.

123. B:1:19   Notebook 5. (Untitled). Holograph. Black
              notebook. 88 l. with 2 torn l. At front of
              notebook: "Professor Harold Wyoming Dedicates
              a New Waxworks Museum". At end of book is an
              "Address by Garley Macdowell to the Has-beens
              Club, Chicago"; also a selection form Augie's
              conversations with Mintouchian.·

124. B:1:20   Notebook 6. (Untitled). Holograph. Black
              notebook. 110 l. Front of notebook includes
              plot outlines, list of characters, and drafts
              of Chapters IX, X, XI, beginning with the end
              of Chapter IX when Augie escapes from Lake
              Erie to Chicago. Chapter X is complete and
              similar to the final version. Chapter XI is
              similar to the first half of Chapter XI in the
              final version. At back of notebook is "A
              Visitor Decides to Steal a Photo of the
              Professor in a Jinnicksha".

125. B:1:21   Notebook 7. "Auigie March - last of Georgie -
              first of Einhorn Sr." "Augie XI - XII".
              Holograph. Light brown University of Minnesota
              notebook. 24 l. .Chapter XI begins with Simon's
              engagement to Charlotte, and continues to the
              end of Chapter XI in the final version. Chapter
              XII begins with the formal wedding of Charlotte
              and Simon, and continues to Augie's attempt to
              persuade Lucy Magnus to elope.

126. B:1:22   Notebook 8. "Augie XII cont'd". Holograph
              Light brown notebook. 16 l. with 1 l torn out.
              Continuation of Notebook 7, beginning with
              Augie's visit to Charlotte and Simon in their
              apartment after their marriage. The chapter is
              incomplete.

127. B:2:1   Notebook 9. "Augie ch. XI - 2" Holograph.
              Dark brown notebook. 37 l. Similar to the
              second half of Chapter XII in the final version.
              Begins with Augie's visit to Mimi in hospital
              where she had hoped to have an abortion, and
              continues to the end of the chapter.

128. B:2:2   Notebook 10. (Untitled). Holograph. Dark
              brown notebook. 47 l. Contains Chapter XIII
              and Chapter XIV. Chapter XIII is similar to
              the final version, except for verbal changes,
              and Chapter XIV has only one page, which is
              an early version of the chapter's opening page.

129.   B:2:3   Notebook 11. (Untitled). Holograph.
                         Light brown notebook without front cover.
                         104 l. Contains Chapter XIV which is similar
                         to the final version.

130.   B:2:4   Notebook 12. (Untitled). Holograph. Dark
                         brown notebook. 50 l. Contains Chapters XV,
                         XVI, and XVII. Chapters XV and XVI are similar
                         to the final versions, but the introduction to
                         Chapter XVII is substantially different from the
                         final version. The Chapter is also incomplete,
                         ending with Christmas fiesta before Sylvester's
                         arrival.

131.   B:2:5   Notebook 13. "XVII cont'd." Holograph. Dark
                         brown notebook. 47 l. Similar to Chapters XVII
                         and IX of the final version. "Millicent" here is
                         Stella in the final version. Also collected are
                         pages of Chapter XXVI which is similar to the
                         final version.

132.   B:2:6   Notebook 14. (Untitled). Holograph. Dark
                         brown notebook. 33 l. with 1 torn l. Contains
                         Chapter XX, which is similar to Chapter XX of the
                         final version, but "Taxco" here is Acatla in the
                         final version.

133.   B:2:7   Notebook 15. (Untitled). Holograph. Dark
                         brown notebook. 34 l. with 1 loose l. Similar
                         to Chapter XX of the final version. Begins with
                         Augie's visit to George after his return from
                         Mexico, and continues to Augie's visit with Simon.
                         Then follows a section from Chapter XX which
                         involves Draja Paslavitch, and the back of the
                         notebook contains a later draft of Chapter XXI,
                         including Augie's visits to Simon and Robey.
                         This draft does not include the episode when
                         Simon rips off Mrs. Magnus' clothes.

134.   B:2:8   Notebook 16. (Untitled). Holograph. Dark
                         brown notebook. 25 l. Chapter XXI, is similar
                         to the final version, but without the episode
                         in which Simon and Augie meet. Also includes
                         draft of Chapter XXII, similar to the final
                         version, although the order of events differs.

135.   B:2:9   Notebook 17. (Untitled). Holograph. Dark
                         brown notebook. 32 l. Chapter XXII, which
                         is similar to Chapters XXIII and XXIV of the
                         final version. Also a draft of Chapter XXIII

which becomes Chapter XXV in the final version.

136.   B:2:10   <u>Notebook 18.</u> (Untitled). Holograph. Dark brown notebook. 44 1. Contains incomplete drafts of Chapters XXII-XXV.

137.   B:2:11   <u>Notebook 19.</u> (Untitled). Holograph. Dark brown notebook. 30 1. with 12 loose 1. Notebook begins with "English 3" notes, and also contains Bellow's analysis of Mr. Young's study of Ernest Hemingway, and Bellow's review of Sholom Aleichem's <u>Adventures of Mottel the Cantor's Son.</u> At the end are 12 loose 1., white, lined paper, containing an incomplete draft of Chapter XXVI.

138.   B:2:12   <u>Notebook 20.</u> "Augie XXV continued". Holograph. Dark brown notebook. 36 1. with 1 torn 1. Includes drafts of Chapters XXV-XXVII, but incidents which were not included in the final version of the novel. They are mostly concerned with Augie's travels in Europe before going to Paris.

139.   B:2:13   <u>Notebook 21.</u> (Untitled). Holograph. Dark brown notebook. 32 1. Front of notebook begins: "By which means I saw a fairly tall person..." and back of notebook begins"... and said the Communists couldn't last in power...". Neither of these drafts is included in the final version.

140.   B:2:14   <u>Notebook 22.</u> (Untitled). Holograph. Dark brown Spiral notebook. 12 1. with 1 torn 1. Miscellaneous notes.

The following pages are moderately late fragmented drafts composed at various stages in the development of <u>The Adventures of Augie March,</u> which have been arranged according to the sequence of chapters in the finished novel. They are all typewritten leaves with holograph corrections on white paper, unlined. 282 1. Consists of:

141.   B:3:1   Chapter IX. pp. 1-47 (47 1)

142.   B:3:2   Chapters IX and X. pp. 298-308 (11 1.)

143.   B:3:3   Chapter XIX. pp. 3-4 (various versions) (7 1.)

144.   B:3:4   Chapter XIX. pp. 692-696, 698-702 (10 1.)

This is a complete final draft of <u>The Adventures of Augie March</u>
as it was sent to the printers in 1953.　The manuscript itself
is typewritten, with corrections and marks by Bellow and the
printers.　928 l.　Consists of:

Included in Box B:4 are the following foreign language editions of The Adventures of Augie March.

163. B:4:6 Augie March Aventyr. Stockholm: Albert Bonniers Forlag. 1955. 2 copies. Collections of Contemporary American Literature, vol. 19, Tokyo: Arechi Shuppa Sha, 1969. 3 copies.

SEIZE THE DAY: novel; published in 1956 by Viking Press. The only material relating to this novel in this collection consists of a play by the same name, adapted from the novel by Saul Bellow and Mary Otis, along with certain clippings about the novel. (For additional Mss, see entries 935-43).

164. B:5:1 "Seize the Day, a play". Multilith draft with corrections in different hands. White paper in a red Hart Stenographic Bureau binding. 92 l. Consists of: Introductory pages. (3 l.) "Act One" pp. 1-43 (43 l.) "Act Two" pp. 1-46 (46 l.)

165. B:5:2 Miscellaneous American newspaper clippings.

HENDERSON THE RAIN KING: novel; published in 1959 by Viking Press. The following 12 notebooks are drafts of Henderson the Rain King. In general the notebooks are very early versions of the novel, which apparently was originally going to be entitled "Bariri", a name which became the Wariri people of the published book. The chapter numbering of these notebooks seldom corresponds to that of the final version. The notebooks are thus arranged approximately according to this early numbering, and each notebook has been assigned a number.

166. B:5:3 Notebook 1. "Bariri I". Holograph. Beige Jewel notebook. 35 l. with loose l. Front of notebook covers the section as far as Henderson's arrival among the Wariri. Back of notebook contains notes on Henderson's children and on "Trembling".

167. B:5:4 Notebook 2. "Bariri III". Holograph. Dark brown Maple Leaf notebook. 23 l. This later becomes part of Chapter XII.

168. B:5:5 Notebook 3. "Bariri III and IV". Holograph. Red Spiral notebook. 43 l. Chapters III-VI: this portion of Chapter III is an early version of the last part of Chapter XII. Chapter IV becomes Chapter XII, and Chapter V, XIV. Chapter VI is unidentified.

169. B:5:6 Notebook 4. (Untitled). Holograph. Dark
           brown notebook. 87 1. Chapters VI and VII.
           Chapter VI contains elements of Chapter XIV
           and XV, and Chapter VII has episodes which
           appear in Chapter IV of the published novel,
           together with unidentified episodes about the
           painting of Henderson and Henderson's des-
           cription of King Dahfu's palace.

170. B:5:7 Notebook 5. (Untitled). Holograph. Green
           Joredco notebook. 59 1. with 2 loose 1.,
           one holograph and one typewritten. Contains
           parts of Chapters VI and VII, which are similar
           to Chapters V and VI of the final version. Also
           includes drafts of a speech on writing fiction.

171. B:5:8 Notebook 6. (Untitled). Holograph. Blue
           Spiral notebook. 48 1. with 3 loose 1.
           Contains elements of Chapters XIV and XVI of
           the final version. Also included are an
           unidentified episode about Riverside Drive and
           material similar to Chapter XVII in the final
           version.

172. B:5:9 Notebook 7. (Untitled). Holograph. Dark
           brown Maple Leaf notebook. 37 1. with 1 torn
           1. Includes episodes similar to those of
           Chapters XVI and XX of the final version.
           Chapters VIII and IX are unidentified episodes
           about Dahfu collecting lions, the death of his
           brother, and intrigues against the king.

173. B:5:10 Notebook 8. (Untitled). Holograph. Yellow
           Easywrite notebook. 65 1. Contains episodes
           similar to Chapter XX of the final version.
           Also unidentified letter from Fiolet Simmons,
           who became Lily in the final version, and early
           versions of Chapters II, XVI, and XX.

174. B:5:11 Notebook 9. (Untitled). Holograph. Red
           Easywrite notebook. 62 1. with 1 torn 1.
           Contains an early version of Chapter XV and
           unidentified fragments on scorpions, amazons,
           a conference with King Dahfu, Henderson's fever
           and dreams, and an episode about the wife of the
           Rain King.

175. B:5:12 Notebook 10. (Untitled). Holograph. Blue
           Easywrite notebook. 75 1. Early versions of
           Chapters XVII and XVIII, and two versions of
           the letter to Lily in Chapter XIX.

176. B:5:13   Notebook 11. (Untitled). Holograph. Black
              notebook. 73 l. Contains unidentified
              episode with King Dahfu; Henderson is left to
              meditate alone in bed; early versions of
              Chapter II; various short sections of unidentified
              notes, and an episode about the stealing of
              Henderson's hat.

177. B:6:1   Notebook 12. (Untitled). Holograph. Black
              notebook. 74 l. Early version of Chapter IX
              probably. Also includes 4 l. of another story
              about three convicts, Dan Affler, Ivan Straub,
              and Dominick Alpo.

178. B:6:2   Notebook 13. (Untitled). Holograph. Black
              notebook. 74 l. with 1 loose l. Story about
              "Hattie"; unidentified episode entitled "Part
              II (after flogging)".

The following holograph fragments are early versions of the text
of Henderson the Rain King. As far as possible they have been
arranged according to the sequence of chapters in the final version.
They are all in the author's own hand. 156 l. Consists of:

179. B:6:3   "Henderson the Rain King I". White paper,
              lined (12 l.) Miscellaneous pages from
              beginning of text.

180. B:6:4   "Bariri II". Yellow paper, unlined. pp. 1-
              51 (51 l.) Early version of Chapter II.

181. B:6:5   (Untitled). Yellow paper, unlined. pp. 37-
              50 (14 l.)

182. B:6:6   Chapter VIII. Yellow paper, unlined. pp. 8-
              7, 8-21 (15 l.) Similar to Chapter VIII of
              the final version.

183. B:6:7   Chapter XVIII. Yellow paper, unlined. pp. 1-
              12 (12 l.) Became Chapter XIX in final version.

184. B:6:8   "Continuing red notebook" (Notebook 8).
              Yellow paper, unlined. pp. 1-21 (21 l.) Be-
              came part of Chapter V where Henderson meets
              Romilayu; and the letter to Lily in Chapter
              XIX.

185. B:6:9   (Untitled). White paper, lined. (11 l.)
              Unidentified episode of Henderson with Horko
              and Bunam.

186. B:6:10   (Untitled). Various sorts of paper. (20 l.)
              Miscellaneous notes.

The following pages are early typewritten drafts of <u>Henderson the Rain King</u>, and several of them are extracts which appeared in the <u>Hudson Review</u> and <u>Botteghe Oscure</u>. The chapter numbering used here, although not always supplied by Bellow, is that of the early version. All the pages are typewritten with occasional holograph corrections. 459 l. Consist of:

187.   B:6:11   Chapters I-V. Yellow paper, lined and white paper, unlined. pp. 1-89 (91 l.) From the beginning to take Henderson through the Arnewi.

188.   B:6:12   Chapters I-IV. White paper, unlined. pp. 1-45 (45 l.) From the beginning to Henderson's departure for Africa. pp. 1-28 of this version appeared in the <u>Hudson Review</u>, Vol. XI no. 1, Spring, 1958.

189.   B:6:13   Chapters X-XIII. White paper, unlined. pp. 31-128 (also numbered 185-285) (99 l.) From Henderson's arrival with the Wariri to Henderson's dance with the amazons after lifting the idol; pp. 42-117 are a slightly different version of an extract which appeared in <u>Botteghe Oscure</u>, Vol. XXI, 1958.

190.   B:6:14   Chapters X-XIII. White paper, unlined. (99 l.) Carbon copy of B:6:13.

191.   B:6:15   Chapters I-V. White paper, unlined. pp. 1-123, with title pages (125 l.) From the beginning to Henderson's dance with the amazons. pp. 48-114 are a slightly different version of an extract which appeared in <u>Botteghe Oscure</u>, Vol. XXI, 1958. (For details, see entry 21.)

The following folders contain a complete typewritten (with the exception of B:7:4) draft of the novel, with holograph corrections. There is also a carbon copy of Chapters I-XVIII. There are minor changes throughout the whole text, but only those variations which show a marked difference from the final version are indicated. 458 l. (and 400 l. of carbon copy). Consists of:

192.   B:6:16   Chapters I-III. White paper, lined. pp. 1-26 (26 l.)

193.   B:6:17   Chapters IV-VI. White paper, lined. pp. 27-105 (78 l.) Chapter V contains a long section which is an early version of Chapter VII in the final version; and Chapter VI contains episodes which are part of Chapter V in the final version.

194. B:6:18 Chapters VII-IX. White paper, lined. pp. 106-180 (75 l.) Chapter VII is an early version of Chapter X; Chapter VIII contains an unidentified episode about rain-making ceremony of the Arnewi; Chapter IX contains episodes in Chapters VIII-X of the published text, but the major episode about the killing of a snake is unidentified.

195. B:7:1 Chapters X-XII. White paper, lined and unlined, and yellow paper, lined. pp. 181-274 (94 l.) Chapter X contains episodes in Chapters VIII, X, and XI of the final version; Chapter XI is an early version of Chapter XII of the published text.

196. B:7:2 Chapters XIII-XV. White paper, unlined. pp. 275-327 (53 l.) Chapters XIII-XV are early versions of Chapters XIV-XVI of the final version.

197. B:7:3 Chapters XVI-XVIII. White paper, unlined. pp. 328-401 (74 l.) Chapter XVI is an early version of Chapter XVII, with the exception of an unidentified episode on the killing of a German in Italy. Chapters XVIII and XIX are early versions of Chapters XIX and XX.

198. B:7:4 Chapters XIX-XXI. Holograph. Yellow paper, unlined. pp. 402-417, 436-437, 441-507. (85 l.) Chapters XIX-XXI are an early version of Chapters XX-XXII. Although these pages are holograph, they seem to form a part of this section and the numbering follows consecutively from B:7:3.

199. B:7:5 Carbon copy of Chapters I-VI.

200. B:7:6 Carbon copy of Chapters VII-X

201. B:7:7 Carbon copy of Chapters XI-XIV.

202. B:7:8 Carbon copy of Chapters XV-XVIII.

Second Typewritten Draft.
This is another early draft of Henderson the Rain King covering only Chapters I-IX, but apparently later than the previous one. The pages are all typewritten with holograph corrections. The chapter numbering, as previously indicated, is that of the early version and in no way corresponds to the final version. 479 l. Consists of:

203. B:7:9   Chapters I-II. White paper, unlined. pp. 1-
            85 (85 l.) Early version of the beginning of
            the novel in which there are two women in
            Henderson's life in addition to his first wife.
            These women, Joanna and Selma, are later
            combined as Lily. Chapter I covers the time
            until Henderson's departure for Africa, and
            Chapter II, until his arrival with the Bariri.

204. B:7:10 Chapters I-II. Yellow paper, unlined. pp. 7,
            8, 18, 19, 20-24, 51-55 (14 l.) Carbon copy of
            B:7:9.

205. B:7:11 Chapters I-II. Yellow paper, unlined, pp. 1-
            46 (46 l.) Carbon copy of B:7:9.

206. B:7:12 Chapters III-V. White paper, unlined, pp. 86-
            141 (56 l.) Chapters III-V are early versions
            of Chapters XII, XIII, and XIV.

207. B:7:13 Chapters VI-VII. White paper, unlined. pp. 142-
            195 (54 l.) Chapter VI is an early version
            of Chapter XV of the final version. Chapter VII
            contains unidentified episodes about Henderson's
            fever and the women who came to him, his trip
            to France and his affair with Joanna Lily, and
            his trip through the village as Rain King
            dispensing water.

208. B:8:1   Chapters VI-VII. Yellow paper, unlined, pp.
            142-195 (54 l.) Carbon copy of B:7:13.

209. B:8:2   Chapters VIII-IX. White paper, unlined and
            yellow paper, lined. pp. 196-230 (35 l.)
            Chapters VIII-IX contain unidentified episodes
            about a lion hunt and the arrest of Romilayu.

210. B:8:3   Chapters VIII-IX. Yellow paper, unlined. pp.
            196-230 (35 l.) Carbon copy of B:8:2.

Third Typewritten Draft.
This draft is a later version than the two previous ones but
covers only Chapters I-VII. The pages are all typewritten with
holograph corrections. The chapter numbering corresponds to
that of the final version. 257 ,. Consists of:

211. B:8:4   Chapters I-VI. Yellow paer, unlined. pp. 1-
            75 (75 l.)

212. B:8:5   Chapters I-V. White paper, unlined. pp. 1-78
            (78 l.) Appears to be a carbon copy of the
            corrected manuscript from B:8:4.

| 213. | B:8:6 | Chapters V-VII. White paper, unlined. pp. 50-101 (52 l.) |
| 214. | B:8:7 | Chapters V-VII. Yellow paper, unlined. pp. 50-101 (52 l.) Carbon copy of B:8:6. |

Miscellaneous Typewritten Pages.
The following folders contain short portions of the text rewritten by the author at various stages during the composition of the novel. An attempt has been made to collate them approximately with the published text, but no attempt has been made to place them in the order in which they were written. They are all typewritten or carbon copies of the original with holograph corrections. 194 l. Consists of:

215.	B:8:8	Yellow paper, lined. pp. 1-5 (5 l.) Early version of beginning of text.
216.	B:8:9	Yellow paper, lined. pp. 1-5 (5 l.) Early version of beginning of text.
217.	B:8:10	White paper, unlined. pp. 1-3, 5 (4 l.) Early version of beginning of text.
218.	B:8:11	Yellow paper, unlined. pp. 1-7 (7 l.) Early version of beginning of text.
219.	B:8:12	Yellow paper, lined. pp. 5-8 (4 l.) Early version of beginning of text.
220.	B:8:13	White paper, unlined. pp. 8-9 (2 l.) Early version of killing of the cat.
221.	B:8:14	Yellow paper, unlined. pp. 10-13 (4 l.) Early version about Henderson's meeting with Lily.
222.	B:8:15	White paper, unlined. pp. 39-43, 48 (6 l.) Early version about the rug, Ricey, and the baby.
223.	B:8:16	Yellow paper, unlined. pp. 45-47 (3 l.) Early version about Ricey and the baby.
224.	B:8:17	Yellow paper, unlined. pp. 77-83 (7 l.) Early version of a portion of the final Chapter VII.
225.	B:8:18	White paper, lined. pp. 85-100 (16 l.) Early version of parts of the final Chapters V and VI.
226.	B:8:19	White paper, lined pp. 113-117 (5 l.) Early version of episode about Henderson and his son.

227.   B:8:20   Yellow paper, unlined. pp. 113-117 (5 l.)
                Carbon copy of B:8:19.

228.   B:8:21   Yellow paper, lined. pp. 161-163 (3 l.) Early
                version of a portion of the final Chapter XII.

229.   B:8:22   White paper, unlined. pp. 314-326 (13 l.)
                Early version of a portion of the final Chapter
                XVI.

230.   B:8:23   White paper, unlined. pp. 314-326 (13 l.)
                Carbon copy of B:8:22.

231.   B:8:24   White paper, unlined. pp. 341-364 (24 l.) Early
                version of a portion of the final Chapter XVIII.

232.   B:8:25   White paper, unlined. Carbon copy of pp. 24-38
                (15 l.) Early version of the episode about
                Henderson's first meetong with King Dahfu and
                the rain ceremony.

233.   B:8:26   Yellow paper, unlined. Carbon copy of pp. 97-
                101 (5 l.) Early version of the episode about
                Henderson's first meeting with King Dahfu.

234.   B:8:27   White paper, unlined. Carbon copy of pp. 127-
                131 (5 l.) Early version of part of the final
                Chapter XVI.

235.   B:8:28   Yellow paper, unlined. Carbon copy pp. 128-
                130, 132 (4 l.) Early version of parts of the
                final Chapter XVI.

236.   B:8:29   Miscellaneous pages on different sorts of
                paper, (39 l.) Original and carbon copies of
                many different drafts.

Miscellaneous Typewritten Chapters.
The following folders contain chapters of the text rewritten by
the author at various stages during the composition of the novel.
An attempt has been made to collate them with the published text,
but no attempt has been made to place them in the order in which
they were written. They are all typewritten with holograph
corrections, or carbon copies wherever indicated. 539 l.
Consists of:

237.   B:8:30   Chapters I-II. White paper, unlined. pp. 1-19
                (19 l.) Relatively late version of the final
                Chapter I.

238.   B:8:31   Chapters I-II. Yellow paper, unlined. pp. 1-
                19. (19 l.) Carbon copy of B:8:30.

239. B:8:32 Chapters II. Yellow paper, unlined. pp. 7-11
(5 l.) Fairly late version of part of the final
Chapter II.

240. B:8:33 Chapters I-IV. Yellow and white paper, unlined.
pp. 1-68 (68 l.) Carbon copy of an early
version of the novel from the beginning of
Henderson's arrival with the Bariri.

241. B:8:34 Chapter V. Yellow paper, unlined. pp. 47-50
(different versions) (5 l.) Early version of
part of the final Chapter V.

242. B:8:35 Chapter V. White paper, unlined. pp. 50-78
(29 l.) Early version of part of the final
Chapter V.

243. B:8:36 Chapter VI. White paper, unlined. pp. 1-27
(27 l.) Early version of the final Chapter XV.

244. B:8:37 Chapter VII. White paper, unlined. pp. 1-12
(12 l.) Early version of part of the final
Chapter XV.

245. B:9:1 Chapter VIII. White paper, lined. pp. 1-13
(13 l.) Unidentified episodes about Henderson's
tour of the village as Rain King and the theft
of his hat.

246. B:9:2 Chapter VIII. White paper, unlined. pp. 1-29
(29 l.) Fairly late expanded version of the
final Chapter VIII.

247. B:9:3 Chapter VIII. White paper, unlined. pp. 1-18
(18 l.) Fairly late version of the final
Chapter VIII.

248. B:9:4 Chapter IX. White paper, lined. pp. 1-16
(16 l.) Early version of the final Chapter
XVI.

249. B:9:5 Chapter IX. White paper, unlined. pp. 1-13
(13 l.) Relatively late version of the final
Chapter IX.

250. B:9:6 Chapter X. White paper, lined. pp. 1-19
(19 l.) Unidentified episode about the wife of
the Rain King.

251. B:9:7 Chapter X. White paper, unlined. pp. 1-21
(21 l.) Fairly late version of the final Chapter
X.

252.	B:9:8	Chapter XI. White paper, lined. pp. 1-19 (19 l.) Early version of the final Chapter XX.
253.	B:9:9	Chapter XVII. Yellow paper, unlined and unnumbered (4 l.) Early version of the final Chapter XX.
254.	B:9:10	Chapter XVIII. White paper, unlined. pp. 382-397 (16 l.) Early version of the final Chapter XIX.
255.	B:9:11	Chapters VI-XI. Yellow paper, unlined. (106 l.) Carbon copy of B:8:36 and 37; B:9:1, 4, 6, and 8.
256.	B:9:12	Chapters VIII-X. Yellow paper, unlined. (81 l.) Carbon copy of B:9:2, 3, 5, and 7.

Final Draft.
The following folders contain the final typewritten draft as it was sent to the printers. The holograph corrections, mostly stylistic, are mainly those of the printer and editor. This is essentially the published text and is therefore arranged according to the final sequence of chapters. They are all on white, unlined paper. 373 l. Consists of:

257.	B:9:13	Chapters I-IV. pp. 1-47 (47 l.)
258.	B:9:14	Chapters V-VII. pp. 48-98 (51 l.)
259.	B:9:15	Chapters VIII-X. pp. 99-145 (47 l.)
260.	B:9:16	Chapters XI-XII. pp. 146-200 (55 l.)
261.	B:9:17	Chapters XII-XV. pp. 201-242 (42 l.)
262.	B:9:18	Chapters XVI-XVIII. pp. 243-294 (52 l.)
263.	B:9:19	Chapters XIX-XX. pp. 295-340 (46 l.)
264.	B:9:20	Chapters XXI-XXII. pp. 340-372 (33 l.)

Galley Proofs.
The following folders contain three sets of galley proofs. The first is Bellow's own with extensive corrections in his hand, in addition to the occasional editorial corrections and comments. The second set is identical with the first, and with the same corrections, but in a different hand. The final group of galleys is the revised proofs, marked "Revised Galleys - Author's", with further revisions in the author's hand, along with editorial suggestions in the margin by another reader. 396 l. Consists of:

265.	B:10:1	Chapters I-V. pp. 1-24 (24 l.) Also included is a letter from the Viking Press to Bellow, which was sent with the proofs.
266.	B:10:2	Chapters VI-X. pp. 25-30 (26 l.)
267.	B:10:3	Chapters XI-XIII. pp. 51-75 (25 l.)
268.	B:10:4	Chapters XIV-XVII. pp. 76-99 (24 l.)
269.	B:10:5	Chapters XVIII-XXII. pp. 100-132 (33 l.)
270.	B:10:6	Chapters I-V. pp. 1-24 (24 l.)
271.	B:10:7	Chapters VI-X. pp. 25-50 (26 l.)
272.	B:10:8	Chapters XI-XIII. pp. 51-75 (25 l.)
273.	B:10:9	Chapters XIV-XVII. pp. 76-99 (24 l.)
274.	B:10:10	Chapters XVIII-XXII. pp. 100-132 (33 l.)
275.	B:10:11	Chapters I-V. pp. 1-24 (24 l.)
276.	B:10:12	Chapters VI-X. pp. 25-50 (26 l.)
277.	B:10:13	Chapters XI-XIII. pp. 51-75 (25 l.)
278.	B:10:14	Chapters XIV-XVII. pp. 76-99 (24 l.)
279.	B:10:15	Chapters XVIII. pp. 100-132 (33 l.)

Clippings and Reviews

280.	B:11:1	Reviews of Henderson the Rain King collected by Vasiliki of Hill and Wang, and sent to Bellow's son, Gregory, with covering letter which is also enclosed.
281.	B:11:2	English and foreign language clippings, pamphlets and magazines.
282.	B:11:3	English and foreign language clippings, pamphlets and magazines.
283.	B:11:4	English and foreign language clippings, pamphlets and magazines.
284.	B:11:5	English and foreign language clippings, pamphlets and magazines.

285. B:11:6 English and foreign language clippings, pamphlets and magazines.

286. B:11:7 English and foreign language clippings, pamphlets and magazines.

287. B:11:8 English and foreign language clippings, pamphlets and magazines.

288. B:11:9 English and foreign language clippings, pamphlets and magazines.

Foreign Lanuage Editions
Included in the collection are the following translations of Henderson the Rain King.

289. B:11:10 Regnkongen. Oslo: H. Aschehoug, 1960. 2 copies. Henderson o Rei da Chuva. Lisbon: Edicao "Livros do Brasil", n.d. 1 copy. Henderson, el Rey de la Lluvia. Mexico: Joaquin Motiz, 1964. 1 copy.

THE LAST ANALYSIS: play: published in 1964 and 1965 by the Viking Press. An early version of The Last Analysis, produced by Roger Stevens, opened at the Belasco Theatre in New York City in 1964. The play was not a great success, and as a result it was rewritten. It was first published in this form by the Viking Press in 1965. Throughout the whole of this section no attempt has been made to distinguish between the two different versions.

The following 20 notebooks are drafts composed at various stages in the development of The Last Analysis. Although obvious sequences of notebooks have been kept together, no attempt has been made to distinguish between the different versions of the play, or to place them either in the order in which they were written, or in the final order of the play. They are all in the author's own hand and each has been assigned a number.

290. B:12:1 Notebook 1. "Bummidge - I". Blue notebook. ¶ 1. Opening of play, with description of Bummidge and first speeches.
Notebook 2. "Bummidge - II". Blue notebook. ¶ 1. Continues from Notebook I, with scene between Bummidge and Dixon.
Notebook 3. "Bummidge - II". Blue notebook. ¶ 1. Continues from notebook 2, with speech by Bummidge.
Notebook 4. "Bummidge - IV". Blue notebook. ¶ 1. Continues from Notebook 3 and begins with speech by Bummidge.

Notebook 5. "B'dge V". Blue notebook. 4 1.
Continues from notebook 4 with speech by
Bummidge.
Notebook 6. "B'dge VI". Light blue notebook.
4 1. Continues from notebook 5, with speech by
Dixon.
Notebook 7. "VII". Light blue notebook. 4 1.

291.   B:12:2   Notebook 8. "Bummidge 1, Sept. '58". Light
blue notebook. 4 1. Opening of play, with
description of Bummidge on couch.
Notebook 9. "Bummidge 2, Sept. '58". Light
blue notebook. 4 1. Continues from Notebook 8.
Notebook 10. "Bum 3". Light blue notebook.
4 1. Continues Notebook 9, with scene between
Gum and Bum.

292.   B:12:3   Notebook 11. "A, Act II from p. 19". Light
green Examination Book notebook. 4 1. Begins
in mid-sentence "used to have some tiny drill
bits" with dialogue between Bumm and Mott.
Notebook 12. "B, Act II from p. 26". Light
green Examination Book notebook. 4 1.
Continues from Notebook 11 with conversation
between Bumm, Mott, and others.
Notebook 13. "C, Act II from p. 34". Light
green Examination Book notebook. 4 1.
Continues from Notebook 12, with Mott's speech
"Who am I in this enactment".

293.   B:12:4   Notebook 14. (Untitled). Yellow Joredco notebook. 60 1. Opening of play, with character
descriptions, and Act I.

294.   B:12:5   Notebook 15. "Bumm Scene I". Brown Standard
Composition Book notebook. 30 1. Opening of
play beginning with character descriptions and
scene and continuing through Act I.

295.   B:12:6   Notebook 16. (Untitled). Beige National notebook 12 1. with 17 loose 1. Opening of play,
beginning with scene "Half an hour before
broadcast time".

296.   B:12:7   Notebook 17. (Untitled). Blue notebook. 113 1.
Begins with speech by Bummidge in mid-scene,
and pp. 1-6 have been torn out.

297. B:12:8   Notebook 18. White paper, lined (1 1. with 1
               torn 1.) Begins with: "A rapid background
               sketch is now necessary ...." - no names are
               given, but this may be a speech by Bummidge.

298. B:12:9   Notebook 19. White paper, unlined. (1 1.)
               Begins with "Shel: Why am I the bodyguard
               here?".

299. B:12:10   Notebook 20. White paper, unlined (1 1.)
               Begins with: "Attached sheet. The end must
               augur success for B."

300. B:12:11   Notebook 21. Yellow paper, lined. (2 1.)
               Suggestions for revision in a different hand.

The following folders contain typewritten drafts of The Last
Analysis composed at various stages in its development, and
therefore with different titles. They are either complete or
almost complete drafts of the whole play or of an act, and are
all typewritten or carbon copies. No attempt has been made to
collate them with the final version of the play or to place
them in chronological order. The numbering of the acts given
is that of Bellow's in that particular version. 840 1.
Consists of:

301. B:13:1   "The Last Analysis". White paper, unlined, in
               a folder marked "Bummy - early version".
               Act I, pp. 1-52; Act II, pp. 1-36; Act III,
               pp. 1-33 (131 1.) Complete but early version
               of the play.

302. B:13:2   "Bummy". With holograph corrections. Yellow
               paper, unlined. pp. 1-73 (77 1.) Complete
               draft, with covering letter from Stevens Production
               Inc., including "the two places those silly
               typists missed", and with 1 1. of "Clarifications".

303. B:13:3   "The Upper Depths". With holograph corrections.
               White paper, unlined, in grey Russell and
               Volkening covers marked "The Upper Depths, A play
               in two acts by Saul Bellow". Act I, pp. 1-29;
               Act II, pp. 1-29 (59 1.) Includes a page of
               temporary titles: "Bummidge", "Humanitis"
               or "The Upper Depths". Complete draft of the play.

304. B:13:4   "Know Thyself". With holograph corrections.
               Yellow and white paper, unlined. pp. 1-43
               (43 1.) Complete draft of Act I.

305.	B:13:5	"Bumm". With holograph corrections. Yellow paper, unlined. pp. 9-74 (66 l.)
306.	B:13:6	(Untitled). White paper, unlined. pp. 1-38 (38 l.) Begins with: "Bumm: What a night I had - such dreams!"
307.	B:13:7	"Act II". White paper, unlined. pp. 1-28 (28 l.) Incomplete draft of Act II.
308.	B:13:8	(Untitled). With holograph corrections. Yellow paper, unlined. pp. 2-34 (33 l.) Incomplete draft of Act II.
309.	B:13:9	(Untitled). With holograph and other hand-written corrections. White paper unlined. pp. 34-63 (30 l.) Incomplete draft of Act II.
310.	B:13:10	"Bummidge II". With holograph notes. White paper, unlined. pp. 1-49 (49 l.) Complete draft of Act II.
311.	B:13:11	(Untitled). With holograph and other hand-written corrections. pp. 1-33 (33 l.) Complete draft of Act II.
312.	B:13:12	"The Last Analysis. Act II". With holograph corrections. Yellow paper, unlined. pp. 1-34 (34 l.) Complete draft of Act II.
313.	B:13:13	(Untitled). White paper, unlined. pp. 16-43, 43-51 (37 l.) Begins with "Bumm: Oh, torture".
314.	B:13:14	(Untitled). With holograph corrections. Yellow paper, unlined. pp. 35-63 (29 l.) Incomplete draft of Act II.
315.	B:13:15	(Untitled). With holograph corrections. Yellow paper, unlined. pp. 36-63 (28 l.) Incomplete draft of Act II.
316.	B:13:16	"The Last Analysis". With handwritten stage directions. White paper, unlined in a black Hart Stenographic Bureau folder, marked "Bummidge". Act I, pp. 1-63; Act II, pp. 1-48 (115 l.) Includes 4 l. of stage setting. Complete draft of the play.
317.	B:13:17	"The Upper Depths". Yellow paper, unlined. Act I, pp. 1-29; Act II, pp. 1-29 (58 l.) Complete early draft of the play.

The following folders contain miscellaneous typewritten or carbon pages of the various versions of The Last Analysis, composed at many different stages in its development. They are short sections of the play, and as before no attempt has been made to collate them with the final version or to place them in chronological order. The numbering of the acts given is that of Bellow's in that particular version. (242 l.)

318.   B:14:1   Yellow and white paper, unlined, in a folder
                marked "Bumm leftovers". pp. I-39-46, II-19,
                III-20-23, 26-28 (various versions) (23 l.)

319.   B:14:2   Yellow paper, unlined. pp. 1-18 (18 l.) Part
                of Act I of "Bummidge - A Farce in Three Acts".

320.   B:14:3   White paper, unlined. With holograph correc-
                tions. pp. 3-15 (13 l.) Probably part of Act I.

321.   B:14:4   White paper, unlined. pp. 1-4, 8-23, 25, 26,
                28, 29 (24 l.) Part of Act II.

322.   B:14:5   White paper, unlined. pp. 15, 16, 20-37 (20 l.)
                Part of Act II.

323.   B:14:6   White paper, unlined. With handwritten correc-
                tions. pp. 36-43 (8 l.) Part of Act II.

324.   B:14:7   Yellow paper, unlined. With handwritten
                corrections. pp. 36-48, 50-63 (29 l.) Part
                of Act II.

325.   B:14:8   White paper, unlined. pp. 46-50 (5 l.) Part
                of Act II.

326.   B:14:9   Yellow paper, unlined. With holograph correc-
                tions. pp. B-3-10 (8 l.) Part of Act I.

327.   B:14:10 White paper, unlined. pp. 56-58 (3 l.) Part
                of Act II.

328.   B:14:11 White paper, unlined. With handwritten correc-
                tions. pp. 57-72 (16 l.) Part of Act II.

329.   B:14:12 White paper, unlined. With holograph correc-
                tions. pp. 2-6 (5 l.) Part of Act II.

330.   B:14:13 Yellow paper, unlined. With holograph correc-
                tions. pp. 1-7 (7 l.) Part of Act I.

331.   B:14:14 Yellow paper, unlined. pp. 1-5 (5 l.) Act I
                of "Bummidge".

332.   B:14:15   White paper, unlined. pp. 1-2 (2 l.)
                 Beginning of play.

333.   B:14:16   White paper, unlined. pp. 1-7 (7 l.)
                 Part of Act I of "In a Beautiful World (or
                 Off the Couch by Christmas)".

334.   B:14:17   Yellow paper, unlined. pp. 1-8 (8 l.)
                 Part of Act II marked "Crash Program".

335.   B:14:18   Yellow paper, unlined, marked "Copy". pp. 28-
                 34 (7 l.) Part of Act I.

336.   B:14:19   White paper, unlined. With holograph correc-
                 tions. pp. 27-34, 36 (various versions) (10 l.)
                 Part of Act II.

337.   B:14:20   Yellow paper, unlined. With holograph correc-
                 tions. pp. 22-23, 32-38, 40 (various versions)
                 (17 l.) Part of Act II. Some of these pages
                 are carbon copies of pages in B:14:19.

338.   B:14:21   White paper, unlined. pp. 14, 11-24, 11-40,
                 41 (4 l.) Miscellaneous pages, some with hand-
                 written corrections.

339.   B:14:22   White and yellow paper, unlined. (3 l.) Notes
                 on the play and characters.

The following folders contain multigraphs and xerox copies, a
microfilm, and occasional typewritten pages, particularly
relevant to this section, of the different versions of The Last
Analysis. Some of them were used as acting copies during
productions of the play. No attempt has been made to place
them in chronological order.

350.   B:14:23   The Last Analysis Xerox of a typewritten copy,
                 Pink paper, unlined. Act I, pp. 1-52, Act II,
                 pp. 1-36, Act II, pp. 1-28 (116 l.) Early
                 version.

351.   B:14:24   The Last Analysis. Multigraph with holograph
                 corrections. White paper, unlined. Act I,
                 pp. 1-44, Act II, pp. 1-45 (various versions)
                 (96 l.) Almost the same as the final version,
                 with memorandum from the Viking Press.

352.   B:14:25   The Last Analysis. Typewritten with occasional
                 multigraph pages, and with holograph and other
                 handwritten corrections. White paper, unlined.
                 Act I, pp. 1-44, Act II, pp. 1-41 (86 l.)
                 Almost the same as the final version.

343. B:14:26 The Last Analysis. Xerox of a typewritten
copy with holograph and other typewritten
corrections. White paper, unlined. Act I,
pp. 1-44, Act II, pp. 1-36 (80 l.) Almost
the same as the final version.

344. B:15:1 The Last Analysis. Microfilm of the script.

345. B:15:2 The Upper Depths. Multigraph with holograph
corrections. White paper, unlined, in a
green Hart Stenographic Bureau notebook. Act
I, pp. 1-89, Act II, pp. 1-71 (161 l.) Roger
Stevens production copy.

346. B:15:3 Upper Depths. Multigraph, with holograph
corrections. White paper, unlined in a green
Hart Stenographic Bureau notebook. Act I, pp.
1-89 (90 l.) Same version as B:15:2 but with
different corrections. Also in this notebook
are several typewritten pages: White paper,
unlined. Act I, pp. 1-22, Act II, pp. 32-37
(various versions) (31 l.) Also several holo-
graphic pages: White paper, lined. pp. 1-27
(14 l.)

347. B:15:4 Upper Depths. Multigraph. White paper,
unlined, in a green Hart Stenographic Bureau
notebook. Act II, pp. 1-71 (71 l.) Same as Act
II of B:15:2.

348. B:15:5 Upper Depths. Multigraph. White paper,
unlined in a red Hart Stenographic Bureau notebook. Act I, pp. 1-52, Act II, pp. 1-53
(106 l.) Original version of the play, but
different from B:15:2.

349. B:15:6 Bummidge. Multigraph. White paper, unlined in
a dark blue Hart Stenographic Bureau notebook.
Act I, pp. 1-70, Act II, pp. 1-65 (136 l.)
Stevens Productions and David Oppenheim copy.
Also list of Staff and Cast for The Last
Analysis (3 l.) and several revised pages:
typewritten with holograph corrections and
holograph. White paper, unlined and yellow
paper, lined. (11 l.)

350. B:15:7 Bummidge. Xerox of a typewritten copy with
holograph corrections. White paper, unlined.
pp. 1-47 (47 l.) Not the same as the "Bummidge"
of B:15:6.

The following set of galley proofs is the only one in the collection, and is the final version of The Last Analysis. There are holograph corrections, and occasional handwritten comments probably by the editor.

351.   B:15:8   Acts I and II, pp. 2-40 (39 l.)

Clippings and Reviews

352.   B:15:9   "Hoffman's great, condensed outline for In a Beautiful World, It's Bellow's Toes We Tread on". Typewritten, white paper, unlined. pp. 1-7 (7 l.) Unidentified place of publication.

HERZOG: novel; published in 1964 by The Viking Press. The following 27 notebooks are drafts of Herzog, and represent various stages in the development of the novel. No attempt has been made to place them in chronological order, but they are arranged approximately according to the final sequence of events, with miscellaneous notes at the end, and each notebook has been assigned a number. Together with those notebooks are occasional loose holograph and typewritten leaves, which were found when the material was deposited in the Library. Werevere these leaves seem to form an integral part of the notebook, or wherever they show interesting changes or development, they have been left in their original place; otherwise they have been filed elsewhere.

353.   B:16:1   Notebook 1. "Dr. Herzog I". Holograph. Brown notebook. 27 l. with 9 loose holograph l. An early draft, beginning with Amram (later becomes Moses) Herzog's visit to the Trishanskys (later become Sisslers) in Martha's Vineyard, and continuing to Herzog's letter to Carlos (later becomes Sandor) Himmelstein. Much of this material is discarded in later drafts, and Herzog here is a physicist with leanings towards the humanities.

354.   B:16:2   Notebook 2. (Untitled). Holograph. Brown notebook. 23 l. A continuation of notebook 1, including Herzog's return to his apartment in Chelsea, and letters involving Vic and Mary, old friends with marital problems who do not appear in the final version (but reappear in Humboldt's Gift.

355.   B:16:3   Notebook 3. (Untitled). Holograph. Beige notebook. 84 l. Very early version about Brown seeking a divorce, and his friend the lawyer, Ranking. Back of notebook contains

notes about Reichuk's paintings and drawings.

356.   B:16:4   <u>Notebook 4</u>. "Latest I". Holograph. Brown notebook. 25 l. with 1 typewritten l, inserted. Early version of the beginning of the novel.

357.   B:16:5   <u>Notebook 5</u>. (Untitled). Holograph. Yellow Columbia notebook. 27 l. Contains letters to Edie (later becomes Tennie) Pontritter and letter to Smithers. Back of notebook contains notes for essay on film directors.

358.   B:16:6   <u>Notebook 6</u>. "Herzog I". Holograph. Green marbled National notebook. 95 l. with 14 loose typewritten l. inserted, and 1 loose typewritten l, inserted. Fairly late draft of the opening sections of novel.

359.   B:16:7   <u>Notebook 7</u>. "Notebook II". Holograph. Brown Standard Composition Book notebook. 37 l. Includes incidents and letters later discarded, about Herzog's life in Princeton and the problems of his "old friends", George Driver and Irene. (scenes which reappear in <u>Humboldt's Gift</u>).

360.   B:16:8   <u>Notebook 8</u>. (Untitled). Holograph. Brown Standard Composition Book notebook. 38 l. with 3 loose holograph l. Herzog's childhood in Canada; George and Irene of Princeton and George's death.

361.   B:16:9   <u>Notebook 9</u>. (Untitled). Holograph. Brown Champion notebook. 7 l. with 1 loose xerox l. and 1 loose holograph l. Draft of letter to Dr. Edvig, concerning Juliana's (later becomes Madeleine) paranoia.

362.   B:16:10   <u>Notebook 10</u>. "Herzog II". Holograph. Grey notebook. 76 l. Letter to Himmelstein, Geraldine Portnoy's letter, and a letter to Monsignor.

363.   B:16:11   <u>Notebook 11</u>. "Herzog III". Holograph. Light brown Stenographer notebook. 84 l. Begins with Julian's (later becomes Madeleine) preperations for work at Fordham. Life in Ludeyville and flashback to life with Daisy in the country where Herzog was writing his book, <u>Christianity and Romanticism</u>.

364. B:16:12   Notebook 12. "Herzog II (IV)". Holograph.
                Light brown Stenographer notebook. 65 l.
                Continuation of Notebook 11: Daisy leaves
                Ludeyville; Mr. Idwal, a minister and neighbor
                of Herzog at Ludeyville, unsuccessfully attempts
                to convert Herzog; letter to Dr. Mossbach and
                incomplete Nachman episode.

365. B:16:13   Notebook 13. "Herzog V". Holograph. Green
                marbled National notebook. 55 l. Continuation
                of Notebook 12, with Herzog's childhood in
                Canada, telephone call from Ramona, thoughts
                while preparing to see Ramona.

366. B:17:2   Notebook 14. (Untitled). Holograph. Brown
                notebook. 21 l. Herzog's thoughts while going
                to spend the evening with Ramona.

367. B:17:3   Notebook 15. (Untitled). Holograph. Brown
                University of Chicago notebook. 41 l. Herzog's
                thoughts while Ramona prepares breakfast. Back
                of book contains draft of letter to Mr.
                Bloomgarten concerning the play The Interviewer.

368. B:17:4   Notebook 16. (Untitled). Holograph. Red
                Easywrite notebook. 32 l. Begins with Jewish-
                Catholic conflict, and includes Herzog's cab
                drive with Ramona to her florist shop, early
                version of letter and interview with Dr. Edvig.
                Herzog is an ethnologist in this version. Front
                of notebook contains copy of letter to Mr.
                Sackett.

369. B:17:5   Notebook 17. (Untitled). Holograph. Green
                Easywrite notebook. 49 l. with 5 loose holo-
                graph l. and 1 loose typewritten l. Herzog
                addresses George Hoberly, talk with New York
                lawyer, Rubenstein (later becomes Simkin),
                Herzog at the court building in New York,
                flashback to childhood in Canada, and a letter
                to Dr. Edvig.

370. B:17:6   Notebook 18. "Herzog Oct. '63". Holograph.
                Beige National notebook. 26 l. Herzog wakens
                while Ramona sleeps; Herzog talks to his New
                York lawyer.

371. B:17:7   Notebook 19. (Untitled). Holograph. Green
                marbled Compositions notebook. 59 l. with 1
                loose holograph l. Herzog's thoughts in the
                court building; back of notebook contains

Herzog's thoughts while ramona sleeps, break-
fast with Ramona and a talk with a New York
lawyer.

372.   B:17:8   Notebook 20. (Untitled). Beige Alma Mater
notebook. 23 l. with 61 loose holograph l.
Notebook contains Herzog's thoughts about his
mother's death, and the loose pages contain
the flight from New York to Chicago after the
court scene; flashback to New York where Herzog
found the letter from Geraldine Portnoy; and
Herzog's arrival in Chicago when he walks by his
home on Harper Avenue and visits Asphalter's
apartment.

373.   B:17:9   Notebook 21. (Untitled). Holograph. Green
marbled Compositions book. 59 l. with 9 loose
holograph l. Herzog's return to Chicago and
walk by his home. He stays the night in a hotel,
rather than in Asphalter's apartment, as in the
final version.

374.   B:17:10   Notebook 22. (Untitled). Holograph. Brown
National notebook. 23 l. with 11 loose holograph l. and 2 loose typewritten l. Details of
the car accident.

375.   B:17:11   Notebook 23. (Untitled). Holograph. Brown
notebook. 39 l. with 1 loose l. Trip to the
museum with June, car accident, police station,
and Herzog's return to Ludeyville.

376.   B:18:1   Notebook 24. (Untitled). Holograph. Brown
Vernon Memo notebook. 69 l. Back of notebook
contains notes for Herzog, including a
description of Juliana (later becomes Madeleine).
Front of notebook contains names and addresses,
and some notes for The Last Analysis.

377.   B:18:2   Notebook 25. (Untitled). Holograph. Brown
Gregg Memo notebook. 31 l. Random Herzog
fragments and notes for a lecture delivered at
Wellesley College.

378.   B:18:3   Notebook 26. (Unitiled). Holograph. Red
Paper King Memo notebook. 21 l. Miscellaneous Herzog and personal notes.

379.   B:18:4   Notebook 27. (Untitled). Holograph. Brown
                  Royal Memo notebook. 30 l. Miscellaneous
                  Herzog and other personal notes.

The following manuscript pages are either short portions of
the text, or miscellaneous notes connected with the writing of
Herzog which have not been arranged in a specific order. They
are all holograph. 49 l. Consists of:

380.   B:18:5   White paper, linèd. 8 l. Begins "corrupt.
                  It is angry. A forces is going on ...", and
                  continues with the scene where Herzog goes to
                  visit his old friend Libbie. Last page also
                  includes miscellaneous notes.

381.   B:18:6   White paper, lined. 5 l. Some paragraphs about
                  Grensbach and some about Ramona; other
                  miscellaneous notes.

382.   B:18:7   White paper, unlined. 12 l. Herzog thinks
                  about his ex-wife Daisy.

383.   B:18:8   White paper, lined. 5 l. Fragments about
                  Daitch; Isak helps the drunken Daitch upstairs,
                  a description of Daitch, along with other
                  miscellaneous notes.

384.   B:18:9   Miscellaneous fragments. 19 l.

The following folders contain typewritten, carbon, or xerox
drafts of Herzog composed at different stages during its development. They are all fairly long portions of the novel, but no
attempt has been made to place them in chronological order.
1063 l. Consists of:

385.   B:18:10   "Hertzog. Saul Bellow". Xerox of a type-
                  written draft. Pink paper, unlined. pp. 1-83
                  (83 l.) Early draft from beginning of novel
                  to episodes concerning friends from Princeton
                  and Herzog's ex-wife, Daisy.

386.   B:18:11   (Untitled). Carbon with holograph correc-
                  tions. White paper, unlined. pp. 3-113
                  (various versions). (113 l.) From the
                  beginning of the novel to the letter to
                  Eisenhower.

387.   B:18:12   "Herzog: Revised Version". Carbon, with some
               xerox pages. White and yellow paper, unlined.
               pp. 1-153 (various version) (190 l.) From the
               begginning of the novel to the letter to Nachman
               which is written while Ramona sleeps.

388.   B:18:13   "Herzog. Saul Bellow. New version". Type-
               written, with handwritten comments. White
               paper, lined. pp. 1-112 (various versions)
               (113 l.) From the beginning of the novel to
               letters to Carlos (later becomes Sandor)
               Himmelstein, and Eisenhower.

389.   B:18:14   (Untitled). Typewritten with holograph correc-
               tions. White paper, lined and unlined. pp.
               3-63 (various versions) (65 l.) From the
               beginning of the novel to Herzog's visit with
               the Sislers.

390.   B:18:15   "Herzog". Typewritten with holograph correc-
               tions. White paper, unlined. pp. 1-60 (60 l.)
               Beginning of the novel to episode with Axel
               Johannes, Herzog's friend and former student,
               who here informs him of Juliana's (later
               becomes Madeleine) affair with Valentine.

391.   B:18:16   (Untitled). Typewritten with holograph correc-
               tions. White paper, lined. pp. 1-57 (57 l.)
               Opening sections of the novel.

392.   B:18:17   "Alas and Hurray". Typewritten with holograph
               corrections. White paper, lined. pp. 1-66
               (66 l.) From the beginning of the novel to the
               letter to Hillel (later becomes Nachman). Here
               Herzog is the author of the textbook Contemporary
               Humanities.

393.   B:18:18   (Untitled). Typewritten with holograph correc-
               tions. White paper, lined. pp. 15-277 (263 l.)
               Herzog buying clothes for the trip to Martha's
               Vineyard, to his visit with Ramona in New York.

394.   B:19:1   "Alas and Hurray". Typewritten with holograph
               corrections. White paper, lined. pp. 1-81
               (various versions) (113 l.) to letter to Dr.
               Schonbaum.

395.   B:19:2   (Untitled). Carbon with holograph corrections,
               and occasional xerox pages. White, yellow, and
               pink paper, unlined. pp. 1-48 (various versions)
               (40 l.) Opening sections of the novel.

The following folders contain short typewritten or carbon
portions of the text rewritten by the author at various stages
during the composition of the novel. No attempt has been made
to place them in order in which they were written, but they
are grouped approximately according to the general sequence of
events in the final version.

a) Opening pages of Herzog, and Herzog riding to Martha's
    Vineyard.
b) Letters to Dr. Edvig.
c) Herzog's visit with the Sisslers in Martha's Vineyard.
d) Letter to Monsignor, and life with Juliana (later becomes
    Madeleine) before marriage.
e) Herzog's life in Princeton and his ex-wife Daisy.
f) Herzog's childhood in Canada.
g) Letter to Eisenhower and Sono.
h) Ramona.
i) Herzog's day in court.
j) The car accident.
k) Herzpg's final visit to Ludeyville.
l) Miscellaneous.

Because this is only a rudimentary division, and because it
represents a period of extensive revision on the part of the
author, there is much overlapping from one category to another.
Occasional holograph leaves have been left in order to retain
the sense of the draft. 1746 l. Consists of:

a) Opening pages of "Herzog," and Herzog riding to Martha's
    Vineyard. 393 l. Consists of:

396. B:19:3   White paper, lined. Typewritten. pp. 2-16
               (15 l.) Opening pages, including Juliana's
               (later becomes Madelaine) car accident, an
               episode discarded in subsequent revisions.

397. B:19:4   White paper, unlined. Carbon. pp. 1-6a
               (various versions) (13 l.) Opening pages.

398. B:19:5   White paper, lined. Typewritten with holo-
               graph corrections. pp. 1-6a (various versions)
               (10 l.) Opening pages.

399. B:19:6   White paper, unlined. Carbon. pp. 3-6
               (various versions) (7 l.) Opening pages:
               same as part of B:19:5.

400. B:19:7   White paper, lined. Typewritten. pp. 3-6
               (3 l.) Opening pages.

401. B:19:8   White paper, lined. Typewritten. pp. 3-5f
               (various versions) (9 l.) Opening pages.

402. B:19:9   White paper, lined. Typewritten with holo-
                graph corrections. pp. 8-13 (6 l.) Opening
                pages.

403. B:19:10 White paper, lined. Typewritten, with holo-
                graph corrections. pp. 1-9 (various versions)
                (12 l.) Opening pages.

404. B:19:11 White paper, lined. Typewritten with holo-
                graph corrections. pp. 10-30 (various
                versions) (22 l.) Opening pages.

405. B:19:12 White paper, unlined. Typewritten with holo-
                graph corrections. pp. 14-20 (7 l.) Letter
                to Edie (later becomes Tennie) Pontritter and
                memo to Smithers.

406. B:19:13 White paper, lined. Typewritten with holo-
                graph corrections. pp. 19-24 (6 l.) Letter
                to Pontritter and memo to Smithers.

407. B:19:14 White paper, unlined. Carbon. pp. 22-39
                (17 l.) From letter to Aunt Shortie to letter
                to the Times.

408. B:19:15 White and yellow paper, unlined. Carbon.
                pp. 19-43 (25 l.) Letters to Pontritter, Aunt
                Short, Dr. Strawforth, Dr. Bhave, Shapiro, and
                others.

409. B:19:16 White paper, unlined. Carbon. pp. 17-48,
                50-60 (43 l.) Letters written in the cab and
                the train, including one to Axel Johannes
                (later becomes Asphalter). In this early
                version he is considerably less sensitive than
                Asphalter, and in contrast to Asphalter's
                slovenly appearance, has "beautifully cut fair
                hair", wears a suede jacket, and drives a
                Jaguar.

410. B:19:17 White paper, lined. Typewritten with holo-
                graph corrections and some complete holograph
                l. pp. 24b-30 (various versions) (18 l.) Memo
                to Smithers, letter to Aunt Short, flashback
                to Juliana's (later becomes Madeleine) outbreaks
                of temper and car accident.

411. B:19:18 White paper, unlined. Typewritten. pp. 22-24,
                31(4 l.) Letter to Aunt Short, etc.

412. B:19:19 White paper, unlined. Carbon and multigraph, with holograph and other handwritten corrections. pp. 54-69 (various versions) (21 l.) Fairly late draft of letter to Asphalter.

413. B:19:20 White paper, unlined. Carbon. pp. 34-35 (2 l.) Flashback to Valentine Grenzbach (later becomes Gersbach).

414. B:19:21 White paper, unlined. Typewritten. pp. 38-40 (3 l.) Early version of letter to Dr. Strawforth.

415. B:19:22 White paper, lined. Typewritten with holograph corrections. pp. 31-35, 38 (6 l.) Letters to Aunt Short, Dr. Strawforth, Dr. Bhave, and the Credit Department of Marshall Fields.

416. B:19:23 White paper, lined. Typewritten with holograph corrections. pp. 30-42 (13 l.) Letters to Dr. Strawforth, Dr. Bhave, Shapiro, Marshall Fields, and a quarrel with Juliana (later becomes Madeleine) about money.

417. B:19:24 White paper, lined, Typewritten with holograph corrections. pp. 40-41 (2 l.) Fragment of letter.

418. B:19:25 White paper, unlined. Carbon. pp. 40-41 (2 l.) Fragment of letter.

419. B:19:26 White paper, unlined. Carbon and multigraph with holograph corrections. pp. 78 (2 l.) Letter to Stevenson.

420. B:19:27 White paper, lined. Typewritten with holograph corrections. pp. 83-93 (10 l.) Herzog's letter to Himmelstein.

421. B:19:28 White paper, unlined. Carbon. pp. 48-57, 60-70 (21 l.) Letter to Dr. Bhave, Marshall Fields, etc.

422. B:19:29 White paper, lined. Typewritten with holograph corrections. pp. 82-107 (26 l.) Letters to Sono and Himmelstein.

423. B:19:30 White paper, lined. Typewritten. pp. 65-72 (8 l.) Description of Daitch.

424. B:19:31 White paper, lined. Typewritten with holograph corrections. pp. 95-102 (8 l.) Letter to Hillel (later becomes Nachman); a letter to Shura.

425.   B:19:32   White paper, lined. Typewritten with holograph
                   corrections. pp. 63-66 (4 l.) Herzog in his
                   Chelsea apartment.

426.   B:19:33   White paper, lined. Typewritten. pp. 64-65
                   (3 l.) Letter to Marcus etc. White paper,
                   unlined. Carbon. pp. 64-65 (3 l.) Copy of
                   above pages.

427.   B:19:34   White paper, lined. Typewritten. pp. 85-94
                   (10 l.) Letter to Bakeless.

428.   B:19:35   White paper, unlined. Typewritten with holo-
                   graph corrections. pp. 101-132 (32 l.) Herzog's
                   thoughts about Juliana (later becomes Madeleine)
                   and the problems of his friends George Driver
                   and Irene (later becomes Humboldt and Kathleen).

b)   Letters to Dr. Edvig. 156 l. Consists of:

429.   B:19:36   White paper, lined. Typewritten with holograph
                   corrections. pp. 106-126, 156, 159-163, 165,
                   169, 173-178, 181, 187-194 (various versions)
                   (65 l.) Letter to Dr. Edvig.

430.   B:19:37   White paper, lined and unlined, and yellow
                   paper, unlined. Carbon. pp. 150-183 (34 l.)
                   Letter to Dr. Edvig, which includes life with
                   Juliana (later becomes Madeleine) in New York
                   before marriage, and in Ludeyville.

431.   B:19:38   White paper, unlined. Carbon. pp. 85, 119,
                   137, 138, 149 (5 l.) Letter to Dr. Edvig.

432.   B:19:39   White paper, unlined. Carbon. pp. 173-177
                   (5 l.) Letter to Dr. Edvig.

433.   B:19:40   White paper, unlined. Carbon. pp. 174-178
                   181 (6 l.) Letter to Dr. Edvig.

434.   B:19:41   White paper, unlined. Carbon. pp. 156, 161,
                   162, 165, 174, 175, (7 l.) Letter to Dr. Edvig.

435.   B:19:42   White paper, unlined. Carbon. pp. 175-178
                   (4 l.) Letter to Dr. Edvig.

436.   B:19:43   White paper, unlined. Xerox of a typewritten
                   copy, with holograph corrections. pp. 199-223
                   (25 l.) Letter to Dr. Edvig, written while
                   Herzog visits Ramona in her New York apartment.

437.   B:19:44   White paper, unlined. Typewritten. pp. 274b-278 (5 l.) Letter to Dr. Edvig, written while Herzog is in New York Court Building.

c)   Herzog's visit with the Sisslers in Martha's Vineyard. 95 l. Consists of:

438.   B:20:1   White paper, lined. Typewritten with holograph corrections. pp. 3-7 (5 l.) Early draft when Herzog meets Libbie Sissler in New York and she invites him to spend a weekend at Martha's Vineyard.

439.   B:20:2   White paper, unlined. Carbon. pp. 59-60 (2 l.) Libbie meets Herzog on his arrival at Martha's Vine yard.

440.   B:20:3   White paper, lined. Typewritten with holograph corrections. pp. 45-46 (3 l.) Herzog talks with Libbie at Martha's Vineyard.

441.   B:20:4   White paper, lined. Typewritten with holograph corrections. pp. 54-60 (7 l.) Early draft of dinner with the Sisslers, and letter to Shapiro.

442.   B:20:5   White paper, lined. Typewritten with holograph corrections. pp. 64-72a (10 l.) Scenes with Miss Thurnwald which have been deleted from final version.

443.   B:20:6   White paper, unlined. Carbon. pp. 71-126 (56 l.) Dinner with the Sisslers and letter to Himmelstein.

444.   B:20:7   White paper, lined. Typewritten with holograph corrections. pp. 74-83 (12 l.) Herzog's return to New York after visit with the Sisslers, and letter to Himmelstein.

d)   Letter to Monsignor Hilton, and life with Juliana (later becomes Madeleine) before marriage. 132 l. Consists of:

445.   B:20:8   White paper, lined. Typewritten with holograph corrections. pp. 58-83 (26 l.) Letter to Monsignor and life with Juliana.

446.   B:20:9   White paper, unlined. Carbon. pp. 132-136 (5 l.) Letter to Monsignor.

447.   B:20:10   White paper, unlined. Carbon. pp. 139-148 (10 l.) Life with Juliana.

448.   B:20:11   White paper, lined. Typewritten with holograph corrections. pp. 149-151 (3 l.) Letter to Sunny, Juliana's roommate in New York.

449.   B:20:12   White paper, lined. Typewritten with handwritten grammatical corrections. pp. 127-148 (22 l.) Letter to Monsignor and recollections of life with Juliana in New York.

450.   B:20:13   White paper, lined. Typewritten with holograph corrections. pp. 135-137 (3 l.) Fragment of letter to Monsignor.

451.   B:20:14   White paper, lined, and yellow paper, lined. Typewritten with holograph corrections, and 1 holograph l. pp. 95-105 (11 l.) Letter to Monsignor.

452.   B:20:15   White paper, lined. Typewritten with holograph and other handwritten corrections. pp. 113-126 (14 l.) Letter to Sono about Juliana, and letter to Monsignor.

453.   B:20:16   White paper, unlined. Carbon. pp. 110-112, 122-135 (also numbered 115-117, 127-140) (17 l.) Copy of part of B:20:15.

454.   B:20:17   White paper, lined. Typewritten. pp. 167-172 (5 l.) Letter to Monsignor.

455.   B:20:18   White paper, lined. Typewritten with holograph corrections. pp. 143-149 (7 l.) Letter to Monsignor.

456.   B:20:19   Miscellaneous pages all connected with the letter to Monsignor. Typewritten and carbon. (9 l.)

e)   <u>Herzog's life in Princeton, and his ex-wife Daisy.</u> 159 l. Consists of:

457.   B:20:20   White paper, lined. Typewritten with holograph corrections. pp. 69-100 (32 l. with 1 holograph l.) Begins with letter to Monsignor and recounts Herzog's life in Princeton, including flashback to Daisy's visit to Herzog who is in hospital with pneumonia.

458.   B:20:21   Yellow paper, unlined. Carbon. pp. 198-224 (27 l.) Herzog's life in Princeton, thoughts about Driver.

459. B:20:22 Yellow paper, unlined. Carbon. pp. 213-221
(9 1.) Similar to portions of B:20:21.

460. B:20:23 White paper, lined. Typewritten with holograph
corrections. pp. 196-226 (31 1.) Life in
Princeton, and George Driver.

461. B:20:24 White paper, lined. Typewritten. pp. 198-229
(32 1.) Letter to Hoberly, life in Princeton,
and episodes with George Driver.

462. B:20:25 White paper, lined. Typewritten. pp. 222-236
(various versions) (17 1.) Life in Princeton.

463. B:20:26 White paper, unlined. Carbon with holograph
corrections. pp. 139-143 (also numbered 144-
148) (5 1.) Daisy visits Herzog.

464. B:20:27 Yellow paper, unlined. Carbon. pp. 225-229
(5 1.) Daisy visits Herzog.

f) Herzog's childhood in Canada. 14 1. Consists of:

465. B:20:28 White paper, lined. Typewritten with holograph
corrections. pp. 67-69 (8 1.) Childhood
in Canada.

466. B:20:29 Yellow paper, unlined. Carbon. pp. 68-72
(various versions) (6 1.) Herzog's childhood
in Canada.

g) Letter to Eisenhower and Sono. 18 1. Consists of:

467. B:20:30 White paper, lined. Typewritten with holograph
corrections. pp. 93a-94 (2 1.) Fragment of
letter to Eisenhower.

468. B:20:31 White paper, unlined. Carbon. pp. 127-131
(5 1.) Letter to Eisenhower.

469. B:20:32 Yellow paper, unlined. Carbon with holograph
corrections. pp. 189-191 (3 1.) Fragment of
letter to Eisenhower.

470. B:20:33 White paper, unlined. pp. 189-191 (3 1.)
Xerox copy of B:20:32

471. B:20:34 White paper, lined. Typewritten. pp. 127-131
(5 1.) Letter to Sono.

h)   Ramona. 466 l. Consists of:

472.   B:20:35   White paper, lined. Typewritten with holograph corrections. pp. 9-11 (3 l.) Description of Ramona while Herzog buys new clothes at her suggestion.

473.   B:20:36   White paper, unlined. Carbon. pp. 9-11 (3 l.) Description of Ramona.

474.   B:20:37   White paper, lined. Typewritten. pp. 96-107 (12 l.) Entitled "Herzog Visiting with Ramona".

475.   B:20:38   White paper, lined. Typewritten. pp. 132-137 (6 l.) Entitled "Herzog Visiting with Ramona".

476.   B:20:39   White paper, lined. Typewritten. pp. 101-102 (2 l.) Description of Ramona. Yellow paper, unlined. pp. 101-102 (2 l.) Carbon copy of B:20:39.

477.   B:20:40   White paper, lined. Typewritten with hand-written grammatical corrections. pp. 149-245 (97 l.) Entitled "Herzog's Visit with Ramona".

478.   B:20:41   White paper, unlined. Carbon. pp. 184-228 (45 l.) Beginning of visit with Ramona to letters written while Ramona sleeps.

479.   B:20:42   White paper, lined. Typewritten with holograph corrections. pp. 145-171 (27 l.) From dinner with Ramona to letters written while she sleeps.

480.   B:20:43   White paper, lined. Typewritten with holograph corrections. pp. 110-123 (14 l.) Description of Ramona.

481.   B:20:44   White paper, lined. Typewritten with holograph corrections. pp. 138-144 (7 l.) Description of Ramona.

482.   B:20:45   White paper, lined. Typewritten with holograph corrections. pp. 172-186 (15 l.) Mainly about Nachman.

483.   B:21:1   White paper, lined. Typewritten with holograph corrections. pp. 124-141a (18 l.) Description of Ramona.

484.   B:21:2   White paper, lined. Typewritten with holograph
                 corrections. pp. 142-157 (16 l.) Letters written
                 while Ramona sleeps.

485.   B:21:3   Yellow paper, unlined. Carbon. pp. 215-233
                 (19 l.) Description of Ramona.

486.   B:21:4   Yellow paper, unlined. Carbon. pp. 136-141
                 (6 l.) Herzog's thoughts while Ramona prepares
                 for bed.

487.   B:21:5   White paper, lined. Typewritten. pp. 137a-
                 139 (3 l.) Herzog's thoughts while Ramona
                 prepares for bed.

488.   B:21:6   White paper, lined. Typewritten with holograph
                 corrections. pp. 193-195 (3 l.) Herzog leaves
                 Ramona after awakening in the middle of the
                 night.

489.   B:21:7   White paper, lined. Typewritten with holograph
                 corrections. pp. 136-138, 140-141 (5 l.)
                 Letters written while Ramona sleeps.

490.   B:21:8   White paper, lined. Typewritten with holograph
                 corrections. pp. 175-189 (15 l.) Letters written
                 while Ramona sleeps.

491.   B:21:9   White paper, unlined. Typewritten. pp. 246-
                 250, 261, 266, 272-274 (various versions) (11 l.)
                 Letters written while Ramona sleeps.

492.   B:21:10   White paper, unlined. Carbon. pp. 246-251,
                 258-260, 266 (various versions) (11 l.) Letters
                 written while Ramona sleeps.

493.   B:21:11   Yellow paper, unlined. Carbon with holograph
                 corrections. pp. 217, 220-224, 226 (7 l.)
                 Letters written while Ramona sleeps.

494.   B:21:12   White paper, unlined. pp. 217, 220-224, 226
                 (7 l.) Xerox of B:21:11.

495.   B:21:13   White paper, unlined. Typewritten with holograph
                 corrections. pp. 246-281 (36 l.) From letters
                 and thoughts while Ramona sleeps to the cab drive
                 to the Court Building.

496.   B:21:14   White paper, lined. Typewritten with holograph
                 corrections. pp. 196-204 (10 l.) Letters while
                 Ramona sleeps, including letter to Monsignor.

497.   B:21:15   White paper, lined. Typewritten with holograph
               corrections. pp. 190-195 (6 l.) Ramona awakes
               to find Herzog writing letters.

498.   B:21:16   White paper, lined. Typewritten. pp. 179-
               181 (3 l.) Ramona's discovery.

499.   B:21:17   Yellow paper, unlined. Carbon. 273-277 (5 l.)
               Ramona's discovery.

500.   B:21:18   White paper, unlined. Carbon. pp. 170-190
               (12 l.) Letter written while Ramona sleeps,
               and telephone call from George Hoberly.

501.   B:21:19   White paper, lined. Typewritten. pp. 182-
               184 (3 l.) After George Hoberly's call.

502.   B:21:20   White paper, lined. Typewritten. pp. 206-
               208 (3 l.) After Hoberly's call.

503.   B:21:21   White paper, lined. Typewritten with holograph
               corrections. pp. 213-223 (11 l.) Thoughts
               addressed to Hoberley. Yellow paper, unlined.
               Carbon copy of B:21:21 (8 l.)

504.   B:21:22   White paper, lined. Typewritten. pp. 183-
               187 (5 l.) Entitled "To George Hoberley".

505.   B:21:23   White paper, lined. Typewritten with holograph
               corrections. pp. 188, 207, 214, 215, 231-233
               (7 l.) Herzog leaves Ramona after taking her to
               work.

506.   B:21:24   Yellow paper, unlined. pp. 231-233 (3 l.)
               Carbon copy of part of B:21:23.

i)   Herzog's day in court, and his return to Chicago   219 l.
     Consists of:

507.   B:21:25   White paper, lined.   Typewritten with holograph
               corrections. pp. 209-233 (25 l.) Entitled
               "Herzog's Day in Court".

508.   B:21:26   White paper, lined. Typewritten. pp. 278-284
               (7 l.) Entitled "Herzog's Day in Court".
               Yellow paper, unlined. pp. 278-284 (7 l.)
               Carbon copy of B:21:26.

509.   B:21:27   White paper, unlined. Typewritten with holo-
               graph corrections. pp. 241-261 (21 l.) Morning
               with Ramona, and Herzog's call to New York
               lawyer, Rubenstein (later becomes Simkin).

510. B:21:28 Yellow paper, unlined. Carbon. pp. 241-279
                (39 l.) Copy of B:21:27.

511. B:21:29 White paper, unlined. Typewritten with holo-
                graph corrections. pp. 242-245, 254-256, 259,
                263, 264, 266, 268, 270, 272-280 (various
                versions) (21 l.) Herzog leaves Ramona at the
                florist shop, court scene and letter to Dr.
                Edvig written at Court Room.

512. B:21:30 Yellow paper, unlined. Carbon. pp. 242-259,
                272-274, 280 (22 l.) Part is the same as part
                of B:21:29.

513. B:21:31 White paper, lined and unlined. Typewritten
                pp. 246-260 (various versions) (22 l.) Court
                scenes.

514. B:21:32 White paper, lined. Typewritten. pp. 230-236
                (7 l.) Lunch at Tracey's Bar after leaving
                Ramona. Yellow paper, unlined. Carbon. pp.
                230-236 (7 l.) Copy of B:21:32.

515. B:21:33 White paper, unlined. Typewritten with hand-
                written comments. pp. 253-254 (2 l.) Herzog
                talks to Rubenstein (later becomes Simkin).

516. B:21:34 White paper, unlined. Typewritten with holo-
                graph corrections. pp. 246-258 (13 l.) Herzog
                talks with Simkin.

517. B:21:35 White paper, unlined. Typewritten with holo-
                graph corrections. pp. 271-273, 278-280
                (6 l.) Court scenes

518. B:21:36 Yellow paper, unlined. Carbon, with 1 xerox l.
                pp. 254-256, 272-280 (various versions)
                (12 l.) Court scenes.

519. B:21:37 White paper, unlined. Carbon. pp. 279-281
                (3 l.) Court scenes.

520. B:21:38 Yellow paper, unlined. Carbon with holograph
                corrections. pp. 309, 316, 319-320 (4 l.)
                Herzog's talk with Phoebe and Asphalter on his
                return.

521. B:21:39 White paper, unlined. Typewritten. (1 l.)
                Herzog's thoughts on the plane.

j)   The car accident. 118 1. Consists of:

522.   B:21:40   White paper, unlined. Typewritten with holo-
                   graph corrections. pp. 333-356a, 367, 391a-
                   400 (various versions) (38 1.) Car accident
                   and at the police stations.

523.   B:21:41   White paper, unlined. Xerox of a typewritten
                   copy. pp. 330, 332-339, 342-398 (66 1.) Copy
                   of some of B:21:40.

524.   B:21:42   Yellow paper, unlined. Carbon with holograph
                   corrections. pp. 334-346 (3 1.) Carbon of some
                   of B:21:40.

525.   B:21:43   Yellow paper, unlined. Carbon with holograph
                   corrections. pp. 338-342, 353-355, 367 (various
                   versions) (11 1.) Ride in squad car and at
                   police station.

k)   Herzog's final visit to Ludeyville. 28 1. Consists of:

526.   B:21:44   White paper, unlined. Typewritten with holo-
                   graph corrections. pp. 372-378, 382, 388-
                   389 (10 1.) Letter writing in Ludeyville.

527.   B:21:45   Yellow paper, unlined. Carbon with holograph
                   corrections. pp. 372-377, 391-398 (15 1.)
                   Copy of some of B:21:44.

528.   B:21:46   Yellow paper, unlined. Carbon. pp. 382, 388-
                   389 (3 1.) Will's arrival at Ludeyville.

l)   Miscellaneous. 107 1. Consists of:

529.   B:21:47   Miscellaneous typewritten, carbon and xerox
                   fragments. 40 1.

530.   B:22:1   "Pages replaced, in ribbon copy before setting,
                   by revised pages newly typed by authour. Thus
                   these pages valuable, as indicate revisions
                   made for final setting copy. cc9/66". (51 1.)

531.   B:22:2   "Pages retyped for setting copy. Some correx.
                   in Bellow's hand, others cc transferred from
                   carbon. cc 9/66". (16 1.)

First Final Draft.
The following folders contain a complete carbon copy of the
final draft of Herzog with holograph corrections, as used
by the printers. There are occasional xerox and typewritten
pages included, and also comments by the editors. Entitled
"Herzog A Novel by Saul Bellow. Author's revised Ms. copy III".
423 1. Consists of:

532. B:22:3 pp. 1-100 (107 1.)

533. B:22:4 pp. 101-200 (109 1.)

534. B:22:5 pp. 201-300 (104 1.)

535. B:22:6 pp. 301-400 (103 1.)

Second Final Draft.
The following folders contain a second complete draft of Herzog,
a xerox copy with occasional carbon and typewritten pages
included, all with holograph and editorial corrections, which
was sent to the press. 417 1. Consists of:

536. B:22:7 pp. 1-100 (108 1.)

537. B:22:8 pp. 101-200 (100 1.)

538. B:22:9 pp. 201-300 (106 1.)

539. B:22:10 pp. 301-400 (103 1.)

Third Final Draft
The following folders contain a third complete draft of Herzog,
the setting copy of typewritten and xerox pages, with holograph
and editorial corrections. 4 1. Consists of:

540. B:22:11 pp. 1-100 (115 1.)

541. B:23:1 pp. 101-200 (108 1.)

542. B:23:2 pp. 201-300 (105 1.)

543. B:23:3 pp. 301-400 (113 1.)

Galley Proofs
The following folders contain the galley proofs for Herzog:
first is a complete set with Bellow's own corrections; then
xerox copies of portions of this set and pages for insertion
and replacement in this set; and finally the remaining
editorial and miscellaneous galleys. 346 1. Consists of:

544. B:23:4 Galleys 1-125 (125 1.) Complete copy of
              Herzog, with holograph corrections.

545. B:23:5 Galleys 100 and 116 (9 1.) Typewritten and
              xerox pages for insertion in the set of proofs
              in B:23:4.

61

546. B:23:6 Galleys 1-73 and 108-121 (87 1.) Galleys with
                transcriptions of the corrections in B:23:4.

547. B:23:7 Galleys 74-107 and 122-125 (83 1.) Xerox copies
                of portions of the author's corrected set of
                galleys.

548. B:23:8 Galleys 27, 55, 71, 74-91, 85-86, 88, 92-100,
                106, 111, 113, 116-120, 122-125 (42 1.) Galley
                proofs with editorial corrections and comments.

549. B:23:9 Envelope containing torn pieces of corrected
                galley proofs (possibly galleys 74-108 and 122-
                125).

Miscellaneous Material.

550. B:24:1 Galley proofs, unnumbered, which represent
                the selection of Herzog which appeared in the
                Saturday Evening Post. 30 1. (See entry 22).

551. B:24:2 Esquire, July, 1963. Contains "Letter to Dr.
                Edvig" by Saul Bellow. (See entry 26).

552. B:24:3 Dictabelts. A reading of pp. 1-169 of Bellow's
                handwritten manuscript.

Clippings and Reviews.
The following section consists of a small collection of English
language reviews, and an extensive collection of German clippings
and reviews which Verlag Keipenheuer & Witsch, publishers of
Bellow's novels in Köln-Marienburg, sent to him in February,
1966. These 113 clippings were taken from German newspapers and
magazines from the last few months of 1965 and reveal Herzog's
popularity in Germany. They are not in folders, but a list of
clippings follows.

553. B:24:4 English Language clippings and reviews.

554. B:24:5 1.Nordpress - Feuilleton. Der preisgekrönte
                "Herzog" - Saul Bellow Roman.

                2.Civis: Magazin fur Kultur und Politik, p. 29.

                3.Neue Wege: Kulturzeitschrift junger Menschen.
                  p. 44.

                4.Zürcher Woche, 10 Dezember 1965. Sensibler Tor.

                5.Wiesbadener Kurier. 4 Dezember 1965. Der
                  preisgekönte, Herzog.

6. Studio Radio Bern 6 Jan. 1966. "Was haben Sie im verganenen Jahr gelesen".

7. Der Spiegel 27 Oktober 1965. "Der Beschamte Rebell" p. 154.

8. Film und Frau 11. Januar 1966. Drei amerikanische Romance p. 32.

9. Bücherschiff Dezember 1965. p. 19.

10. Der Leihbuchandler. advertisement p. 133.

11. Allgemeine 7 Januar 1966. "Die Passion des Moses E. Herzog.

12. A-Z - Feuilleton 9 Dezember 1965. "Von Sartre bis Hemingway".

13. "Ein Griff in unsere Bücherkiste".

14. Munchener Literatur Dienst. Saul Bellow/Herzog.

15. Zeitschritt für Verisicherungswesen. Herzog von Saul Bellow.

16. Deutschlandsender, Berlin-Ost. Saul Bellow: "Herzog".

17. Afrika Januar/Februar 1966. Romane.

18. Der Abend, Berlin.

19. Bücher im Gespräch. Saul Bellow: Herzog.

20. Literaturbeobachter Dezember 1965 Saul Bellow Herzog. p. 1276.

21. "Geschenk für IHN"

22. Bücher und Leser. November 1965. Ein Mann spricht mit sich selbst.

23. Der Buecherwurm Dezember 1965. Saul Bellow: Herzog.

24. Blick vom Hochhaus Januar 1966.

25. Westermanns Monatshefte Nr. 2 1966. "Herzog" -- ein grosser Roman.

26. Landes-Kriminalblatt November 1965. Saul Bellow: Herzog.

27. Wiener Wochenblatt Dez. 25, 1965. Neue Romane:

28. JCTVS 1965. Saul Bellow "Herzog" p. 15.

29. Bellow; "Herzog" Günter Blöcker

30. Saul Bellow: "Herzog" by R.H. Strand

31. Hessischer Rundfunk, Frankfurt am Main. Tendenzen und Erfahrungen" Ein Bericht von Henrich Vormweg.

32. Januar 9, 1966. "Das Amerika der russischjüdischen Inteliganz" by Salcia Landmann

33. Solothurner Nachrichten Nr. 280 2 Dezember 1965. Neue Bücher.

34. Neue Zeit 11 Dezember 1965. Romane im Schaufenster.

35. De Periscoop Januar 1966 Henderson de Regenkoning p. 13.

36. Aktuelles Feuilleton July 24, 1965 Buch-besprechung: "Herzog" von Saul Bellow

37. Spandauer Volksblatt 22 Sept. 1965.

38. Westdeutsche Allgemeine Zeitung. Rätsel um Bestseller.

39. "Kraft und Krise eines Intellektuellen"

40. Christ und Welt 15 Oktober 1965. "Die Leiden eines Individualisten".

41. Literaturbeilage 15 Oktober 1965. Vom Sweifel am Menschen.

42. Runschau um Wochenende/Literatur 18 September 1965. Der Held aber lebt nicht

43. Artikel aus der Kultur 12 August 1965. Die Passion des Moses Elkanah Herzog.

44. Junge Stimme Sep. 25 1965. Professor Herzog

45. Ebbenburener Volkszeitung 3 Jul 1965 Romane sind Spiegel des Lebens.

46. Frankfurter Allgemeine Zeitung 26 Juni 1965. Aus dem Redaktionsprogramm.

47. Die Weltwoche, Zürich. Drei amerikan-ische Bestseller.

48. AZ - Feuilleton 8/9 Mai 1965. Kein Happy-End für Moses Herzog.

49. Bücherei und Bildung Saul Bellow: Herzog Koval, Alexander. Saul Bellows neuester Roman: Herzog.

64

50. Koval, Alexamder. Saul Bellow neuester
    Roman: Herzog

51. Die Leseprobe "Herzog" Aus dem gleichnamigen
    Roman von Saul Bellow

52. Badische Zeitung 2/3 Oktober 1965. Das
    schwierige Leben des Moses E. Herzog

53. Abend Zeitung, München. Von Sartre bis
    Hemingway

54. Arbeiter Zeitung 7 November 1965. Der Don
    Quichotte unserer Zeit

55. Kultur 18 December 1965. Der Buchhändler
    empfielht

56. Bremer Nachrichten 12 Dezember 1965.
    Monolog eines Intellektuellen

57. Nordsee - Zeitung 18 Dezember 1965. Die
    Passion des Moses Elkanah Herzog

58. Rheinische Post 13 November 1965. Bellows
    grosser Wurf

59. Offenbach-Post 10 November 1965. Romane und
    Erzählungen

60. Rheinische Post. Die ersten Zwölf

61. Die Bücherkommentare 15 Sept. 1965. Saul
    Bellow. Herzog

62. Bellow, Saul: Herzog von Hanns-Hermann
    Kersten

63. Saarbrücker Zeitung 16/17 Oktober 1965.
    Lieber Herr Nietzsche

64. Kölnische Rundschau 8 Oktober 1965.
    Liebeserklärung an einen Roman

65. Frankfurter Buchmesse 13 Oktober 1965.
    Mein liebstes Buch

66. Die literarische Tat Schach der Verweiflung
    von Robert von Berg

67. Frankfurter Buchmesse. Hochgeehrter Herzog
    aus den USA

68. Der Buchanzeiger. Literatur aus Amerika

69. Hessischer Rundfunk. Herzog/Roman

70. Die Passion des Moses Herzog von Walter
    Alexander Bauer

71. Verzicht auf die Beschreibungsmanie:
    Saul Bellows neuer Roman "Herzog" in einer
    Vorbesprechung

72. Hamburger Abendblatt 16 November 1965.
    Verstrickt in die Gefühle.

73. Berliner Morgenpost 12 November 1965. Im
    Streit mit der Wirklichkeit

74. NRZ an Rhein und Ruhr 9 November 1965.
    Der mitteilsame Moses

75. Stuttgarter Nachrichten. Keine Jedermanns-
    lektüre

76. Frankfurter Neue Presse. Herzog

77. Mittag 29 Oktober 1965. Das Buch des Jahres
    pp. 10-11

78. Darmstädter Echo 9 Sep 1965. Lieber Herr
    Nietzche

79. Saarbrücker Allegemeine Zeitung 20 Dezember
    1965. Herzog

80. Wetzlarer Neue Zeitung 11 Dezember 1965.
    Die Passion des Moses Elkanah Herzog

81. Westdeutscher Rundfunk. Saul Bellow:
    "Herzog"

82. Neue Zürcher Zeitung 25 November 1965.
    Herzog

83. Süddeutscher Rundfunk. Ein Buch und eine
    Meinung: Wolfgang Weyrauch spricht über den
    Roman "Herzog" von Saul Bellow

84. Wiener Wochenausgabe. Unsere Buchecke

85. RIAS Berlin Kulturelles Wort. Von Büchern
    und Schriftstellern

86. Neue Tagespost. Saul Bellow: Herzog

87. Feuilleton 22 Oktober 1965. Pech mit
    Namen

88. Werk und Leben 25 September 1965. Das
    Bücherbrett p. 26

89. Die Presse 30/31 Oktober 1965. Grüsse
    und Hinfälligkeit des Menschen

90. Literaturblatt 30 Oktober 1965. Moses
    Herzogs Passion

91. Hessische Allgemeine 22 Oktober 1965.
    Bücher: von denen man spricht

92. Westdeutsche Allgemeine Zeitung 30 Oktober
    1965 Herzog - der traurige Amerikaner

93. Deutsche Tagespost 29/30 Oktober 1965. Mit
    sich und der Welt in Fehde

94. Herzogs Briefe

95. Die Weltwoche 3 Dezember 1965.
Schrifsteller raten den Lesern der
Weltwoche

96. Die Bark Heft 3 1965. p. 3

97. Industriekurier. Wuz und Ulysses in einem

98. Das Neue Buch. Bellow, Saul: Das Geschäft

99. Das Neue Buch. Ein Erzähler von Weltrang

100. Litteraturblatt. Katalog der Irrungen

101. "Erfolgreiche angelsächsische Autoren"

102. Zeitschrift für Versicherungswesen. Die
Abenteuer des Augie March p. 844.

103. Wiesbadener Kurier. Des Gestrandete von
Saul Bellow

104. Zeit 30 April 1965. Professor Herzog -
in amerikanischer Gantenbein

105. Frankfurter Allgemeine Zeitung 5 mai 1965.
Saul Bellow ausgezeichnet

106. Die Welt der Literatur 29 April 1965.
Schrecken, Lachen, Hilflosigkeit

107. Der Volsbote 11 Dezember 1965. Zwei
Romanciers vorwiegend für Intellektuelle

108. Die Zukunft Oktober 1965. p. 31 Einer de
letzen Menschen

109. Lübecker Nachrichten 25 November 1965.
Herzog

110. Harzburger Zeitung 23 November 1965.
"Herzog"

111. Kirche der Heimat Nr. 22/1965. Bestseller -
kritisch gelesen

112. Sozialpolitische Korrespondez November 1965.
Bücher fur den Weihnachtstisch p. 16.

113. Die Weltwoche, Zurich. Bestseller-Liste
der Weltwoche Oktober 1965

Foreign Language Editions
Contains the following foreign language editions of Herzog.

555   Herzog, um homem do nosso tempo. Lisbon:
Editorial Estudios Cor, n.d. 1 copy
Herzog. Ljubljani: Cankarjeva Zlaozba, 1966.
1 copy.
Herzog. Zagreb: Matica Hrvatska, 1966. 1 Copy.

Herzog. A Treasury of World Literature, vol.
51. Tokyo: Charles E. Tuttle Co. Inc., 1967
2 copies

SERIES C: MINOR WORKS

LEAVING THE YELLOW HOUSE

The following folders contain notebooks and other miscellaneous
pages for this short story which appeared in Esquire, vol. XLIX
no. 1 (Jan. 1958). The material has not been arranged in any
specific order, although the notebooks have been assigned a
number. (For details of the published version, see entry 25).

556.   C:1:1   Notebook 1. "Hattie's Will. Hattie I".
                 Holograph. Beige National notebook. 80 1.
                 Beginning of story abou Hattie and her
                 neighbors.

557.   C:1:2   Notebook 2. "Hattie II". Holograph. Beige
                 National notebook. 78 1. Continuation of
                 C:1:1.

558.   C:1:3   Holograph fragments. Yellow paper, lined.
                 pp. 1-8, 5-10, and unnumbered pp. (12 1.)
                 Miscellaneous pages.

559.   C:1:4   Typewritten pages with holograph corrections.
                 White and yellow paper, unlined. pp. 1-7,
                 1-16, 21 (24 1.) Different drafts of part of
                 the story.

560.   C:1:5   Carbon draft. "Leaving the Yellow House".
                 White paper, unlined. pp. 1-57 (57 1.)
                 Complete draft of story.

561.   C:1:6   Typewritten draft with holograph corrections.
                 "Leaving the Yellow House". White paper,
                 unlined. pp. 1-57 (57 1.) Complete draft
                 of the story, as it was published in Esquire.

A TALK WITH THE YELLOW KID.

The following folder contains the material for the article,
"A Talk with the Yellow Kid", which was publishes in The Reporter,
vol. XV (Sept. 6, 1956). (For details, see entry 90).

562   C:1:7   Holograph draft. White paper, lined.
                 Unnumbered (9 1.) Apparently one of the first
                 manuscripts. Typewritten draft with holograph
                 corrections. "A Talk with the Yellow Kid".
                 pp. 1-10 (10 1.) Complete draft of the work.
                 (Also see entry 944.)

MEMOIRS OF A BOOTLEGGER'S SON.
The following folders contain notebooks and other material for
the story "Memoirs of a Bootlegger's Son". The notebooks appear
first, each having been assigned a number, but not in any specific
order, followed by the holograph and typewritten pages.Unpublished.

563.   C:1:8   Notebook 1. "Jews I^2". Holograph. Brown
                 notebook. 36 1. Begins: "Viewing myself I
                 perceive I am a strange kind..." and continues
                 to Chapter VIII.

564.   C:1:9   Notebook 2. "Jews III". Holograph. Brown
                 Champion notebook. 27 1. with 2 loose 1.
                 Begins: "The bakery failed..." Back of note-
                 book contains notes about Dr. Adler and Wilhelm.

565.   C:1:10   Notebook 3. "I. Men owe us what we imagine
                 they will give us. We must forgive them this
                 debt". Pink University Exercise Book notebook.
                 26 1. Begins with a scene about Sugarman, and
                 back of notebook begins: "But when he saw me
                 playing cops and robbers..."

566.   C:1:11   Notebook 4. "Joshua II". Holohraph. Yellow
                 University Exercise Book notebook. 26 1.
                 Begins with "15. pp. 173 Aunt Julia was ready
                 for us...".

567.   C:1:12   Notebook 5. (Untitled). Holograph. Brown
                 notebook. 102 1. Begins: "What Do You Think
                 Your're Doing?" and continues to Chapter VI.

568.   C:1:13   Holograph fragments. White paper, lined. pp.
                 63-64 and unnnumbered (4 1.) Begins: "Every
                 city-born man...".

569.   C:1:14   Holograph fragments. White paper, lined.
                 Unnumbered (11 1.) Begins: "This argument was
                 a standard one...".

570.   C:1:15   Holograph fragments. White paper, lined.
                 Unnumbered (114 1.) Begins: "As the store in
                 Point St. Charles...", and continues with
                 pages marked Chapters VIII and XII.

571.   C:1:16   Typewritten draft with holograph corrections.
                 "Memoirs of a Bootlegger's Son". White paper,
                 unlined. pp. 1-172 (various versions) (174 1.)
                 Complete draft of the story.

572.   C:1:17   Carbon copy of C:1:16, without corrections.
                 White and yellow paper, unlined. (175 1.)

DON JUAN'S MARRIAGE.
The following folders contain a notebook and some typewritten
meterial for this unpublished short story.

573.   C:2:1   Notebook. "Don Juan's Marriage I". Holograph
                Brown notebook. 85 l. with 2 loose l. Contains
                Chapters I-IV.

574.   C:2:2   Notebook. (Untitled). Holograph. White
                University Filler Pad notebook. 31 l. Contains
                Chapter III, and notes on Pa and Cousin Ilona.

575.   C:2:3   Typewritten pages with holograph corrections.
                White and yellow paper, unlined, in a folder
                marked "Don J.". pp. 1-38., 17-52 and carbon
                of pp. 45-52 (81 l.) Covers Chapters II-V.
                p. 14 entitled "Lover from America".

FOREWORD TO DOSTOIEVSKY'S "WINTER NOTES".
The following folders contain three drafts of Bellow's preface
to Dostoievsky's Winter Notes, which was published by the
Criterion Press of New York. (For details, see entry 52).

576.   C:2:4   Typewritten draft with holograph corrections.
                Yellow and white paper, unlined. pp. 1-13
                (13 l.) The draft sent to the printers.

577.   C:2:5   Typewritten draft with editorial corrections.
                White paper, unlined. pp. 1-16 (16 l.) The
                printer's copy of the final version. Also:
                Yellow paper, lined. Handwritten. 1 l. Notes
                of Dostoievsky's The Brothers.

578.   C:2:6   Carbon copy of C:2:5.

ARTICLES ON LITERATURE AND WRITERS.
The following folders contain a variety of articles on literature
and writers, definitely or probably by Bellow. Both published
copies and reprints, and manuscripts, are included in this section.
Publication information is given whenever certain, and other
articles may or may not have been published. The articles have
not been arranged in any specific order, except that printed
articles are to be found at the end.

579.   C:2:7   "The Writer as Moralist". Published in The
                Atlantic, March, 1963. Holograph and type-
                written pages with holograph corrections.White
                and yellow paper, unlined. (Various versions)
                40 l. (See entry 102.)

580. C:2:8 "Writers and Morals". Xerox of a typewritten copy with holograph corrections. Pink paper, in a grey Russell and Volkening folder marked "Writers and Morals", by Saul Bellow". pp. 1-6 9-15 (13 l.)

581. C:2:9 (Untitled). Marked: "St. Louis Post Dispatch, Dec. '60". Carbon with holograph corrections. Yellow paper, unlined. pp. 1-5 (5 l.) About the novelist, his solitude, and his relations with the outside world.

582. C:2:10 (Untitled). Typewritten with holograph corrections. White paper, unlined. pp. 4. (1 l.) About "deep readers".

583. C:2:11 "Deep Readers". Carbon. Yellow paper, unlined. pp. 1-5 (5 l.) p. 4 is a copy of B:2:10.

584. C:2:12 "Distractions of a Fiction Writer". Typewritten with holograph corrections. White and yellow paper, unlined. (Various versions) 32 l. (For details, see entry 50.)

585. C:2:13 "The Writer and the Welfare State". Multigraph. White paper, unlined. pp. 1-7, (7 l.) Paper for a seminar.

586. C:2:14 (Untitled). Notebook. Holograph. Black Cuaderno notebook. 200 l. Draft of a lecture about the role of the writer and the university.

587. C:2:15 "Writers and Universities". Typewritten. White paper, unlined. pp. 1-7 (7 l.) Later draft of B:2:14.

588. C:2:16 (Untitled). Notebook. Holograph. Brown UCLA Bruins notebook. 90 l. Lecture notes about the modern novel.

589. C:2:17 "Where do we go from here: the future of fiction". Typewritten with holograph corrections. White paper, unlined. pp. 1-15 (16 l.) Includes introduction to the talk. Almost certainly a later draft of C:2:16.

590. C:2:18 "Where do we go from here: the future of fiction". Carbon with holograph corrections. White paper, unlined. A different draft of the same speech as C:2:17. (See entry 97.)

591.   C:2:19   "Notes on The White House and The Artists". Typewritten with holograph corrections, and carbon of the same draft. pp. 1-4 (8 l.)

592.   C:2:20   "Books 1962". Typewritten with holograph corrections. White paper, unlined. pp. 1-61 (61 l.)

593.   C:2:21   "Appearance". Published as the foreward to Isaac Rosenfeld's An Age of Enormity (Cleveland: World, 1962). Holograph. Yellow paper, lined pp. 1-8 (8 l.) Draft of a character sketch of Isaac Rosenfeld. (See entry 59.)

594.   C:2:22   (Untitled). Typewritten with holograph corrections, and holograph. White paper, lined, and white and yellow paper, unlined. (Various versions) 17 l. Different drafts of an essay on the novelist and truth.

595.   C:3:1   (Untitled). Notebooks. Holograph. 3 blue notebooks. 12 l. Marked II, III, and IV, and containing an essay on the fiction writer, the journalist and the historian.

596.   C:3:2   (Untitled). Holograph. Yellow paper, lined 4 l. About the writer and his readers.

597.   C:3:3   (Untitled). Carbon with holograph corrections. White paper, unlined. pp. 1-19 (19 l.) About Flaubert.

598.   C:3:4   (Untitled). Holograph. White paper, lined. Unnumbered. 1 l. Notes about reading novels.

599.   C:3:5   (Untitled). Typewritten. White paper, lined. Unnumbered. 2 l. About the connection between the aesthetic and the political-historical, with references to Thomas Mann.

600.   C:3:6   (Untitled). Holograph. White paper, lined. 1 l. About American writers.

601.   C:3:7   (Untitled). Typewritten with holograph corrections. White paper, lined. 1 l. About literature.

602.   C:3:8   The New York Review of Books. September 26, 1963 Article on the poet, Yevtushenko. Also: carbon. Yellow paper, unlined. pp. 1-3 (3 l.) Draft of the article. (See entry 81.)

603. C:3:9   The Times Literary Supplement, July 1, 1960.
                "The Sealed Treasure". 2 copies. (See entry 57.)

604. C:3:10   Partisan Review, n.d. "Spanish Letter".
                Reprint. (See entry 88.)

605. C:3:11   The Reporter, August, 1959. Review of Five
                Families, B Oscar Lewis. Also letter from
                The Reporter to Bellow, August 21, 1959.
                Galley proofs. (See entry 96.)

606. C:3:12   Commentary, March, 1951. "Looking for Mr.
                Green". Reprint. (See entry 27.)

ARTICLES ON POLITICAL FIGURES
The following folders contain articles about political figures
written by Bellow; they are not in any specific order.

607. C:3:13   "Writing about Presidents". Published in the
                New York Herald Tribune Book Review.
                Holograph and typewritten with holograph
                corrections. Yellow paper, lined, and white
                paper, unlined. pp. 1-5, and unnumbered.
                (11 l.) (See entry 103).

608. C:3:14   "Literary Notes on Krushchev". The article
                published in Esquire, March 1961.(See entry 66.)

609. C:3:15   "Reflections on Mr. K.". Typewritten with
                holograph corrections. White paper, unlined.
                pp. 1-3 (3 l.) Early draft of C:3:14.

610. C:3:16   "Reflections on Mr. K.". Carbon with holograph
                corrections. Yellow paper, unlined. pp. 1-9
                (9 l.) Different draft from C:3:15.

611. C:3:17   (Untitled). Typewritten. White paper, lined.
                2 l. Notes on Krushchev.

MISCELLANEOUS MANUSCRIPTS
The following folders contain the remaining manuscripts written
by Bellow, either parts of longer works or complete in themselves,
but more or less unidentified. At the end are to be found three
poems, probably written by Bellow. The manuscripts have not been
placed in any specific order.

612. C:3:18   "Golub". Holograph. White paper, lined, in a
                folder marked "Golub". Unnumbered. 15 l.
                Probably a short story.

613. C:3:19   "Lines Written by Toto Galfoniere to an
                American Friend and Patron". Holograph
                Brown notebook. 39 l. Also a letter from

Toto Rinieri to Maury, presumably used as a
basis for Bellow's story in the notebook.
Notebook also contains other miscellaneous notes
on novels.

614.   C:3:20   "Jews - notes - hospitals". Holograph.
Beige Spiral notebook. 9 l. About Mrs.
Lunie, Jacob, Hugo and a hospital.

615.   C:3:21   "Distractions". Typewritten with holograph
corrections. White paper, unlined. pp. 1-2
(2 l.) Beginning of a short story probably.

616.   C:3:22   (Untitled). Holograph. Brown notebook. 21 l.
About Mr. T. and Eugene Nail Hendrickson.

617.   C:3:23   (Untitled). Typewritten with holograph corrections
White paper, unlined. pp. 1-6 (6 l.) About film
directors.

618.   C:3:24   "Gonzaga". Holograph. Brown Standard
Composition Book notebook. 41 l. A short
story called "The Gonzaga Manuscripts" which
was printed in Seize the Day (1956, the Viking
Press). (For further details, see entry 20).

619.   C:3:25   (Untitled). Holograph. White paper, lined.
6 l. Part of a short story about Don Affle,
Dominick Apollo and Pops Vieder, three convicts.
Compare B:6:1.

620.   C:3:26   (Untitled). Typewritten. White paper, unlined.
pp. 23-24, 27-29 (5 l.) About Robert, who is
watching a play rehearsal.

621.   C:3:27   (Untitled). Carbon. Yellow paper, unlined.
1 l. About Selma, Dr. Vergras, Dr. Dorothy,
and others.

622.   C:3:28   (Untitled). Holograph. Brown Maple Leaf notebook. 18 l. About belief in others and love;
also notes about Mrs. Tannes, Basconi, and
others.

623.   C:3:29   (Untitled). Carbon with holograph corrections.
Yellow paper, unlined. pp. 1-8 (8 l.) Reply
to an article by Harold Rosenberg, who had
commented on a previous article by Bellow on
the attitudes of modern writers towards the
Self.

633.	C:3:30	"Millionaire". Holograph. white paper, lined. Unnumbered. 2 l. The beginning of a play about the poet, Brazen and Rallo.
634.	C:3:31	Miscellaneous notes. 7 l.
635.	C:3:32	Brown notebook. Miscellaneous notes.
636.	C:3:33	"Mechanism vs Functionalism". Holograph. White paper, unlined. 1 p. Poem. (Inc. in entry 4).
637.	C:3:34	"American Lights, Seen From Off Abroad". Carbon. White paper, unlined 2 l. Poem.
638.	C:3:35	Typewritten. White paper, unlined. 1 l. Poem beginning: "Go, world, roar without me".

CORRESPONDENCE
Deposits 26, 27, 28, 30, 31, 32, 34. (1967)

639. Box 1:1-9	Correspondence A-G.
640. Box 2:1-10	Correspondence H-R.
641. Box 3:1-7	Correspondence R-F; Folder 8: Unidentified.

THE VICTIM
Deposits 30, 32. (1967)

Clippings and Reviews.

| 642. Box 4:1 | 24 German clippings and reviews of Das Ofer, The Victim. |
| 643. Box 4:2 | 2 English language clippings. |

SEIZE THE DAY
Deposits 27, 28, 30, 32. (1967)

644. Box 4:3	Holograph fragments. White paper, unlined. 1l. Miscellaneous notes for the play version.
645. Box 4:4	Typewritten fragments. White paper, unlined. Act I, p.8, Act II, p.37, and one unnumbered (3 l.) Different drafts of the play.
646. Box 4:5	Typewritten draft. White paper, unlined. Typewritten with holograph corrections. Probably part of the last act.
647. Box 4:6	Reviews. "The Theme of Seize the Day" by James C. Mathis. (For details, see entry 1402.)

648. Box 4:7   "CIA (classified) Read & Destroy". Commentary
                by an unknown person on certain aspects of the
                play. White paper, unlined. Typewritten. 1 l.

THE LAST ANALYSIS.
Deposits 31, 32. (1967).

649. Box 4:8   Notebook. (Untitled). Holograph Beige "National"
                notebook. 107 l. Unidentified part of the play,
                also including other miscellaneous notes.

650. Box 4:9   Holograph fragments. White paper, lined. pp.
                28-52 (13 l.) Part of the play, possibly Act
                I (?), beginning with scene between Mott, Wink,
                Imogen etc.

651. Box 4:10   Typewritten fragments. White paper, unlined. pp.
                11-38 (1 l.) Scene between Bumm, Max, etc.

652. Box 4:11   One English language book review of The Last
                Analysis.

HERZOG.
Deposits 27, 32, 34. (1967).

653. Box 4:12   Holograph fragments. White paper, lined 1 l.
                Unidentified draft of novel.

654. Box 4:13   English language clippings, including Herzog
                book jacket.

MANUSCRIPTS FOR MINOR WORKS.
Deposits 28, 29, 30, 31, 32, 33, 34. (1967)

THE ORANGE SOUFFLÉ.

655. Box 4:14   Typewritten drafts. White paper, unlined, pp.
                1-13 (13 l.) Complete draft of the play.

656. Box 4:15   Yellow paper, unlined. Carbon. pp. 1-13 (2
                drafts) and pp. 2-15 (40 l.) The first 2 drafts
                are carbon copies of Box 4 Folder 14: and the
                third draft is a carbon copy of a different
                version of the play.

657. Box 4:16   C'e speranza nel sasso? ed Giangiacomo
                Feltrinelli, Milan, 1967. Italian version of
                Bellow's three one act plays: "Orange Souffle",
                "Out From Under", and "The Wen".

OUT FROM UNDER.

658. Box 4:17   "Out From Under". Yellow paper, unlined.
Carbon. pp. 1-19 (19 l.) Complete draft of
the unpublished play.

659. Box 4:18   "Hitting Back". Yellow paper, unlined. pp.
1-18 (18 l.) Complete draft of the play, but
an early version with different title, and with
Harry as Marco.

THE FUTURE MOON.

660. Box 4:19   (Untitled). Holograph. Yellow Penworthy notebook. 57 l. Begins with part of this story,
but also includes part of "Out From Under",
and miscellaneous notes.

661. Box 4:20   White paper, unlined. Typewritten with holograph corrections. pp. 1, 3, 10, 29 (various
versions). (6 l.)

THE OLDE SYSTEM.

662. Box 4:21   "Saul Bellow 1967". Holograph. Grey notebook.
76 l. Incomplete draft of this short story; back
of notebook also includes part of another short
story, beginning "The poet Jonas Hamilcar...".

663. Box 4:22   "Isaac and Tina". White paper, unlined. Typewritten draft with holograph corrections. pp.
1-44 (44 l.) January 1968. Includes covering
letter from Playboy with certain queries.

OUT OF BOUNDS.

664. Box 4:23   White paper, unlined. Typewritten with holograph corrections. pp. 1-30 (30 l.) Incomplete
draft of the story. Unpublished.

NOTHING SUCCEEDS.

665. Box 4:24   Typewritten fragments. White paper, unlined.
pp. 2, 3, 6, (3 l.)

666. Box 4:25   Typewritten drafts. White paper, unlined.
Carbon. pp. 1-11 (11 l.) Incomplete draft of
the story. Unpublished.

667. Box 4:26   White paper, unlined. Carbon. pp. 1-18 (18 l.)
Complete (?) draft of the story.

SAMSON.

668. Box 5:1   White paper, unlined. Typewritten with holo-
                graph corrections. pp. 1-3 various versions
                (6 l.) Incomplete drafts of the unpublished
                short story, beginning "In a dream I saw Igor
                Stravinsky...".

OLVUVAI.
Typewritten darfts.

669. Box 5:2   "Olduvai". White paper, unlined. pp. 1-10
                (10 l.) Incomplete draft of the unpublished
                short story.

670. Box 5:3   Olduvai. White paper, unlined. pp. 1-10
                (10 l.) Carbon copy of Box 5 Folder 2.

671. Box 5:5   "Olduvai George". White paper, unlined. Type-
                written with holograph corrections. pp. 1-4
                (various versions) (6 l.) Has the same title as
                in the previous three folders, but appears to be
                a completely different story, beginning with
                "A longer life span...".

THE POET JONAS AMILCAR.
Notebook.

671. Box 5:6   (Untitled). Holograph. Brown Filller Note-
                book. 79 l. with 5 loose l. Back of notebook
                also includes part of Samson, beginning with "In
                a dream I saw Igor Stravinsky...". (cf. Box
                5:Folder 1, entry 668).

672. Box 5:7   White paper, lined. Holograph fragments. Un-
                numbered. 47 l. Many different versions, some
                starting with "The Poet Jonas Amilcar...",
                some with "When I board the plane..." etc.

673. Box 5:8   Yellow paper, lined. Holograph. Unnumbered.
                2 l.

674. Box 5:9   White paper, unlined. Typewritten fragments.
                pp. 1-8 (8 l.) Incomplete draft of part of the
                story.

675. Box 5:10   White paper, unlined. Typewritten with holograph
                corrections. pp. 1-20 (20 l.)

676. Box 5:11   White paper, unlined. Typewritten with holograph
                corrections. pp. 1-20 (20 l.)

677. Box 5:12   Yellow paper, unlined. Carbon with holograph
                 corrections. pp. 1-10 (10 l.)

678. Box 5:13   Yellow paper, unlined. Carbon. pp. 1-8 (8 l.)

679. Box 5:14   White paper, unlined. Typewritten with holo-
                 graph corrections. pp. 1-5, 7 (6 l.)

680. Box 5:15   White paper, unlined and lined. Typewritten
                 with holograph corrrections. pp. 1-8, 14-19,
                 24 (various versions) (46 l.)

681. Box:5:16   Yellow paper, unlined and carbon. pp. 3, 14,
                 23, 24, 25 (5 l.) Unpublished.

ARTICLES ON LITERATURE AND WRITERS.

682. Box 5:17   "Skepticism and the Depth of Life". Xerox and
                 Carbon with holograph corrections. pp. 1-24
                 (24 l.) (see entry 84).

683. Box 5:18   (Untitled). Typewritten with holograph correct-
                 ions. pp. 1-14 (14 l.) A different version of
                 the same article in Box 5 Folder 17.

684. Box 5:19   (Untitled). Holograph. Yellow paper, lined.
                 pp. 1-22 (11 l.) Draft for a speech (?) on
                 the modern religious novel.

685. Box 5:20   (Untitled). Typewritten with holograph correct-
                 ions. White paper, unlined. p. 2 (1 l.)
                 Formerly attached to Box 5 Folder 19, though
                 seems to have little to do with it, and begins
                 "There is an art...".

686. Box 5:21   (Untitled). Holograph. White paper, lined.
                 pp. 12-20 (5 l.) Begins "But let us now turn
                 from the judgments....and seems to be part of
                 a speech or article on modern literature.

687. Box 5:22   (Untitled). Typewritten with holograph correct-
                 ions. White paper, unlined. pp. 1-10 (10 l.)
                 A series of questions on modern literature,
                 probably for an interview with Bellow's answers.

688. Box 5:23   (Untitled). Carbon. White paper, unlined. pp.
                 1-8 (8 l.) Different version from Box 5 Folder
                 22. (For final published version, see entry 1249.)

689. Box 5:24   (Untitled). Typewritten with holograph correct-
                 ions. White paper, unlined. pp. 1-6 (6 l.)

Speech or article on literary intellectuals, and the use of literature today.

690. Box 5:25   (Untitled). Typewritten with holograph correct-ions. White paper, unlined. pp. 1-8 (8 1.) Apparently the same article as Box 5:Folder 24, but with major alterations.

691. Box 5:26   Carbon copy of Box 5:Folder 25.

692. Box 5:27   (Untitled). Xerox copy of pages from a note-book 16 1. Probably notes for the same article as Box 5:Folder 24.

693. Box 5:28   (Untitled). Holograph. Yellow paper, lined. Notes for the same article as Box 5:Folder 24.

694. Box 5:29   (Untitled). Typewritten. White and yellow paper, unlined. 6 1. Miscellaneous pages probably connected with the articles in Box 5: Folder 24.

695. Box 5:30   "The Next Necessary Thing". Typewritten with holograph corrections. White paper, unlined. pp. 1-19 (19 1.) (see entry 76.)

696. Box 5:31   "The Next Necessary Thing". Typewritten with holograph corrections. White paper, unlined. pp. 1-6 (6 1.) Different draft from Box 5 Folder: 30, and incomplete.

ARTÍCLES OF POLITICAL CONTENT.

697. Box 5:32   Xerox of "The Great Society is a Sick Society" by Senator J.W. Fulbright from the New York Times Magazine, August 20, 1967. Back of article contains holograph notes by Bellow about this article.

698. Box 5:33   (Untitled). Typewritten. White paper, unlined. pp. 1, 4, 5, (various versions) (5 1.) Differ-ent drafts of Bellow's article.in Box 5 Folder 30 beginning "I assume when Senator Fulbright says America is a sick society...".

699. Box 5:34   Holograph. White paper, lined. 4 1. Draft of a letter to President Johnson accepting an invitation to the White House Festival of the Arts.

700. Box 5:35   Typewritten with holograph corrections. White paper, unlined. pp. 1-2 (various versions)

	(3 l.) Two more drafts of the letter to President Johnson accepting the invitation to the White House.
701. Box 5:36	"To the Editor of the Chicago Daily News". Typewritten with holograph corrections. White paper, unlined. Unnumbered. 2 l. Letter about Anti-Vietnam demonstrations. Undated.
702. Box 5:37	"McIlwaine Newsday Tuesday's Junket". Carbon. White paper, unlined. pp. 1-8 and 1-4 (12 l.) An article on the Israeli war Bellow wrote for Newsday.
703. Box 5:38	"Tel Aviv June 8th. Telex to Newsday". Carbon White paper, unlined. pp. 1-3 (3 l.) Report on the Israeli war for Newsday.
704. Box 5:39	"Tel Aviv June 10th". Carbon. White paper, unlined. p. 1. (1 l.) Report for Newsday on the Israeli war.
705. Box 5:40	Letter of introduction from Newsday for Bellow's report on the Israeli war; also 5 l. of miscellaneous holograph notes about the war.
706. Box 5:41	(Untitled). Typewritten with holograph corrections. White paper, unlined. 1-7 (8 l.) Draft of an article (presumably written much later) on Bellow's trip to Tel Aviv concerning the Israeli war for Newsday. (For details, see entry 60.)

MISCELLANEOUS MANUSCRIPTS.

707. Box 6:1	(Untitled). Typewritten with holograph corrections. White paper, unlined. pp. 1, 2, 7, 9, 10, 12, 24 (8 l.) Part of a short story beginning "On heavy paper Goodknins daughter Patsy...".
708. Box 6:2	(untitled). Typewritten with holograph corrections. White paper, unlined. pp. 52-57, and carbon of pp. 52-56 (11 l.) seems to be part of a short story abou Vera, George, Meeker, etc.
709. Box 6:3	(Untitled). Holograph. White paper, lined. Unnumbered. 5 l. Part of a play scene between Sab and Zis.
710. Box 6:4	"Draft from Bellow to the Trustees". Xerox of a typewritten copy. White paper, unlined. pp.

1-6 (6 l.) Letter about the proposal theatre for the University of Chicago.

711. Box 6:5   (Untitled). Typewritten with holograph corrections. White paper, unlined. pp. 36, 38-46, 49, 53, 62, 67 (various versions) (18 l.) Part of a story about Chancellor and D.S. Hutchins.

712. Box 6:6   (Untitled). Carbon. White and yellow paper, unlined. pp. 38-46, 49, 53, 62, 67 (various versions) (17 l.) Partly the same as Box 6 Folder 5.

713. Box 6:7   Notebook. Holograph. Brown notebook. 36l. Front of notebook has part of a play called "A Mausoleum in One Act;" back of notebook contains part of short story beginning "my friend H.R.....".

714. Box 6:9   Notebook Holograph. Light brown University notebook. 62 l. with 4 loose l. Part of a short story beginning "A passion for old bones...".

715. Box 6:10   Large brown envelope with "The Next Necessary Thing" on one side; and miscellaneous holograph notes on the other. (See entry 76.)

716. Box 6:11   Miscellaneous pages of various sorts, with unidentifiable notes. Holograph. 18 l.

717. Box 6:12   (Untitled). Carbon. Yellow paper, unlined. pp. 1-2 (2 l.) Notes of Bellow's on certain books of modern authors.

718. Box 6:13   (Untitled). Typewritten with holograph corrections. White paper, unlined. pp. 9-10 (2 l.) Part of an article on American writers and universities.

719. Box 6:14   Miscellaneous typewritten pages, some with holograph corrections. 11 l. Unidentified notes.

REVIEWS OF BELLOW.
Deposits 28, 32, 33. (1967)

720. Box 7:1   Saul Bellow by Tony Tanner. Writers and Critics, Oliver and Boyd Ltd., Edingburgh, 1965. (See entry 1459 .)

721. Box 7:2   Saul Bellow: A Critical Essay by Robert
                Detweilter. Contemporary Writers in Christian
                Perspective, 1967. (See entry 1312).

722. Box 7:3   Smith's Trade News, August, 1966.

723. Box 7:4   The Rialto: The Return of Saul Bellow, Play-
                wright. Newspaper clipping.

724. Box 7:5   Bellow Triple Bill Gets London Raves. Newspaper
                clippings from the Times, and Xerox copy.

725. Box 7:6   Two Original Short Plays by a Novelist. News-
                paper clippings from the Times.

726. Box 7:7   3 Bellow Plays are Appreciated. Newspaper clippings
                from the New York Times. 3/8/1966.

MISCELLANEOUS ITEMS (collected by Bellow, along with personal
artifacts) 28, 29, 30, 32, 33, 34. (1967)

727. Box 7:8   "The New Chicago" by Arnie Karlen C. Holiday,
                March 1967, uncorrected galley prooofs,
                including covering letter from Kovier to Bellow,
                December 22, 1966.

728. Box 7:9   "A Runaway War or a Deadlocked Peace". by
                Howard Schomer. Mimeographed. pp. 1-5 (5 l.)

729. Box 7:10   National Translation Center information
                pamphlet.

730. Box 7:11   Berkeley Daily Gazette, December 15, 1964.

731. Box 7:12   "English 10 Mrs. Bellow". Mimeographed
                English test, May 23, 1962.

732. Box 7:13   Bellow's 1966 Income Tax Returns.

733. Box 7:14   Newspaper clippings "The Creation and the End of
                the World Will Take Place in York on June Tenth
                at 8 p.m.

734. Box 7:15   "The Mihajlov Affair:" pp. 22 Xerox copy of
                magazine.

735. Box 7:16   "Memorandum of Collision". Yellow paper, unlined.
                Carbon copy of Bellow's report of a car collision
                in which Bellow and his wife were involved.

736. Box 7:17   Announcement of Norman Rosten in a series of four
                "Poetry Colloquia" to be held at the Polytechnic
                Institute of Brooklyn.

737. Box 7:18   "A Year of Contemporary Writers" calender for 1968.

738. Box 7:19   List some schools in New York.

739. Box 7:20   Announcement of series of talks sponsored by l'Associazione Culturale Italiana.

740. Box 7:21   "Existentail Psychoanalysis and Metaphysics" by George A. Schrader. Reprint from The Review of Metaphysics vol. XIII no.1 (September, 1959)

741. Box 7:22   Stein, Roe & Farnham: Quarterly Report, September 30, 1964; and 15th Annual Report, December 31, 1964.

742. Box 7:23   Amities Stendhaliennes en Belgique, by Jules Dechamps (La Renaissance du Livre, 1963) With typewritten note attached: "A 10 cents bargain is irresistable".

743. Box 7:24   "Political Reporting Trends". by Thomas Donovan. Xerox of article in the Foreign Service Journal, November 1913.

744. Box 7:25   List of "Publications since last promotion" of Professor Lemont.

745. Box 7:26   "Rockefeller Foundation Proposed Garantees 1966-1967 Literature Program". Xerox of typewritten list.

746. Box 7:27   Dietary instructions by J.S Golden, M.D.

747. Box 7:28   Brochure from the First National Bank of Chicago.

748. Box 7:29   "Greenie Goodbye". by Kelly Morris. Reprint from Juggler, Winter, 1965 and Fall of 1964.

749. Box 7:31   "The Great Obsession" by Edward Shils. Xerox of and unidentified clipping.

750. Box 7:32   "Connaisance du Theatre Contemporain Francais et Etranger". Carbon of 2 1. of notes.

751. Box 7:33   Page from the Jewish Floridian, May 8, 1964.

752. Box 7:34   Page from the New York Post, February 23, 1955.

753. Box 7:35   Page from The Times, June 6, 1967.

754. Box 7:36   Le Monde, June 15, 1967.

755. Box 7:37   Criticism of Miss Arendt's work on the conduct
                 of the European rabbinate, from an unidentified
                 source.

756. Box 7:38   Jackson Shore Cooperative Apartments Corporation.
                 Note to shareholders.

757. Box 7:39   "List of workshops 1967" mimeograph.

758. Box 7:40   Carbon copy of Retail Installment Contract, for
                 payment of car.

759. Box 7:41   Hand-coloured lithograph caricatures of a
                 soldier.

760. Box 7:42   Hermes Baby Rocket Typewriter instructions.

761. Box 7:43   Check Book Stubs, two of Bellow's and one
                 unidentified.

762. Box 7:44   Invitation from Academy Associates to dinner in
                 honor of Samuel Bellows, the elder brother of
                 Saul Bellow.

763. Box 7:45   Two American Express invoices.

764. Box 7:46   Membership cards, etc.

765. Box 7:47   Scraps of paper with names and addresses.

766. Box 7:48   Half a birthday card.

767. Box 7:49   Jewish New Year Card.

768. Box 7;50   University National Bank deposit receipt.

769. Box 7:51   Freifield and Corepary card.

1968 Deposit:

770. Box I: Correspondence: Consists of 230 letters to Saul
                 Bellow; one letter from Saul Bellow. (35, 36, 37,
                 38 (part), 39, 40, 41,)

Manuscripts and Galleys of Mosby's Memoirs and Other Stories.   New
York: Viking Press, 1968.

771. Box II:1   (Preliminary pages) White paper, unlined.
                 Typewritten with printer's notation. (4 l.)
                 Xerox copy of printed page. (1 l.)

772. Box II:2   "Leaving the Yellow House." Typewritten draft, white paper, unlined. With holograph emendations in pencil and printer's notations in ink. pp. 1-48 (48 1.)

773. Box II:3   "Leaving the Yellow House". Typewritten draft, white paper, unlined. Carbon copy, with holograph emendations. pp. 1-48 (48 1.) (Indentical to draft in folder 2 above, without printer's notations.)

774. Box II:4   "Leaving the Yellow House". Galley proofs with holograph emendations. Viking Press. Galleys 1-14 (14 1.)

775. Box II:5   "The Old System." Typewritten draft, white paper, unlined. With holograph emendations in pencil and printer's notations in ink. pp. 49-99 (51 1.)

776. Box II:6   "The Old System." Typewritten draft, white paper, unlined. Carbon copy with holograph emendations. pp. 1-51, also numbered 49-99. (51 1.) (Indentical to draft in folder 5 above, without printer's notations.)

777. Box II:7   "The Old System." Galley proofs with holograph emendations. Viking Press. Galleys 15-28 (14 1.)

778. Box II:8   "Looking for Mr. Green." Typewritten draft, white paper, unlined. With printer's notations. pp. 100-118, 118A-128 (30 1.)

779. Box II:9   "The Gonzaga Manuscripts." Typewritten draft, white paper, unlined. With printer's notations. pp. 129-162 (34 1.)

780. Box II:10   "The Gonzaga Manuscripts." Galley proofs with holograph emendations. Viking Press. Galleys 38-48 (11 1.)

781. Box II:11   "A Father-to-be." Typewritten draft, white paper, unlined. With printer's notations. pp. 163-176 (14 1.)

782. Box II:12   "Mosby's Memoirs." Notebook, beige stenographer's. Holograph early version of the story (63 1.) Also contains one leaf white paper, unlined, typewritten, p. 26 of the story.

783. Box II:13   "Mosby's Memoirs. Typewritten draft, white paper, unlined. With holograph emendations. pp. 1-27 (27 1.)

784. Box II:14   "Mosby's Memoirs." Typewritten draft,
white paper, unlined. pp. 1-32 (32 l.)
Marked "superseded" at the top of p.1.

785. Box II:15   "Mosby's Memoirs." Galley proofs, unmarked
except for autograph on p.1. New Yorker
magazine. Galleys 1-23 (23 l.)

786. Box II:16   "Mosby's Memoirs." Galley proofs, distinguished
from proofs in folder 15 above by printer's
notations and some holograph emendations. New
Yorker magazine Galleys 1-23, also numbered 177-
199 (23 l.)

787. Box II:17   "Mosby's Memoirs." Galley proofs. With
holograph emendations. Viking Press. Galley's
54-63 (10 l.)

Other Works: Plays.

788. Box III:1   "The Wrecker" and "The Orange Soufflé."
Mimeograph copy in a black Hart Stenographic
Bureau cover. pp. 1-21, 1-20 (45 l.) (See
1967 Gift. Box 4:14-16, for Ms drafts and
translations of "The Orange Souflé", entries
655-57.

Other Works: Short Fiction.

789. Box III:2   "Don Juan's Marriage." (Unpublished.) Chapter I.
White paper, unlined. Carbon. pp. 1-8 (8 l.)
(See also Series C:2:1-3. entries 573-75.)

790. Box III:3   "Don Juan's Marriage." Chapter II. White paper
unlined. Carbon. pp. 9-16 (8 l.)

791. Box III:4   "Don Juan's Marriage." Chapter III. White paper,
unlined. Carbon pp. 17-32 (16 l.)

792. Box III:5   "Don Juan's Marriage." Chapter IV. White paper.
Unlined. Carbon. pp. 17-32 (16 l.)

Other Works: Non-fiction.

793. Box III:6   "Introduction to a Volume on the Mississippi
Freedom Workers Murders." Xerox copy of typewritten Ms with holograph corrections. Stapled
in green covers of literary agent. pp. 1-6 (6 l.)
(Unpublished. Written at the request of Congress
on Racial Equality.)

794. Box III:7   "The Public and the Writer." Deep yellow paper,
unlined. Typewritten with holograph corrections.

pp. 1-6 (6 l.) (Published Sept. 15, 1968 in
Bookweek, later in the Observer; see entry 80.

Miscellaneous

795. Box III:8   One legal-sized unidentified sheet. White paper,
unlined. Holograph, sic. One mock-up of Cason
Old Face type sample: "Saul Bellow/The Adventures of Augie March (sic)".

796. Box III:9   (Untitled). White paper, unlined p. II-19 (a)
Scene between Wilhelm and Tamkin.

797. Box III:10 Galley proofs of preliminary pages of Herzog.
Viking Press. On verso holograph Ms of
conversation between Luke and Moses Herzog. 2 l.

798. Box III:11 Literature on "Sound Seminars." Lists of names
(1 l.) white unlined paper. (Authors, books,
students.) Interviews, appointments: students
for winter quarter course. (1 l.)

Printed Works In Translation (Not in folders)

799. Box IV: Dangling Man ed. with notes by the Taiyosha
Editorial Department. Tokyo: Taiyosha Press,
1967.

800. Box IV: Herzog. translated into Italian by Letizia
Ciotti Miller. Milano: Feltrinelli, 1967.

801. Box IV: Herzog. translated by Zeljko Bujas. Zagreb:
Matica Hrvatska, 1966.

802. Box IV: Herzog. translated into Portuguese by Luia Dluca
Soares. Lisboa: Estudios Cor, 1966.

803. Box IV: Japanese translation of The Adventures of Augie
March, in Selections from Contemporary American
Literature, Vol. 2, pp. 5-417, Tokyo; Charles
E. Tuttle.

Working Materials Deposit - November 15, 1968 (from Deposit 38)

804. Box I:1   ("The Poet Jonas Hamilcar") or "A Hole in the
Forum." Notebook, light brown "Champion".
Holograph (63 l.) Three sections:

leaves 2-27 Untitled work beginning "Richard
thought he was safe ..."

leaves 28-45 Untitled work beginning "The
poet Jonas Hamilcar ...." See also leaves 61-62

805. Box I:2   "Olduvai George." Typewritten draft, titled
                    "A Hole in the Forum." White paper, unlined.
                    pp. 1-3 (3 1.) Begins "Mr. Orlansky, boarding
                    a plane, needed a drink .." (later becomes
                    Charles Citrine).

806. Box I:3   "Olduvai George." Typewritten draft, entitled
                    "A Hole in the Forum," yellow paper, unlined.
                    Carbon copy of folder 2 above. pp. 1-3 (3 1.)

807. Box I:4   "Olduvai George." Typewritten draft, untitled.
                    white paper, unlined. With holograph emendations.
                    pp. 38, 58-62, 61 (7 1.)

808. Box I:5   Typewritten draft, untitled, yellow paper, unlined.
                    With holograph emendations. pp. 12 36. (2 1.)

809. Box I:6   "Olduvai George." Typewritten draft, untitled,
                    white paper, unlined. With holograph emendations.
                    pp. 1-16, 13-26, 28-32, 29-32 (41 1.)

810. Box I:7   "Olduvai George." Typewritten draft, untitled,
                    white paper, unlined. Xerox copy with holograph
                    corrections. pp. 3-12 (10 1.) Begins "Certain
                    parallels: my father also was struck down in a
                    public place ..."

811. Box I:8   "Olduvai George". Typewritten draft, untitled,
                    white paper, unlined. with holograph emendations.
                    pp. 3-22, (21 1.) Begins "As it happened, my
                    father was struck down in public ..."

812. Box I:9   "Olduvai George." Typewritten draft, untitled,
                    white and yellow paper, unlined. Carbon copy
                    with holograph emendations. pp. 11-28 (18 1.)
                    Begins "You mean Hamilcar is dead."(becomes Humboldt).

813. Box I:10   "Olduvai George". Typewritten draft, untitled,
                    yellow paper, unlined. Carbon copy with holograph
                    emendations. pp. 13-18 (6 1.) Begins "The
                    teetering of the 727, the flexibility of the
                    wings..."

814. Box I:11   "Olduvai George." Typewritten draft, untitled,
                    deep yellow paper, unlined. pp. 66, 75, 81
                    (3 1.) Later appears in Humboldt's Gift.

815. Box I:12   "Olduvai George", Ty'ewritten draft, untitled,
                    light yellow paper, unlined. Carbon copy. pp.
                    66-67 of draft in folder 11 above. (1 1.)
                    (The carbons are superimposed upon one another to
                    the point of being nearly illegible.)

<u>Mr. Sammler's Planet</u>:

Deposits 42-47, amalgamated. n.b. <u>Mr. Sammler's
Planet</u> (originally entitled, <u>Future of the Moon</u>)
was published by the <u>Atlantic Monthly</u> in November
and December, 1969. The entire novel was then
published by Viking Press; There are differences
in the <u>Atlantic Monthly</u> and Viking versions; the
latter contains the more elaborate revisions. (See
entry 30.)

816. Box I:1   Notebook 1. "Future of the Moon I." Holograph
                Black notebook. 184 l. with text.

817. Box I:2   Notebook II. "Moon II." Holograph Black note-
                book. 75 l., including last, with text.

818. Box I:3   Notebook III. "Moon III." Holograph. Brown spiral
                notebook. 83 l. with text.

819. Box I:4   Notebook IV. "Moon Notebook IV." Holograph.
                Brown spiral notebook. 140 pages with text.

820. Box I:5   Holograph fragments. 24 leaves.

821. Box I:6   Typescript fragments. 24 leaves

822. Box I:7   Typescript draft. 41 leaves. Various versions
                of pp. 5-9.

823. Box I:8   First typescript draft, corrected. pp. 1-59
                (60 leaves).

824. Box I:9   First typescript draft, corrected. pp. 60-119
                (60 leaves).

825. Box I:10   First typescript draft, corrected. pp. 120-146
                (29 leaves).

826. Box I:11   First typescript draft, corrected. pp. 147-188
                (50 leaves).

827. Box I:12   First typescript draft, corrected. pp. 189-238
                (90 leaves).

828. Box I:13   Partial typescript draft, (a copy made to be sent
                to publishers). pp. 1-122 (122 leaves). (Part
                xeroxed).

829. Box I:14   Second typescript draft, (only p. 85 corrected).
                pp. 1-111 (111 leaves).

830. Box II:1   Second typescript draft, corrected. pp. 112-287
                (178 leaves).

90

831. Box II:2-4 Second typescript draft, xerox copy. Annotated
by Edward Shils. pp. 1-287 (289 leaves).

832. Box II:5 Atlantic Monthly galley proofs, Chapter 1,
uncorrected. 18 leaves.

833. Box II:6 Atlantic Monthly galley proofs, Chapter I,
"Uncorrected author's proof," (galley 57
uncorrected.)

834. Box II:7 Atlantic Monthly gallery proofs, Chapters III
and IV (partial), uncorrected. 16 leaves.

835. Box II:8 Atlantic Monthly galley proofs, Miscellaneous
galleys, uncorrected. 7 leaves.

836. Box II:9 Atlantic Monthly galley proofs, Chapter VI
(partial), galleys 124-6, corrected. 8 leaves.

837. Box II:10 Synopsis of the work for Atlantic Monthly,
holograph, 2 leaves, with typescript copy,
2 leaves.

838. Box II:11 Viking Press galley proofs. Title and preliminary
pages. 2 leaves.

839. Box II:12 Viking Press galley proofs, "Duplicates" galleys,
corrected, but not in Saul Bellow's hand. 94
leaves.

840. Box II:13 Viking Press galley proofs. "Author's proof"
partial xerox, partial duplicate of folder
12 above, corrected by Saul Bellow. 156 leaves.

841. Box II:14 Viking Press galley proofs, Chapter I, galley
12 only, 2 copies. One corrected by Saul Bellow,
the other corrected in another hand and corrected again by Saul Bellow, marked "Discard". 2
leaves.

842. Box II:15 Viking Press, galley proofs, Galleys 13-25,
uncorrected duplicates of part of folder 12
above. 13 leaves.

843. Box II:16 Draft of Chapter VI, partially typescript,
partially galleys (from Atlantic Monthly galleys),
all corrected and xeroxed, with covering letter
from Teresa Egan of Viking. 37 leaves.

844. Box II:17 Chapter VI, typewritten fragments. pp. 1-12
various versions, corrected. 59 leaves.

845. Box II:18   "About Mr. Sammler's Planet and Its Proprietor"
                  by Denver Lindley, Viking Press. Typescript
                  (part xerox, part carbon copies). 7 leaves.

846. Box II:19   Editorial correspondence and comments: July-
                  October, 1969. 17 leaves, 22 leaves.

Mr. Sammler's Planet: Deposit 48.

847. Box III:1   Viking Press galley proofs, "For Author".
                  Corrected and reviewed partially by Saul Bellow
                  partially by an editor. 96 leaves.

848. Box III:2   Viking Press galley proofs. Duplicates of
                  folder 1 above, corrected and revised partially
                  by Saul Bellow, partially by an editor. 96
                  leaves.

                  (n.b. All revisions in the two sets are identical,
                  alternating between Saul Bellow's and the editor's
                  hands. The galleys in folder 2 contain some
                  revisions in Saul Bellow's hand which were later
                  deleted, presumably by Saul Bellow, and not copied
                  onto the set in folder 1).

849. Box III:3   Viking Press galley proofs, Part VI, uncorrect-
                  ed. 19 leaves.

850. Box III:4   Typescript fragment, Part VI, page 1. Late
                  revision, after galleys. 1 leaf.

Miscellaneous.

851. Box III:5   Northwestern University. Diploma for Bachelor
                  of Science with honors awarded to Saul Bellow
                  June 12, 1937.

852. Box III:6   The Friends of Literature: Certificate of
                  Distinguished Service to Literature to Saul
                  Bellow for Henderson, The Rain King, awarded
                  on April 23, 1960.

Mr. Sammler's Planet: Deposit 49.

853. Box IV:1   Second typescript draft, corrected. Carbon copy
                  of 1969 Deposit Box I, folder 16 and part of Box
                  II, folder 1 above. Chapters I-IV. (In Russell
                  and Volkening, Inc. folder) 164 leaves.

854. Box IV:2-4   Second typescript draft, corrected. Xerox copy
                  of folder 1 above, with printer's proofmarkings.
                  (Marked "Nov. Atlantic".) 164 leaves.

855. Box IV:5   "What has happened thus far," synopsis of
                Chapters I-IV. Typescript with corrections,
                2 leaves.

856. Box IV:6   Second typescript draft, carbon copy with
                printer's proofmarkings.

857. Box IV:7   Second Typescript draft, carbon copy with
                printer's proofmarkings. Chapter VI (Marked
                "November Atlantic".) 55 leaves.

858. Box IV:8-10 Atlantic Monthly galleys, Chapters I-IV. (Marked
                "Corrections transferred".) 61 leaves.

859. Box IV:11 Atlantic Monthly galleys, Chapter V. (Marked
                "Revised galleys".) 25 leaves.

860. Box IV:12 Atalntic Monthly galleys, corrected. Xerox
                copy. Chapter V. (Marked "author's correct-
                ionstransferred".) 51 leaves.

861. Box IV:13 Draft of Chapter VI, typescript with correct-
                ions. Xerox copy. (Marked "xerox of original
                pages 173-183".) 9 leaves.

862. Box IV:14 Draft of Chapter VI, typescript, carbon copy,
                with Printer's proofmarkings. (Different from
                folder 13 above.) 11 leaves.

863. Box IV:15 Atlantic Monthly galleys, corrected. Xerox copy.
                Chapter VI. (Marked "184-214"). 30 leaves.

Mr. Sammler's Planet: Deposit 50.

864. Box IV:16-7 First typescript draft, uncorrected. Xerox
                copy (cf. 1969 Deposit, Box I, folders 10-14.)
                235 leaves.

Correspondence: Deposit 51.

865. Box V:1   Letters from Bellow. A.L. Draft to Sanchez,
                n.d. 1p. A.L. draft to Gerald Freund n.d. 1p.
                A. note. 4 lines (on envelope postmarked
                December 2, 1966).

866. Box V:2   A-C, including family correspondence.

867. Box V:3   D-F, including letters from Ruth Dayan and Gerald
                Freund (Rockefeller Foundation).

868. Box V:4   G-K, including correspondence from Michael
                Harrington and Mark Harris.

869. Box V:5   L-N.

870. Box V:6   P-S, including letters from Norman Rosten and
                Edward Shils.

871. Box V:7   T-Z, including Eli Wallach and enclosure from
                Isaac B. Singer in letter from Dan Wickenden.

872. Box V:8   Unidentified last name correspondence.

873. Box V:9   Miscellaneous financial and other notes.   32
                items.

Reviews.

874. Box V:10   Reviews of Bellow's works, clippings and copies.
                Articles about Bellow clippings and copies.

875. Box V:11   Listing of Bellow Papers in the University of
                Chicago Library, and accompanying correspon-
                dence.

Works.

876. Box V:12   "Mosby's Memoirs," excises from the New Yorker,
                July 20, 1968.

877. Box V:13   "The Old System", excised from Playboy, January
                1968.

878. Box V:14   Seize the Day - correspondence and cartoons,
                from and unknown source.
                - annotated copy of 1966, revised, screenplay
                   (Mimeographed).
                - another annotated copy of the above.

879. Box VI:1   Seize the Day - another annotated copy of the
                above.

880. Box VI:2   Seize the Day - unannotated copy of the above
                with one insertion of 2 pages and covering letter.

881. Box VI:3   "Samson", typescript, 3 leaves. Unpublished.

882. Box VI:4   "A Report from Existence", typescript, 21 leaves.

Unidentified Works.

883. Box VI:5   Re: Pawlyk and Rosa, typescript and holograph,
                6 leaves.

884. Box VI:6   Re: Harry Pomfret, typescript 7 leaves.

885. Box VI:7   Three unrelated works:
                  a) beginning "I parked on Division Street...".
                  b) discussion of "The Old System".
                  c) discussion of the vularisation of culture
                  notebook, 29 leaves with writing, plus 5 loose
                  from two notebooks.

886. Box VI:8   Re: the vulgarisation of culture, typescript
                  and holograph, 25 leaves.

887. Box VI:9   Re: the 1967 Israeli war, typescript, 6 leaves.

888. Box VI:10   Re: Hamilcar, Humboldt, Orlansky etc. Beginning,
                  "The poet Jonas Hamilcar.." notebook, 30 leaves
                  with writing, plus 2 loose leaves.

889. Box VI:11   Re: "The poet Jonas Hamilcar..." typescript,
                  28 leaves.

890. Box VI:12   Re: holograph fragments, 3 leaves.

391. Box VI:13   Re: "In the long corridors of O'Hare Airport..."
                  typescript. 26 leaves.

392. Box VI:14   Re: "Then as the 727 teetered..." typescript.
                  11 leaves.

393. Box VI:15   Re; "When I board the plane..." typescript
                  14 leaves.

394. Box VI:16   Re: "When I board the plane..." typescript.
                  10 leaves.

395. Box VI:17   Re: "He then wanted to go..." typescript. 17
                  leaves.

396. Box VI:18   Re: "...encountering the real McCoy..." type-
                  script, 8 leaves.

397. Box VI:19   Re: "What for," typescript 4 leaves.

398. Box VI:20   Re: "The tears rose..." typescript. 21 leaves.

399. Box VI:21   Re: "...in him to be shocked..." typescript
                  41 leaves.

400. Box VI:22   Re: "He was heavy..." typescript, 12 leaves.

401. Box VI:23   Re: Hamilcar, Humboldt, Orlansky, etc. "Terribly
                  suffering..." typescript, 2 leaves.

902. Box VII:1   Re: "... made. Over the great prairies..." typescript, (xeroxed), 14 leaves.

903. Box VII:2   Re: "...youthful, natural..." typescript, 9 leaves.

904. Box VII:3   Re: "...After this..." typescript 11 leaves.

905. Box VII:4   Re "Considering in the room..." typescript, 18 leaves.

906. Box VII:5   Re: "Conrad Aiken..." typescript, 2 leaves.

907. Box VII:6   "The mansard roofing..." four typescript drafts, 23 leaves.

908. Box VII:7   "...and she was thinking..." typescript, 14 leaves.

909. Box VII:8   "Brooding from..." typescript, 21 leaves.

910. Box VII:9   Re: Miscellaneous writings, notebook, 13 leaves with writing, plus 3 loose leaves.

Works by Others: originals, xeroxed copies and excised copies from printed works, etc.

911. Box VII:10   Thomas A. Donovan.

912. Box VII:11   Theodore Hoffman.

913. Box VII:12   Edward B. Hungerford.

914. Box VII:13   Aron Krich.

915. Box VII:14   Irving Kristol.

916. Box VII:15   Benjamin Nelson.

917. Box VII:16   Harold Rosenburg.

918. Box VII:17   Peter Selz.

919. Box VII:18   Edward Shils.

920. Box VII:19   Stanley Warren and Tobie Zion. Harris.

921. Box VII:20   Unidentified, "Our condition is a hubbub..."

Correspondence, 1966-70: Deposit 52.

922. Box I:1-7   Letters collected alphabetically A-G.

923. Box II:1-14 Letters collected H-G; Folder 15 contains
                  miscellaneous and unidentified correspondence
                  to Bellow.

924. Box II:16   Clippings and reviews of various works by Bellow.

Miscellaneous.

925. Box II:17   Szkockie Pozegnania, by Przemyslaw Bystrzycki,
                  Poland, 1963. Inscribed copy.

926. Box II:18   "The Bellow-Gallo Letters," 1961, carbon, 68
                  pages.

927. Box II:19   "Dana" by Douglas Cater, copy of galley proofs,
                  154 pages. Unidentified.

928. Box II:20   Bellow Gift 1973: Collection of foreign editions
                  of Bellow's major works from Brazil, Chile,
                  Germany, Czechoslavakia, Denmark, Italy, Japan,
                  Netherlands, Romania, Russia, and Sweden. For
                  further details see the section devoted to
                  translations, entries 946-985.

In addition to the extensive holdings of <u>Bellow Papers</u> in
Chicago a minor collection of working materials can be found in
the Humanities Research Center at the University of Texas, Austin.
The following listing describes briefly the items housed in the
Center. Permission from the author is required to examine the
manuscripts.

929.　　　Ms　(Bellow, S) Works.
　　　　　　　Speech accepting National Book Award for Herzog,
　　　　　　　Typed manuscript duplicated pages (3 pp.)
　　　　　　　1965 (March 9).

930.　　　Ms　(Bellow, S) Works.
　　　　　　　<u>Mosby's Memoirs</u> (32 pp.)　Typed carbon copy of
　　　　　　　manuscript.

931.　　　Ms　(Bellow, S) Works.
　　　　　　　<u>Mosby's Memoirs</u> Page proofs for <u>New Yorker</u>; xerox
　　　　　　　copy (16 pp.) 1968 (July 20).

932.　　　Ms　(Bellow, S) Works.
　　　　　　　"Mosby's Memoirs" and other stories: "A Father-
　　　　　　　to-be" (and front matter) Galley proofs (7
　　　　　　　sheets). Undated.

933.　　　Ms　(Bellow, S) Works.
　　　　　　　"Mosby's Memoirs" and other stories. Galley
　　　　　　　proofs with A note (61 sheets). Uncorrected
　　　　　　　proof copy (186 pp.) Undated. Unbound.

934.　　　Ms　(Bellow, S) Works.
　　　　　　　"Mosby's Memoirs" and other stories: "Looking
　　　　　　　for Mr. Green". Galley proofs (9 pp.). Undated.

935.　　　Ms　(N.M. Coll.) Miscellaneous.
　　　　　　　<u>Seize the Day</u> Typed manuscript with autograph,
　　　　　　　printer's marks, and notes (140 pp.) Undated.
　　　　　　　(p. 2. missing).

936.　　　Ms　(Bellow, S) Works.
　　　　　　　(Seize the Day) <u>Here and Now - Here and Now</u>,
　　　　　　　alternative title. Typed manuscript with auto-
　　　　　　　graph emendations (61 pp.). Undated.
　　　　　　　Title deleted: <u>One of Those Days</u>.

937.　　　Ms　(Bellow, S) Works.
　　　　　　　(<u>Seize the Day</u>). <u>Here and Now - Here and Now</u>.
　　　　　　　Typed manuscript with Author's revisions (38 pp.)
　　　　　　　Undated.

938. Ms (Bellow, S) Works.
          (Seize the Day). Here and Now - Here and Now.
          Typed carbon copy of manuscript including
          Author's revisions and typed insertions (72 pp.)
          Undated.

939. Ms (Bellow, S) Works.
          (Seize the Day) Here and Now - Here and Now.
          Typed carbon copy of manuscript including typed
          emendations (44 pp.).

940. Ms (Bellow, S) Works.
          (Seize the Day). One of Those Days. Manuscript
          with Author's revisions (2 exercise books).
          Undated. Early version. Bound.

941. Ms (Bellow, S) Works.
          (Seize the Day) One of Those Days. Holograph
          fragments with Author's emendations (24 pp.)
          Undated.

942. Ms (Bellow, S) Works.
          (Seize the Day). Typed manuscript with Author's
          revisions (71 pp.) Undated. Boxed with Seize
          the Day; typescript and typed carbon copy of
          manuscript fragments with Author's notes. (118
          pp.).

943. Ms (Bellow, S) Works
          Seize the Day. Typescript and typed carbon
          copy manuscript fragments with autograph notes
          (118 pp.). Boxed with Seize the Day, (Typed
          manuscript including) Author's revisions
          (71 pp.)

944. Ms (Bellow, S) Works.
          "A Talk with the Yellow Kid". Typed carbon
          copy of manuscript (12 pp.). Undated.

945. Ms (Pritchett, V.S.) Works. (Collected with Bellow
          Ms) Bellow, Saul; Herzog.
          Pritchett, V(ictor) S(awdon), 1900 - (Review of)
          Herzog by Saul Bellow. Holograph with Author's
          revisions (6 pp.). Typed carbon copy of
          manuscript (6 pp.). Undated.

Works in Translation

Dangling Man

946.   Por um Fio. Rio de Janeiro, Brasil Edicoes Bloch, 1967.

947.   Hombre en Suspenso, Santiago, Chile, Zig-Zag, 1968.

948.   Mann in der Schwebe. Köln, Kiepenheuer and Witsch, 1969.
       Mann in der Schwebe. Hamburg, Rowohlt, 1971.

The Victim

949.   Offeret, Oslo, Norway; H. Aschenbourg, 1967.

950.   Zrtva, Beograd, Yugoslavia; trans. Branko Bosnjak, 1973.

951.   Zrtva, Zagreb, Yugoslavia; trans. Marta Frajd, 1965.

The Adventures of Augie March.

952.   Augie March Aventyr. Stockholm, Sweden; Albert Bonniers Forlag, 1955.

953.   Augie March, Tokyo, Japan; Arechi Shuppa Sha, 1959.

954.   Dogodovscine Angieja Marcha, Maribor, Obzorja, Yugoslavia; trans. Herbert Grun, 1961.

955.   Dozivljaji Anagie Marcha, Zagreb, Yugoslavia; trans. Mignon Mihaljević and Frida Subić, 1965.

Seize the Day

956.   Ne Propusti Dan, Sarajevo, Svjetlost; trans. Jara Ribnikar, 1963.

Henderson the Rain King

957.   Regnkongen, Oslow, Norway; H. Aschenbourg, 1960.

958.   Henderson o Rei da Chuva, Lisbon: Edicao "Livros do Brasil".

959.   Henderson, el Rey de la Lluvia, Mexico; Joaguin Motiz, 1964.

960.   Henderson, Kralj Kise, Subotica; Beograde, Yugoslavia; trans. Jara Ribnikar, 1962.

Herzog

961.   Herzog, Bratislava, Tatran, (Czechoslovakia) 1968.

962.   Herzog, Kobenhavn, (Denmark) Det Schonbergske Forlag, 1971.

963.   Herzog, Milano, (Italy) Feltrinelli Editore, 1971.

964.   Herzog, Japan, Hayakawa Shobo and Co., 1970.

965.   Herzog, Amsterdam, Uitgeverij De Bezige Bij, 1969.

966.   Herzog, Bukarest, (Romania) Kriterion Konyvkiado, 1970.

967.   Herzog, Tallinn, (U.S.S.R.) Kirjastus Eesti Raamat, 1972.

968.   Herzog, un Homan do Nosso Tempo, Lisbon, Portugal; 1966.

969.   Herzog, Llubljana: Cankarjeva Založba; trans. Mira
        Miheličeva, 1966.

970.   Herzog, Zagreb: Matica Hrvatska, trans. Zeljko Bujas,
        1966.

971.   Herzog, Tokyo: Charles E. Tuttle Co. Inc., 1967.

972.   Herzog, Paris: Gallimard; trans. Jean Rosenthal, 1966.

The Last Analysis

973.   L'Ultime Analyse, in Pierre Dommergues' Saul Bellow
        (Paris: Grasset) trans. Rosette Lamont, 1967.

Mosby's Memoirs

974.   Mosbys Eridringer, Denmark, Gyldendals, Bekkasinboger,
        1970 paperback.

975.   Mosby's Memoirs, Tokyo, K. Yano, 1970.

976.   Mosbys Memoarer, Stockholm, Albert Bonniers Forlag, 1970.

Mr. Sammler's Planet

977.   Mr. Sammler's Planet, Denmark, Gyldendals Bogklub, 1970.

978.   Mr. Sammler's Planet, Denmark, Gyldendals, 1970 paperback.

979.   Mr. Sammlerin Planeetta, Helsinki, Kustannusosakeyhtio
        Tammi, 1970.

980.   Mr. Sammler's Planet, Köln, Kiepenheuer and Witsch, 1971.

981.   Il Pianeta de Mr. Sammler. Milano, Feltrinelli, 1971.

Down From Under: Three one-act plays.

982.   C'e speranza del sesso, Giangiacomo Fettrinelli, Milan,
        1967.

983.   "Le souffle a l'orange" and "Un grain de beauté" ("The
        Wen") in Pierre Dommergues' Saul Bellow, Paris, 1967.

"The Wrecker"

984.   "Le démolisseur" in Au jour le jour (Seize the Day),
        trans. Danielle Planel, Paris, 1962.

"Father-to-be"

985.   "Koga bi bil tatko", trans. V. Cretkovski, Razvitok,
        Yugoslavia, 1972.

Reviews of Individual Works

Dangling Man

986.   Chamberlain, John, New York Times, 25 (March 1944), 13.

987.   De Vries, Peter, Chicago Sun Bookweek, 9 (April 1944), 3.

988.   Fearing, Kenneth, New York Times Book Review, 49 (26 March 1944), 5, 15.

989.   Hale, Lionel, Observer, (January 1947), 3.

990.   Heppenstall, Rayner, New Statesman and Nation, 32 (December 1946), 488-89.

991.   Kristol, Irving, Politics, 1 (June 1944), 156.

992.   Kupferberg, Herbert, New York Herald Tribune Book Review, 20 (April 1944), 11.

993.   Mayberry, George, New Republic, 110 (April 1944), 473-74.

994.   O'Brien, Kate, Spectator, 178 (January 1947), 27.

995.   Rothman, N.L., Saturday Review of Literature, 27 (April 1944), 27.

996.   Schorer, Mark, Kenyon Review, 6 (Summer 1944), 459-61.

997.   Schwartz, Delmore, Partisan Review, 11 (Summer 1944), 348-50.

998.   Time, 43 (8 May 1944), 104.

999.   Times Literary Supplement, (11 January 1947), 21.

1000. Trilling, Diana, Nation, 158 (15 April 1944), 455.

1001. Wilson, Edmund, The New Yorker, 20 (1 April 1944), 78, 81.

The Victim

1002. Downer, Alan S., New York Times Book Review, 52 (30 November 1947), 29.

1003. Farrelly, John, New Republic, 117 (8 December 1947), 27-28.

1004. Fielder, Leslie, Kenyon Review, 10 (Summer 1948), 519-27.

1005. Gibbs, Wolcott, The New Yorker, 28 (10 May 1952), 58.

1006.   Greenberg, Martin, Commentary, 5 (January 1948), 86-
        87.

1007.   Hale, Lionel, Observer, (12 June 1948), 3.

1008.   Hardwick, Elizabeth, Partisan Review, 15 (January 1948),
        108-17.

1009.   Match, Richard, New York Herald Tribune Book Review,
        24 (November 1947), 10.

1010.   Poore, Charles, New York Times, 22 (November 1947), 13.

1011.   Smith, R.D., Spectator, 180 (4 June 1948), 686, 688.

1012.   Straus, Ralph, Sunday Times, (London), 6 June 1948, 3.

1013.   Time, 50 (1 December 1947), 111-12.

1014.   Trilling, Diana, Nation, 166 (3 January 1948), 24-25

1015.   Wilson, Edmund, The New Yorker, 23 (13 December 1947),
        139-40.

The Adventures of Augie March

1016.   American Scholar, 23 (Winter 1953-54), 126.

1017.   Amis, Kingsley, Spectator, 192 (21 May 1954), 626.

1018.   Cassidy, T.E., Commonweal, 58 (2 October 1953), 636.

1019.   Connole, John, America, 90 (October 1953), 133.

1020.   Crane, Milton, Chicago Sunday Tribune Magazine of Books,
        (20 September 1953), 4.

1021.   Davis, Robert Gorham, New York Times Book Review, 58
        (20 September 1953), 1, 36.

1022.   Finn, James, Chicago Review, 8 (Spring-Summer 1954), 104-11.

1023.   Geismer, Maxwell, Nation, 177 (14 November 1953), 404.

1024.   Harwell, Meade, Southwest Review, 39 (Summer 1954), 273-
        76.

1025.   Hicks, Granville, New Leader, 36 (21 September 1953),
        23-24.

1026.   Hughes, Riley, Catholic World, 178 (December 1953),
        233-34.

1027.   Kristol, Irving, Encounter, 3 (July 1954), 74-75.

1028.   Mizener, Arthur, New York Herald Tribune Book Review,
        30 (20 September 1953), 2.

1029.   Newsweek, 42 (21 September 1953), 102, 104.

1030.   Pickrel, Paul, Yale Review, 43 (Autumn 1953), 10.

1031.   Podhoretz, Norman, Commentary, 16 (October 1953), 378-
        80. (For details surrounding the writing and reception
        of the review see entry 1421).

1032.   Popkin, Henry, Kenyon Review, 16 (Spring 1954), 329-34.

1033.   Prescott, Orville, New York Times, 18 September 1953,
        21.

1034.   Priestly, J.B., Sunday Times, (London), 9 May 1954. p.5.

1035.   Rolo, Charles, J., Atlantic, 192 (October 1953), 86-87.

1036.   Rosenberg, Dorothy, San Fransisco Sunday Chronicle, 25
        October 1953, 18.

1037.   Schorer, Mark, Hudson Review, 7 (Spring 1954), 136-41.

1038.   Schwartz, Delmore, Partisan Review, 21 (January-February
        1954), 112-15.

1039.   Time, 62 (21 September 1953), 114, 117.

1040.   Times Literary Supplement, (4 June 1954), 357.

1041.   Walbridge, Earle F., Library Journal, 78 (15 September
        1953), 1529-30.

1042.   Warren, Robert Penn, New Republic, 129 (2 November 1953),
        22-23.

1043.   Webster, Harvey Curtis, Saturday Review of Literature
        36 (19 September 1953), 13-14.

1044.   West Ray B., Jr., Shenandoah, 5 (Winter 1953), 85-90.

1045.   Wilson, Angus, Observer, 9 May 1954, 9.

Seize the Day

1046.   Allen, Walter, New Statesman and Nation, 53 (27 April
        1957), 547-48.

1047.   Alpert, Hollis, Saturday Review of Literature,
         39 (24 November 1957), 18, 34.

1048.   Baker, Robert, Chicago Review, 11 (Spring 1957), 107-
         10.

1049.   Bayley, John, Spectator, 198 (7 June 1957), 758.

1050.   Bowen, Robert, Northwest Review, 1 (Spring 1957), 52-56.

1051.   Crane, Milton, Chicago Sunday Tribune Magazine of Books,
         30 December 1956, 7.

1052.   Fenton, Charles A., Yale Review, 46 (Spring 1957), 452.

1053.   Fielder, Leslie, The Reporter, 15 (13 December 1956),
         45-46.

1054.   Flint, R.W., Partisan Review, 24 (Winter 1957), 139-45.

1055.   Gill, Brendan, The New Yorker, 32 (5 January 1957),
         69-70.

1056.   Gillman, Richard, Commonweal, 78 (29 March 1963), 21
         (drama).

1057.   Gold, Herbert, Nation, 183 (17 November 1956), 435-36.

1058.   Hicks, Granville, New Leader, 39 (26 November 1956),
         24-25.

1059.   Hogan, William, San Francisco Chronicle, 15 November
         1956, 27.

1060.   Hopkinson, Tom, Observer, 21 April 1957, p.11.

1061.   Kazin, Alfred, New York Times Book Review, 61 (18 Nov-
         ember 1956), 5, 36.

1062.   Lynch, John, Commonweal, 65 (30 November 1956), 238-39.

1063.   Manchester Guardian, 95 (15 December 1956), 10.

1064.   Newsweek, 48 (19 November, 1956), 142-43.

1065.   Pickrel, Paul, Harper's, 213 (December 1956), 100.

1066.   Rolo, Charles J., Atlantic, 199 (January 1957), 86-87.

1067.   Rugoff, Milton, New York Herald Tribune Book Review,
         33 (18 November 1956), 3.

1068.   Saturday Review of Literature, 48 (20 November), 40.

1069.   Schwartz, Edward, New Republic, 135 (3 December 1956),
         20-21.

1070.   Stern, Richard G., Kenyon Review, 21 (Autumn 1959),
         655-61.

1071.   Swados, Harvey, New York Post Weekend Magazine, 18
         November 1956, 11.

1072.   Swan, Michael, Sunday Times, (London), 21 April 1957, 7.

1073.   Time, 68 (19 November 1956), 122.

1074.   Times Literary Supplement, (10 May 1957), 285.

1075.   West, Ray B., Jr., Sewanee Review, 65 (Summer 1957),
         498-508.

1076.   Wyndham, Francis, London Magazine, 4 (August 1957), 66.

Henderson the Rain King.

1077.   Atlantic Monthly, 203 (March 1959), 88.

1078.   Baker, Carlos, New York Times Book Review, 64 (22 February
         1959), 4-5.

1079.   Booklist, 55 (15 December 1958), 202.

1080.   Coren, A., Punch, 251 (19 October 1966), 603.

1081.   Cruttwell, Patrick, Hudson Review, 12 (Summer 1959),
         286-95.

1082.   Curley, T.F., Commonweal, 70 (17 April 1959), 84.

1083.   Gilbert, Felix, The Yale Review, XLVIII (March 1959),
         453-56.

1084.   Gold, Herbert, Nation, 188 (21 February 1959), 169-72.

1085.   Hardwick, Elizabeth, Partisan Review, 26 (Spring 1959),
         299-303.

1086.   Hicks, Granville, Saturday Review of Literature, 42,
         (21 February 1959), 20.

1087.   Hogan, William, San Francisco Chronicle, 23 February,
         1959, 25.

1088.   Jacobsen, Dan, Spectator, 202 (22 May 1959), 735.

1089.   Kogan, Herman, Chicago Sunday Tribune Magazine of
         Books, 22 February 1959, 3.

1090.   Levine, Paul, Georgia Review, 14 (Summer 1960), 218-20.

1091.   Maddocks, Melvin, Christian Science Monitor, 26
         February 1959, 11.

1092.   Malcolm, Donald, The New Yorker, 35 (14 March 1959),
         171-73.

1093.   Maud, Ralph, Audit, 2 (22 February 1960), 17-18.

1094.   Newsweek, 53 (23 February 1959), 106.

1095.   Miller, Karl, Listener, 61 (25 June 1959), 1099-1100.

1096.   Perrott, Ray, Manchester Guardian, 29 May 1959, 6.

1097.   Pickrel, Paul, Harper's, 218 (March 1959), 104.

1098.   Podhoretz, Norman, New York Herald Tribune Book Review,
         35 (22 February 1959), 3.

1099.   Prescott, Orville, New York Times, 23 February 1959, 21.

1100.   Price, Martin, Yale Review, 48 (Spring 1959), 453-56.

1101.   Rolo, Charles J., Atlantic, 203 (March 1959), 88.

1102.   Scott, J.D., Sunday Times, (London), 24 May 1959.

1103.   Swados, Harvey, New Leader, 42 (23 March 1959), 23-24.

1104.   Tanasoca, Donald, Library Journal, 84 (January 1959)
         118.

1105.   Thompson, Frank H., Prairie Schooner, 34 (Summer 1960),
         174-75.

1106.   Time, 73 (23 February 1959), 102.

1107.   Times Literary Supplement, 12 June 1959, 352.

1108.   Wain, John, Observer, 24 May 1959, 21.

1109.   Waterhouse, Keith, New Statesman, 57 (6 June 1959), 805-
         6.

1110.   Weales, Gerald, The Reporter, 20 (19 March 1959), 46-47.

1111.   Whittemore, Reed, New Republic, 140 (16 March 1959), 17-
         18.

1112.   Wilson, Angus, Observer, "Books of the Year", 27
        December 1959, 8.

Herzog

1113.   Barrett, William, Atlantic Monthly, 214 (November
        1964), 192, 196.

1114.   Battaglia, Frank, San Fransisco Chronicle, 7 March 1965,
        43.

1115.   Bradbury, Malcolm, Punch, 248 (27 January 1965), 145.

1116.   Burns, R.K. Library Journal, 89 (1 September 1964), 3182.

1117.   Capon, Robert F., America, 112 (27 March 1964). 425-27.

1118.   Casty, A., Antioch Review, 26 (Fall 1966), 399-411.

1119.   Chevigny, Bell Gale, Village Voice, 8 October 1964.17.

1120.   Coren, A., Punch, (19 October 1966), 603.

1121.   Curley, Thomas, Commonweal, 81 (23 October 1964), 137-38.

1122.   Davenport, Guy, National Review, 16 (3 November 1964),
        978-79.

1123.   Edelman, L., Jewish Heritage, 7 (Winter 1964-65), 3-4.

1124.   Elliot, George P., Nation, 199 (19 October 1964), 252-
        54.

1125.   Froncek, Tom, Tablet, (London), (6 February 1965), 154.

1126.   Gill, Brendan, The New Yorker, 40 (October 1964), 218-22.

1127.   Goldreich, G., Hadassah Magazine, 46 (December 1964),
        14-16.

1128.   Goran, L., Chicago Sunday Tribune, 20 September 1964,
        1.

1129.   Gross, B., Chicago Review, 17 (1964), 217-21.

1130.   Gross, J., Encounter, 25 (July 1965), 64-65.

1131.   Klein, Marcus, The Reporter, 31 (22 October 1964), 53-54.

1132.   Lamont, Rosette, Massachusetts Review, 6 (Spring/Summer
        1965), 630-35.

1133.   Lemon, L.J., Prairie Schooner, (Summer 1965), 161-62

1134.   Ludwig, Jack, Holiday, (February 1965), 16-19.

1135.   Maddocks, Melvin, Christian Science Monitor, (24 September 1964), 7.

1136.   Malin, I., Reconstructionist, 30 (16 October 1964), 28-30.

1137.   Moynahan, Julian, New York Times Book Review, 69 (20 September 1964), 1, 41.

1138.   Muggeridge, M., Esquire, 43 (January 1965), 24.

1139.   Newsweek, 64 (21 September 1964), 114.

1140.   Pickrel, Paul, Harper's 229 (October 1964), 128.

1141.   Poirier, R., Partisan Review, 32 (Spring 1965), 264-71.

1142.   Pritchett, V.S., New York Review of Books, 3 (23 October 1964), 4-5 (For manuscript details see entry 945).

1143.   Rahv, Philip, New York Herald Tribune Book Week, 20 September 1964, 1, 14, 16.

1144.   Raider, Ruth, Cambridge Quarterly, 2 (Spring 1967), 172-83.

1145.   Richler, Mordecai, Spectator, (29 January 1965), 139.

1146.   Rubenstein, R.L. Reconstructionist, 30 (22 January 1965), 7-12.

1147.   Rubin, Louis, Southern Review, (Summer 1966), 697.

1148.   Sale, R., Hudson Review, 17 (Winter 1964-65), 608.

1149.   Saturday Review of Literature, 48 (20 November 1965), 40.

1150.   Scott, N.A., Christian Science Century, 81 (16 December 1964), 1562-63.

1151.   Solotaroff, Theodore, Commentary, 38 (December 1964), 63-66.

1152.   Squirru, Rafael, The Americas, (December 1964), 34.

1153.   Steiner, George, Sunday Times (London), 31 January 1965, 48.

1154.   Time, 84 (25 September 1964), 105.

1155.   Times Literary Supplement,(4 February 1965,) 81.

1156.   Toynbee, Philip, Observer, 31 January 1965, 37.

1157.   Trachtman, Paul, Progressive, (November 1964), 43.

1158.   Trevor, William, Listener, 73 (6th February 1965), 201.

1159.   Virginia Quarterly Review. 41 (Winter 1965), 9.

1160.   Webb, W.L., Manchester Guardian, 92 4 February 1965,
        10.

1161.   Weintroub, B., Chicago Jewish Forum, 23 (Winter 1964)
        163-65.

1162.   Zinnes, H., Books Abroad, (Autumn 1965), 460.

Mr. Sammler's Planet.

1163.   Bayley, John, The Listener, 84 (9 July 1970), 51-52.

1164.   Braine, John, National Review, 22 (10 March 1970),
        264-66.

1165.   Broyard, Anatole, New York Times Book Review, (7
        February 1970), 1, 40.

1166.   DeMott, Benjamin, Saturday Review, 53 (7 February 1970),
        25-28, 37.

1167.   Epstein, Joseph, Book World, (1 February 1970), 1.

1168.   Fletcher, Janet, Library Journal, 95 (2 February 1970),
        511.

1169.   Gray, P.E., Yale Review, 69 (March 1970), 432-33.

1170.   Gross, Beverly, Nation, 210 (9 February 1970), 153-55.

1171.   Howe, Irving, Harper's, 240 (February 1970), 106, 108,
        110, 114.

1172.   Katz, Phyllis, R., Best Seller, 29 (2 February 1970),
        409-10.

1173.   Kazin, Alfred, New York Review of Books, 15 (3 December
        1970), 3-4.

1174.   Kiely, Robert, Christian Science Monitor, (5 Febraury
        1970), B-11.

1175.   Lindroth, James R., America, 122 (21 February 1970),
        190.

1176.   Lurie, Alison, New Statesman, 80 (10 July 1970), 19

1177.   Newsweek, 75 (2 February 1970), 77.

1178.   Oates, Joyce C., Critic, 28 (May 1970), 68-69.

1179.   Opdahl, Keith, Commonweal, 91 (13 February 1970), 535-
        36.

1180.   Samuels, C.T., New Republic, 162 (7 February 1970),
        27-30.

1181.   Sissman, L.E., New Yorker, 45 (31 January 1970), 82,
        85-87.

1182.   Stock, Irwin, Commentary, 49 (May 1970), 89-90, 92-94.

1183.   Time, 95 (9 February 1970), 81-84.

1184.   Times Literary Supplement, (9 July 1970), 749.

The Last Analysis.

1185.   Booklist, 61 (15 April 1965), 777.

1186.   Booklist, 61 (1 May 1965), 863.

1187.   Choice, 2 (September 1965), 400.

1188.   Corrigan, R.W., Book Week, (May 23 1965), 4.

1189.   Hudson Review, 17 (Winter 1964/1965), 556-557.

1190.   Hymas, B., Reconstructionist, 30 (November 13, 1964),
        13-15.

1191.   Jones, D.A.N., New Statesman, 71 (June 1966), 819.

1192.   Life, 57 (October 30 1964), 17.

1193.   Nation, 199 (October 19 1964), 256-257.

1194.   New Republic, 151 (October 24 1964), 25-26.

1195.   Newsweek, 64 (October 12, 1964), 105.

1196.   Richler, M., Spectator, (25 March, 1966), 371.

1197.   Rosenthal, T.G., The Listener, (12 May 1966), 697.

1198.   Saturday Review, 47 (17 October 1964), 29.

1199.   Saturday Review, 49 (26 November 1966), 41.

1200.   Time, 84 (9 October 1964), 92.

1201.   Times Literary Supplement, (31 March 1966), 261.

1202.   Vogue, 144 (15 November 1964), 64.

1203.   Winegarten, R., Jewish Observer, 15 (13 May 1966), 17.

Under The Weather.

1204.   Commonweal, 85 (18 November 1966), 199-201.

1205.   Nation, 203 (14 November 1966), 523-524.

1206.   Newsweek, 68 (7 November 1966), 96.

1207.   New Yorker, 42 (5 November 1966), 127.

1208.   Saturday Review, 49 (12 November 1966), 34.

1209.   Time, 88 (4 November 1966), 85.

Mosby's Memoirs and Other Stories.

1210.   Axthelm, Peter, Newsweek, 72 (28 October 1968), 122.

1211.   Katz, Bill, Library Journal, 93 (15 October 1968), 3797.

1212.   Lasson, Robert, Book World, (20 October 1968), 6.

1213.   Richardson, J., New York Review of Books, 5 (28 March 1969), 12-14.

1214.   Samuels, C.T., Atlantic Monthly, 222 (November 1968), 126.

Humboldt's Gift.

1215.   Aaron, Daniel, New Republic 173 (28 September 1975), 28.

1216.   Allen, Bruce, Library Journal, 100 (1 November 1975), 210.

1217.   Bradbury, Malcolm, Encounter, 45 (November 1975), 61.

1218.   Broyard, Anatole, New York Times, 10 September 1975, 20.

1219.   Gilman, Richard, New York Times Book Review, (17 August 1975), 1-3.

1220.   Gornick, Vivian, The Village Voice, (September 1975), 35.

1221.   Leonard, John, New York Times Book Review, (10 September 1975), 3.

1222.   Lodge, David, Times Literary Supplement, (10 October 1975), 1173.

1223.   Mano, D.K., National Review, 27 (7 November 1975), 1246.

1224.   Mayne, Richard, The Listener, (9 October 1975), 996.

1225.   Nault, Marianne, Arnold Bocklin, (December 1975), 20-21.

1226.   Newman, Charles, Harper's 251 (October 1975), 82.

1227.   Newsweek, (1 September 1975), 33-35.

1228.   Nordell, Roderick, Christian Science Monitor, (27 August 1975), 23.

1229.   Pearson, Gabriel, Manchester Guardian, 9 October 1975, 12.

1230.   Raphael, Frederick, Sunday Times, (London), 5 October 1975, 35.

1231.   Rhodes, Richard, Chicago Tribune Book World, 7 (24 August 1975), 1.

1232.   Shattuck, R.R., New York Review of Books, (18 September 1975), 21.

1233.   Sheppard, R.H., Time, 106 (25 August 1975), 62.

1234.   Stern, Daniel, Commonweal, 102 (24 October 1975), 502.

1235.   Toynbee, Philip, Observer, 9 October 1975, 35.

1236.   Updike, John, <u>New Yorker</u>, 51 (15 September 1975), 122-30.

1237.   Waugh, Auberon, <u>Evening Standard</u>, 7 October 1975, 6.

1238.   Wolf, R.G., <u>New York Tribune</u>, 5 September 1975, 64.

Interviews with Saul Bellow

1239.   Boyers, Robert, "Literature and Culture: An Interview
         with Saul Bellow", _Salmagundi_, 30 (Summer 1975), 6-23.
         The interview was conducted at Skidmore College with a
         panel of members of the faculty. The article is an edited
         transcript of the public interview conducted on 8 Nov-
         ember 1973.

1240.   Bragg, Melvin, "Off the Couch by Christmas", _The
         Listener_, 93 (20 November 1975), 675-76. The Interview
         is an edited version of the televised conversation which
         took place in November 1975, on BBC's "Second House"; the
         program also included dramatized portions of Bellow's
         recently released novel _Humboldt's Gift_:

1241.   Breit, Harvey, "Talk with Saul Bellow", New York Times
         Book Review. (20 September 1953), 22.

1242.   Brandon, Henry, "Writer versus Readers : Saul Bellow",
         Sunday Times (London), 18 September 1966, 24. A discussion
         of a lecture to be delivered at the American Embassy in
         London on "The connection between the writer and his
         public in the Anglo Saxon World".

1243.   Cromie, Robert, "Saul Bellow Tells (among other things)
         the Thinking behind Herzog", _Chicago Tribune Books
         Today_, 24 January 1965, 8-9.

1244.   Dommergues, Pierre, "Rencontre avec Saul Bellow",
         Preuves, 17 (January 1967), 38-47.

1245.   Enck, John, "Saul Bellow: An Interview", _Contemporary
         Literature_, 6 (1965), 156-60.

1246.   Galloway, David D., "An Interview with Saul Bellow",
         Audit, 3 (Spring 1963), 19-23.

1247.   Gavris, K. and R. Pešin, "Razgovor sa Knjizevnikom",
         ("A Conversation with the Writer"), _Nova Makedonija_, 16,
         (24 January 1960). A meeting with Yugoslavian journalists.

1248.   Gutwillig, Robert, "Talk with Saul Bellow", _New York
         Times Book Review_, (20 September 1964), 40.

1249.   Harper, Gordon L., "Saul Bellow - The Art of Fiction:
         An Interview", _Paris Review_, 37 (Winter 1965), 48-73..
         Reprinted in _Writers at Work_, ed. A. Kazin (London, 1968),
         175-196.

1250.   Henry, Jim Douglas, "Mystic Trade", _The Listener_,
         (22 May 1969), 705-07.

1251.   Hoge, Alice Albright, "Saul Bellow Revisited at Home
         and at Work", _Chicago Daily News_, 41, 18 February
         1967, 5.

1252.   Howard, Jane, "Mr. Bellow Considers His Planet",
         Life, 68 (3 April 1970), 57-60.

1253.   Illig, Joyce, "An Interview with Saul Bellow", Publisher's
         Weekly, (22 October 1973), 74-77.

1254.   Kulshreshtha, Chirantan, "A Conversation with Saul Bellow",
         Chicago Review, 23, (Fall 1972), 715-20.

1255.   Nash, Jay and Ron Offen, "Saul Bellow", Literary Times,
         (December 1964), 10.

1256.   Pryce-Jones, David, "One Man and His Minyan", The Daily
         Telegraph, 3 October 1975, 26-30.

1257.   Robinson, Robert, "Saul Bellow at Sixty", The Listener,
         93 (13 February 1975), 218-19.

1258.   Steers, Nina A., "Successor to Faulkner", Show, 4 (Sep-
         tember 1964), 36-38.

1259.   Steinem, Gloria, "A Day in Chicago with Saul Bellow",
         Glamour, (July 1965), 98ff.

Criticism of Saul Bellow's
works

1260.   Aldridge, John W., "The Complacency of Herzog", in Time
to Murder and Create, (New York, 1966). Reprinted in
Irving Malin's Saul Bellow and the Critics, (New York,
1967), 207-10.
        Regards Herzog as a "major Establishment work" which
presents the most flattering image of the intellectual
to be found in modern literature. Despite the occupational
disease of suffering, which is apparently commensurate
with the hero's worth as a person and as a dramatic figure,
the cerebral existence emerges as a greater blessing than
a blight on the contemporary scene. Secondary characters
are viewed as grotesques, verbal abstractions, created to
provide a milieu of idiosyncratic preoccupation in which
Herzog would appear superior and saintly. The bucolic
retreat and transcendental conclusion are seen as empty and
disappointing as the hero is said to "heave a fatty sigh
of middle-class intellectual contentment".

1261.   ————"The Society of Three Novels", In Search of Heresy,
(New York, 1956), 126-48.
        Attempts to elucidate the ambiguities present in the
social milieu of serious fiction as opposed to the milieu
fictive artifice, mimesis, and irony by a comparative
analysis of Salinger's Catcher in the Rye, Styron's
Lie Down in Darkness, and Bellow's The Adventures of
Augie March. Augie March is seen as a "spiritual picaresqu
which possesses no dramatic centrality since the
uncommitted, "inner-directed" picaro experiences no real
conflict with society. Diagnoses the weakness of the novel
as characteristic of a trend in recent American fiction
in that the failure of heroic design has repeatedly
resulted in a spasm of futility, both in theme and style,
which stems from an overambitious social responsibility,
as exemplified in Bellow's work, to attend to the issues
of our time.

1262.   Alexander, Edward, "Imagining the Holocaust: Mr. Sammler's
Planet and Others", Judaism, 22 (Winter 1972), 288-300.
        Discusses Sammler's argument with Hannah Arendt's
theory of the "banality of evil" as epitomized in his
first-hand experience of the Nazi concentration camps. An
extensive knowledge of Dr. Arendt's works constitutes
the basis of a comparision of the "woman professor's"
thesis and Sammler's conception of Western society, the
debacle he had witnessed in Europe, and the sexual madness
of twentieth century America. Bellow's involvement in
the 1967 Arab-Israeli conflict (see entry 60) is linked
to Sammler's desire for "credentials", as well as a need
for the author to become as authoritative as possible
about actual historical events. Analogies are drawn
between Sammler's suffering and actual reports of Eli
Wiesel during the Eichmann trial and Auschwitz, as well as
additional historical events.

263. Allen, Michael, "Idiomatic Language in Two Novels by Saul
    Bellow", Journal of American Studies, 1 (October 1967),
    275-80.
        Compares Mark Twain's use of colloquial language and
    rhythms in Huckleberry Finn with Bellow's experimentation
    in The Adventures of Augie March. The distinctive blend
    of Yiddish intonation, syntax, and humor is seen as an
    effective means of characterization in Augie March, where-
    as the attempt to capture the speech patterns and slang
    of a WASP in Henderson the Rain King, while reflecting
    the hero's moral situation, is unsuccessful. Argues that
    Henderson's flamboyantly eccentric idiom fails, becoming
    merely the "variegated language of an idiosyncratic
    individual".

264. Alter, Robert, "A Fever of Ethnicity", Commentary, 53
    (June 1972), 68-73.
        Discusses the literary and social milieu in America
    during the Fifties and Sixties with the emergence of the
    "Yiddishkeit" and its break from Wasp cultural hegemony,
    the Black Power movement, radical protests, and the
    stirrings of women's liberation. Mr. Sammler's Planet
    is viewed as an expression of the peculiar American
    syndrome of perpetual identity crisis, set amid the
    extreme manifestations of the counter-culture.

265. ————"Heirs of the Tradition", in Rogue's Progress:
    Studies in the Picaresque Novel", (Cambridge 1967), 121-
    25.
        Identifies Augie March as the traditional "picaroon"
    who is moved by an adventurous spirit to experience and
    encompass all things possible in the "multiverse". Elements
    of the Bildungsroman introduce problematic aspects in the
    conflict between Augie's serious struggle to realize his
    fate and the general picaresque conception of the novel.
    Augie's limitless curiosity is viewed both as the work's
    major strength and weakness in its encyclopedic richness
    of language, scene, and character which enthralls and
    yet overwhelms the reader.

266. ————"The Stature of Saul Bellow", Midstream, 10
    (December 1964), 3-15.
        Locates the six Bellow novels outside the realm of
    fashionable literature of alienation. Suggests that
    Bellow writes in opposition to the prevailing nihilistic
    trend, exploring the theme of victimized protagonists
    while turning the clichés and conventions of the genre
    inside out. Discusses the oeuvre within the literary-
    historical perspective, concluding with an analysis of
    Herzog which is seen to exhibit a high degree of Bellow's
    responsiveness to innovations of past writers, while
    developing his own inimitable style and inventiveness.

1267. Atchity, John Kenneth, "Bellow's Mr. Sammler: The Last
       Man Given for Epitome", Research Studies, 38 (March 1970),
       46-54.
            Argues that the "plot" in Mr. Sammler's Planet is
       nonexistent in that "ideas" function as theme, mode of
       conveyance, and characterization, thus failing to communica
       the vision of the artist. Asserts that Bellow's control
       of his fictive material is tenuous, appearing only
       parenthetically, and that the author appears as an unwelcom
       intruder upon his character's interminable monologues.

1268. Atkins, Anselm, "The Moderate Optimism of Saul Bellow's
       Herzog", Personalist, 50 (Spring 1959), 117-29.
            Maintains that Herzog's fundamental "innocence" which
       has survived despite his harsh experiences and critical
       self-knowledge constitutes the basis of his eventual
       regeneration. Rejecting the philosophical pessimism of the
       modern reality instructors, Herzog is able to retain his
       childlike naïveté. It is through the confrontation and
       acceptance of evil and his own survival as "post-crisis
       man" that Herzog preserves his sanity and optimism.

1269. Axthelm, Peter M., "The Full Perception: Saul Bellow" in
       The Modern Confessional Novel, (Conneticut, 1967), 128-
       77.
            Traces Bellow's treatment of traditional themes of the
       confessional genre from Dangling Man to Herzog. Considers
       Moses Herzog's painful progress towards the light of self-
       awareness through the five days of his quest as divided
       into five distinctive movements of external action. The
       hero's submission to Madeleine and Gersbach is viewed as
       a dramatic step towards helplessness and humility which end
       in the cathartic episode in the police station. Suggests
       that the epiphany allows Herzog to destroy previous
       "constructions" and to create a new coherent version of
       his "Promised Land". Homeric, Biblical, and Sophoclean
       parallels are drawn in the discussion of Herzog's
       eventual self-knowledge and understanding which are defined
       as the traditional goals of the confessional hero.

1270. Bailey, Jennifer, "A Qualified Affirmation of Saul Bellow's
       Recent Work", Journal of American Studies, 7 (April 1973),
       67-76.
            Suggests that certain stylistic weaknesses of Mr.
       Sammler's Planet and Herzog are symptomatic of Bellow's
       apparent inability to balance his protagonists!
       subjective reality with a palpable: treatment of their
       social milieu. Maintains that Bellow's humanistic,
       optimistic stance, along with the need to assert a positive
       norm in the face of cultural chaos, has caused him to
       mythicize Herzog and canonize Sammler.

271.	Baim, Joseph, "Escape from Intellection: Saul Bellow's
	Dangling Man", University Review, 37 (Autumn 1970),
	28-34.
		A re-examination of Bellow's first novel in the context
	of the "mystical" or intuitive approach to the
	complexities of self-identity. Asserts that the intellect
	alone cannot fathom the depths of man's being, as Joseph
	demonstrates in Dangling Man; self-knowledge is possible
	only when one is spontaneously and intuitively aware
	of the harmony of the individual and the universal creative
	process, when the cerebral activities are abandoned and
	the childlike, non-discriminatory mode of apprehension is
	regained.

272.	Baker, Sheridan, "Saul Bellow's Bout with Chivalry",
	Criticism, 9 (Spring 1967), 109-22.
		Traces the strains of romance through the canon,
	locating subdued and curious manifestations of the "romantic
	fever" tempered by existentialism in the early works
	which later find full expression in Augie March.
	Emphasizes Bellow's happy incongruity of the imagination
	expressed in the characterization of Augie, whose quest
	is seen in terms of chivalric excesses. The later works
	are viewed as a dramatization of the dilemma of a faithless
	age that attempts to formulate a viable solution, a new
	form of humanism, reconciling "a feeling heart curbed and
	empowered by a sympathetic higher will".

273.	Baruch, Franklin, Bellow and Milton: Professor Herzog in His
	Garden", Criticism, 9 (March 1967), 37-61.
		Discusses Herzog's country setting in terms of a post-
	lapsarian Eden, complete with a network of images of ritual
	and symbols which recall Milton's Paradise Lost. Analyzes
	the hierarchical pattern of imagery in nature, combining both
	beauty and decay as part of the apocalyptic vision, which
	provides the shaping force for Bellow's fiction, as it
	had for Milton's poetry.

274.	Baumbach, Johnathan, "The Double Vision: .The Victim",
	(New York, 1965), 35-54.
		Divides the oeuvre into two categories: works of depth
	and introspection and those of breadth and exploration.
	Bellow's second novel is seen as one of the profound moral
	myths of modern times, an exemplary statement of the
	complex concerns explored throughout the canon. Stresses
	the claustrophobic rendering of the urban scene as a
	dramatic reflecter of the hero's psychic suffocation.
	Dostoevskian parallels from The Double are drawn, along
	with the thematic concern with the dark forces that control
	civilization and victimize the individual.

1275.   Bayley, John, "By Way of Mr. Sammler", _Salmagundi_, 30
        (Summer 1975), 24-33.
             Argues that the misanthropic work presents little
        external contact beyond the consciousness of the
        disenchanted central character. Maintains that Bellow
        effectively employs stylistic and linguistic devices,
        even as he depreciates them, rejecting the modern fictional
        image and form while creating a new genre. Proposes that
        the novel succeeds through the dramatic interaction of
        several perspectives which reflect antithetical views of
        reality, thus allowing the author to diminish and refine
        his own judgement, as well as that of his characters.

1276.   Belitt, Ben, "Saul Bellow: The Depth Factor", _Salmagundi_,
        30 (Summer 1975), 57-65.
             Defines the presence of "depth" in the fictive realm
        as an innate attribute of the living work, as the ultimate
        test of functional fiction. Suggests that Bellow elicits
        the poetics of depth through the continuity of his
        "suspended" protagonists' vision of existence. The Bellow
        canon is seen as a vast system of cancellations, reversals,
        and contradictions in which the function of the author's
        imagination is to "create anew" while refusing to commit
        himself or his dangling heroes to any sociological or
        philosophical mandate, existing in a "zone of magical
        immunity".

1277.   Bergler, Edmund, "Writers of Half-Talent", _American Imago_,
        14 (Summer 1957), 155-64.
             A psychoanalytic discussion of a "sub-group" of
        writers who are "neither truly creative nor hacks" includes
        Jessamyn West's _The Witch Diggers_, Marie Baumer's _The
        Seeker and The Sought_, and Bellow's _The Adventures of
        Augie March_. The "half-talented" novelists are seen to
        create a plethora of external events with an emphasis on
        sexual encounters enacted by static, one-dimensional
        characters. Augie March's condition is diagnosed as that
        of a "hyper-passive masochistic character". Accuses the
        author of unduly heavy reliance upon scatalogical details,
        the depiction of his hero's "criminotic actions" which are
        depicted without psychological awareness, and which in turn
        reveal the writer's own "dreaded psychic masochism".

1278.   Bezanker, Abraham, "The Odyssey of Saul Bellow", _Yale Review_,
        58 (Spring 1969), 359-71.
             A re-examination of the canon from a Jewish perspective
        stressing the the heroes' predilection for suffering and
        their essential vulnerability and volubility. Suggests that
        the disproportionate of the characters' responses to crises
        lends substance to the basically plotless novels. Proposes
        that sexual love in Bellow's fiction is a "necessary
        aberration, pleasurable but ambivalent" and views _Herzog_ as
        a brilliant schematic of the conditions and definitions
        of love. Elucidates Bellovian borrowings from Yiddish

literature and the folklore of the fool, tracing the
three types of fools through the six novels: the
schlimiel, schlimazl, and nebbish.

1279. Bolling, Douglass, "Intellectual and Aesthetic Dimensions
of Mr. Sammler's Planet", Journal of Narrative Technique,
4 (September 1974), 188-203.
Acknowledges the critical commentary which stresses
the consistent thematic concerns in Bellow's fiction but
emphasizes the significant differences as proof of the
author's artistry and visionary vitality. Maintains
that Mr. Sammler's Planet is based upon principles of
contrast and opposition, employing a "strategy of
bifurcation" exemplified in the dual nature of the
protagonist. Sammler's complex intellectual and aesthetic
stance suggests analogies from the world of modern art,
in particular that of Paul Klee, from the philosophy of
Schopenhauer, from the "ethical intuitivisits" such as
G.E. Moore, as well as from the Socratic rhetoric of
Logos.

1280. Boroff, David, "Saul Bellow", Saturday Review of Literature,
47 (19 September 1964), 38-39.
A brief biographical sketch in which details of Bellow's
immersion in a new dramatic milieu are provided. Reports
on Lillian Hellman's early unsuccessful attempts to
convince Bellow that Seize the Day should be dramatized.
The author discusses his first full length play The Last
Analysis which explores the "power of metaphor" and
satirizes the cant and hypocrisy of intellectual solemnity.

1281. Boulger, James D., "Puritan Allegory in Four Modern Novels",
Thought, 44 (Autumn 1969), 413-32.
Discusses the themes of Puritan trials of election,
vocation, and glorification explored in The Last Hurrah,
By Love Possessed, Invisible Man, and Herzog. Notes the
absence of dedication to a viable vocation in Herzog's
pastoral retreat as the"great weakness" of the book, in that
his quietism negates any possibility for any fitting
conclusion to his allegorical journey. Although Bellow
and Ellison are seen to possess prophetic and apocalyptic
yearnings, illustrated in the manner in which their heroes
strive to become purely allegorical figures, The Invisable
Man is viewed as the most significant and successful of
the four works.

1282. Boyers, Robert, "Attitudes towards Sex in American 'High
Culture'", Annals of American Academy of Political and
Social Sciences, (March 1968), 36-52.
Analyzes particular themes and attitudes explored in
several works of fiction published during the last decade.
Varieties of "apocalyptic sexuality" are emphasized while

attempting to relate the focus to broader questions of a
political and social nature. Suggests that Herzog offérs
no convincing illumination of nature of "normal" sexual
relations in American society. Argues that the sexual
encounters are bathed either in pathos or quaint senti-
mentality which renders them ineffably idyllic.

1283.   ————"Nature and Social Reality in Saul Bellow's Mr.
          Sammler's Planet", Critical Quarterly, 15 (Autumn 1973),
          34-56.
          Argues that Sammler is intellectually capable of
          apprehending the social reality presented to him by modern
          life in the Sixties. Attributes his failure of insight
          to the hero's affinity with the mystic affirmations of
          Meister Eckhart which is seen as an escape from the harsh
          realities of existence. Sammler's apparent lack of social
          consciousness is viewed as the inherent weakness of the
          novel wich throws the intellectual sensibility of the
          central character into confusion, presenting a series of
          brilliant philosophical fragments without a coherent vision.

1284.   Bradbury, Malcolm, "Leaving the Fifties", Encounter, 45
          (July 1975), 40-51.
          A survey of the historical, political, and literary
          milieu of the frenetic Fifties, a decade of American
          conspicuous consumption. The "crucial decade" is seen to
          be less abhorrent than aberrant, an other-directed,
          bureaucratised, consumerised period which produced an
          affluent mass-society. Explores the fiction which reflects
          the moral concern with meaningful interactions of self
          and society. A brief discussion of Bellow's first two
          novels underlines the exploration of the absurdity of
          modern existence while reaching beyond it, emphasizing
          the heroes' moral need which transcends historical and
          social determinants. "New" American novelists, such as
          Mailer, Salinger, Updike, and Roth, are considered in the
          same context.

1285.   ————"Saul Bellow and the Naturalist Tradition", Review
          of English Literature, 4 (October 1953), 80-92.
          Considers Bellow to be the most substantial writer of
          the post-war era, concerned with posing moral dilemmas
          amid disintegrating value systems, issues which are
          expressed in a wave of Jewish rhetoric, a fine frenzy of
          prose, replete with Bibical illusions, soul-searching,
          and high comedy. Bellow is placed in the company of the
          environmentalist and naturalist writers, such as Dreiser
          and Norris, by virtue of his treatment of the external
          forces of urban life and the social circumstances of his
          heroes. Notes that Bellow looks beyond determinism as
          his protagonists rebel against societal constrictions
          as they confront the gods and thereby realize their
          humanity.

.286.   —————"Saul Bellow's Henderson the Rain King", Listener,
         71 (30 January 1974), 178-87.
              Emphasizes the ironic elements of the novel which
         parodies the romance in its movement from a social world
         into the realm of myth and fantasy. Links the philosophy
         of the Wariri King to Lamarck's version of Darwinism,
         revealing Dahfu as an optimistic determinist who attempts
         to instruct Henderson in a primitive, ritualistic manner
         Mock-epic dimensions are underlined as the absurd hero
         moves steadily but ironically towards the light of self-
         awareness by way of incomplete, abstruse instructions
         from the philosopher king.

.287.   —————"Saul Bellow's Herzog", Critical Quarterly, 7
         (Autumn 1965), 269-78.
              A comparative analysis of Burrough's Naked Lunch and
         Bellow's novel underlines the issue of the dangerous
         prevalence of "modern self-pity" in recent American
         fiction. Burrough's appears to write in a bohemian-
         aesthetic context, celebrating "deviance", a contempt for
         man, and a fundamental world-weariness, whereas Bellow
         decries the "unearned bitterness" of the nihilist approach
         to life and literature. Suggests that Herzog is an attempt
         to achieve the awareness of the complexities of
         contemporary existence, while offering "a full rendering
         of intense and central human experience", as the hero
         boldly strives to define his own humanity through the
         "gladitorial combats" of his mind.

.288.   —————"Saul Bellow's The Victim", Critical Quarterly, 5
         (Winter 1963), 119-28.
              Proposes that the second novel is Bellow's finest
         work in its striking lyrical texture, the masterful use
         of the Jewish vernacular with its metaphysical vocabulary,
         the readiness to articulate intense experience, and the
         level of abstract moral concerns. Bellow's treatment of
         the "accidental" nature of human responsibility is
         emphasized in the plight of the hero who is a product of
         an uncertain world, a mixture of sensitivity and
         aggressiveness necessary to the urban existence.

.289.   Breit, Harvey, "Saul Bellow" in The Writer Observed, (New York,
         1956), 271-74.
              A biographical sketch in which aspects of Bellow's
         university background are explored, along with information
         about the genesis of Augie March. Bellow attributes the
         plight of modern fiction to the fact that "the novel has
         imitated poetry far too much recently in its severity
         and style and devotion to extract form", along with current
         writers' apparent inability to create dramatic scenes
         while concentrating upon making their work durable through
         form", thus insuring their immortality.

1290. Burgess, Anthony, "The Jew as American", Spectator,
       (7 October 1966), 455-56.
           Defines the Jew as American's great urban export,
       emerging from an over-civilized continent crammed with
       neurosis and dialectic, equipped with all of the
       prerequisite materials of a sophisticated literature.
       A brief survey of Bellow's fiction reveals a sustained
       and positive portrait of the Jew as the spokesman for
       all Americans. Stresses the mastery of language which
       not only creates vital charaters but in the natural
       literary dialect contributes an important, additional
       dimension to the language, as well as a pleasing answer
       to the cautious etiolations of writers such as Hemingway.

1291. Burns, Robert, "The Urban Experience: The Novels of Saul
       Bellow", Dissent, 24 (Winter 1969), 18-24.
           A study of the densely realized urban existence of the
       Bellovian hero, with particular emphasis on The Victim.

1292. Brustein, Robert, "Saul Bellow on the Dragstrip" in
       Seasons of Discontent: Dramatic Opinions, 1959-1965,
       (London, 1966), 172-75.
           Comments upon the apparent and efficient direction of
       Bellow's "remarkable play" The Last Analysis which
       presents one of the "most flamboyant comic characters
       ever written for the American stage", the most
       magnificent rhetoric to be heard since Clifford Odets,
       and a drama which ripples with energy and intelligence.
       Enumerates complaints against the various casting
       choices which have resulted in a "vehicular homicide"
       with the playwright as the major victim.

1293. Capon, Robert F., "Herzog and the Passion", America, 112
       (27 March 1965), 425-29.
           Discusses the work from an orthodox Christian
       perspective but notes that "Jews and secularists seem
       to paint so much better the present condition of man".
       Distinguishes Herzog's mystique of suffering, his speculati
       definition of miseries from the true, health-giving Passion
       of Christ, suggesting that Moses' salvation lies
       within the religious realm. Maintains that he will
       endure only when Herzog is able to "offer his passion
       to Christ, and only by an invitation of Christ's Passion
       into his".

1294. Campbell, Jeff, "Bellow's Intimations of Immortality:
       Henderson the Rain King", Studies in the Novel, 1
       (Fall 1969), 323-33.
           Suggests similarities between Henderson's spiritual
       quest and the process of development in the Wordsworthian
       ode, viewing the conclusion as a return to a fundamentally
       romantic affirmation of life. Examines the parodies of

literary quests and burlesques of the contemporary
intellectual milieu as part of Henderson's particular
malaise. The recurring romantic motifs and allusions
are seen as Bellow's central metaphor, obviously drawn
from Wordsworth.

295. Cecil, L. Moffitt, "Bellow's Henderson as American Imago
of the 1950's", Research Studies, 40 (December 1972),
296-300.
    Argues that Henderson must be seen as the exemplificat-
ion of a new American consciousness emerging in the late
Fifties, that of a "wealthy, powerful, progmatic,
unfulfilled" condition. Interprets Henderson's experiences
with the Arnewi and Wariri as a foretelling of the Peace
Corps attempts abroad, and sees the hero's gradual
transformation in terms of Charles Reich's Greening of
America.

296. Chapman, Abraham, "The Image of Man as Portrayed by Saul
Bellow", College Language Association Journal, 10
(Winter 1967), 285-98.
    The typical Bellovian hero is depicted as a long-
suffering individual who strives for success and a
sense of his own identity with increasing awareness of
his own limitations and the inherent senselessness of
contemporary life. Maintains that the dichotomies of
existence, the absurdity of the struggle between
materialistic and idealistic imperatives, can be
transcended by the "tempered soul" of the protagonist
who has endured the trials of the spirit and has
realized a form of salvation or regeneration - however
tentative - which allows him to re-enter the community of
man.

297. Chapman, Sara S., "Melville and Bellow in the Real World",
West Virginia University Philological Papers, 18 (1970),
51-57.
    A comparative analysis of Herman Melville's Pierre
and Bellow's The Adventures of Augie March suggests
various romantic and gothic similarities between the two
protagonists. (Of particular interest is a reply to a
letter from Ms. Chapman concerning the article which is
collected in the Bellow Papers, see entry 922, in which
Bellow acknowledges his admiration for Melville's works
but denies having read Pierre; states that Augie is more
the Sherwood Anderson ingénu than a gothic hero.)

298. Chase, Richard, "The Adventures of Saul Bellow: Progress
of a Novelist", Commentary, 27 (April 1959), 323-30.
Reprinted in I. Malin's Saul Bellow and the Critics,
(New York, 1967), 25-38. Translated into Serbo-Croation
and reprinted under the title, "Dozivljaj Saul Bellow"

in Pregled, 3 (Belgrade, Yugoslavia, 1960), 1-9.
Regards Henderson the Rain King as a romance rather
than a novel, encompassing the virtues of romantic
abstraction, freedom of movement, and expressions of
pathos, beauty, and terror. Suggests that the brutal
yet ennobled character allows the work to transcend the
limitations of a farce or comedy of manners by virtue
of his humor which is permeated with emotion,realism, and
love of human temperament and activated by a fecund and
resourceful imagination. A brief survey of the canon
underlines Bellow's fertile sense of the conversion of
reality and imagination, of fact and legend, which differs
from the traditional practise of American prose romance
but which draws upon the naturalist, realist, and metaphysical traditions, resulting in a unique fictional
experience.

1299. Ciancio, Ralph, "The Achievement of Saul Bellow's Seize
       the Day"in Literature and Theology, ed. Thomas F. Staley
       and Lester F. Zimmerman, (Oklahoma, 1969), 49-80.
           The philosophy of the charlatan Dr. Tamkin is
       identified as the "gauge" of Bellow's primary interest,
       the spiritual landscape of the novella, in his
       pronouncements on the debilitating struggle between the
       real and pretender souls. The patterns of water imagery
       which prevade the work are interpreted as "one subsuming
       metaphor, the Waters of Life, the Stream of Humanity,
       the Fountainhead of the Human Spirit conceived of as God".
       Suggests that the purgative tears in the final scene are
       the outpouring of universal mourning which cleanses the
       hero's soul, identified as the ritualistic bath, Erab
       Yomtob, performed by the Jews in preperation for Yom
       Kippur.

1300. Clayton, John J., Saul Bellow: In Defense of Man,
       (Indiana, 1968).
           Explores the conflict between self and society,
       freedom and acquiescence, brotherhood and alienation
       throughout Bellow's canon with particular attention to
       The Victim, Henderson, and Herzog. Emphasizes the
       psychological and thematic unity of all works in which
       the complex protagonists are depicted as solipsists,
       masochists, or "alienatees" who strive to become truly
       human. Stresses the essentially religious solutions
       of the heroes' problems through a personal redemption
       from the implicit defense of individuality in favor of
       a commitment to the brotherhood of man.

1301. Clurman, Harold, "Saul Bellow: The Last Analysis" in The
       Naked Image: Observations on the Modern Theatre, (New
       York, 1966), 45-47.
           Enumerates the play's intrinsic shortcomings which are
       emphasized by unsatisfactory casting and a mélange of

staging attempts which ranges from vaudevillian
exaggeration to prosaic sincerity. The central character
remains a "figment of verbiage", a gigantic effigy who
achieves no credible identity outside the author's
consciousness. Suggests that the analytic minutiae of
Bummidge's psyche are not only sordid but commonplace
in a drama which is seen as an extravaganza of the
unconscious, full of "serious nonsense", signifying
nothing.

302. Cowley, Malcolm, "Naturalism: No Teacup Tragedies" in
The Literary Situation, (New York, 1954), 74-95.
     Places The Adventures of Augie March firmly in the
naturalist tradition in a discussion of novelists, such
as Crane, Norris, Dreiser, Ellison, Algren, and Bellow,
who explore the "big subjects" of serious fiction.
Considers the fundamental differences between the literary
visions, stressing the modern writer's affirmation of the
individual, "the personalist", in conflict with social
forces.

303. Cohen, Sarah Blacher, Saul Bellow's Enigmatic Laughter,
(Chicago, 1974).
     Stresses the author's own preference of comedy to
complaint, believing the comic mode to be "more
energetic, wiser, and manlier". Although Bellow
unsparingly exposses the enervating, corruptive, and
brutalizing elements in modern life, his underlying
comic vision is seen to oppose any capitulation to
despair. Comedy of character receives the most extensive
treatment in various forms of affection, self-indulgence,
a "tug-of-war between the spiritual and somatic", and
and intellectual and sexual debilitation. While Bellow's
"comedy of ideas" is concerned with the individual's
struggle with life's anomalies, his distinctive blend of
Yiddish humor, intelligence, and wit undermines the
inherent nihilism, pessimism, or "low seriousness" of the
combat and enables his heroes, and his readers, to laugh
at themselves.

304. ─────── "Sex: Saul Bellow's Hedonistic Joke", Studies in
American Fiction, 2 (1974), 223-29.
     Considers Bellow's treatment of interpersonal
relationships as a vehicle for comedy as the various
attitudes towards sex are examined in Augie March,
Herzog, and Mr. Sammler's Planet. Suggests that the prevalent
response is that sexual desire is a denigrating and
enslaving force, a joke which nature, civilization, and
women have played on the vunerable male. Maintains that
sex is portrayed as the "comic leveller" throughout the
canon, with elements of the omnipresent warfare which
exists between the sexes.

1305. Cohn, Ruby, <u>Dialogue in American Drama</u>, (Indiana, 1971),
192-97.
A brief consideration of Bellow's one-act play "The
Wrecker", and his full length drama, <u>The Last Analysis</u>.
Decides that the earlier drama lacks focus in character
portrayal and theme, despite its brevity, whereas the
subsequent attempt is viewed as a "work of voluble
eloquence" that is rarely to be found on the American
stage. Although Bummidge is seen as a larger-than-life
character, he remains a "pygmy" in comparison with the
heroes of the novels.

1306. Cook, Bruce, "Saul Bellow: A Mood of Protest", <u>Perspective</u>
<u>on Ideas and the Arts</u>, (February 1963), 46-50.
Considers the early fiction as dramatic exploration
of the individual's rightful place in society and the
resultant conflict with the victimizing external forces.
Explores the means by which the Bellovian protagonist
registers his dissent, which is articulated in an
atmosphere of solipsism and "low seriousness" in
<u>Dangling Man</u> and <u>The Victim</u>, as well as through the lyrical
excesses of <u>Augie March</u> and <u>Henderson the Rain King</u>.

1307. Coonley, Donald, "To Cultivate, To Dread: The Concept of
Death in <u>The Ginger Man</u> and <u>Herzog</u>", <u>New Campus Review</u>,
2 (Spring 1969), 7-12.
Compares J.P. Donleavy's obsessive concern with death
which is set against the comedy, mockery, and farce of
his rogue hero's response to life with Bellow's mock-
serious fear of death which stems from his unorthodoxi-
cally Jewish protagonist's guilt and lapse in faith.

1308. Crozier, Robert D., "Theme in Augie March", <u>Critique</u>, 7
(Spring 1975), 18-32.
Argues that Bellow's fiction deals with "supra-
psychologiacl, poetic values" which represent the highly
diversified activities of his contemplative heroes. The
theme-complex of <u>Augie March</u> is described as a pentagonal
pattern consisting of the interaction of "character-fate,
power, money, love, and urbanization". Posits a religious
solution to Augie's spiritual dilemma which is viewed as
a void which "demands that God be poured into it,
discovering the silent emptiness of God into which the
self can be poured".

1309. Davis, Robert Gorham, "The American Individualist Tradition:
Bellow and Styron", <u>The Creative Present</u>, eds. N. Balakian
and C. Simmons, (New York, 1963), 111-41.
A chronological analysis of Bellow's canon within the
context of American affirmative response. Notes a
misanthropic streak in <u>Henderson the Rain King</u> which

undermines the hero's optimistic strivings, while
Styron's novels are seen to be marked by falsely prodigious
rhetoric and uninteresting characters.

1310. Demarest, David, "The Themes of Discontinuity in Saul Bellow's
Fiction: 'Looking for Mr. Green' and 'A Father-to-be'",
Studies in Short Fiction, 6 (Winter 1969), 175-86.
Indicates that apparent inconsistencies between the
world's of ideas and experience in the attitudes of the
characters in two "dialectical" short stories. Realistic
social themes in an urban society are treated
metaphorically as part of the broader philosophical tenor
of the fiction. Stresses the fundamental problem basic
to both pieces: the discontinuity of human moods which
undercuts man's expectations that life should provide
any intellectual order.

1311. Detweiler, Robert, "Patterns of Rebirth in Henderson",
Modern Fiction Studies, 12 (Winter 1967), 405-14.
(Collected in Bellow Papers; see entry 721.)
The basic structual and thematic unity of the novel
is elucidated through a discussion of four basic devices
which develop the concept of rebirth and redemption.
Traces the network of animal imagery which reveals
Henderson's ultimate spiritual and physical transformation
from a lower into a "higher being". Considers the quixotic
character as the archetypal hero, humorously incorporating
symbols of psychological reality and mythic patterns.

1312. ————Saul Bellow: A Critical Essay, (Grand Rapids,
Michigan, 1967). Collected in the Bellow Papers; see
entry 721.
Assumes a Christian perspective in a discussion of
Bellow's fiction which is seen as a representative
statement for the spiritual dilemma of the Christian
majority, as well as the Jewish minority. As a novelist
of affirmation Bellow is said to celebrate the marriage
of the spirit and the flesh in his works as part of the
matured act of faith, a reunified consciousness, which is
seen as an outgrowth of personal crisis. Aware of the
dangers of "outrageous theologizing", the Bellovian canon
is not to be read as theology but as an "imaginative
witness to faith that exists in a fruitful tension with
Christian faith.

1313. Dickstein, Morris, "For Art's Sake", Partisan Review, 33
(1966), 617-21.
A vociferous reply to Bellow's keynote address to the
International PEN Congress (see entry 64) during which the
novelist attacked current critical methods. Bellow's
suggestion that critics accept "rooted norms" of literary
analysis, along with his apparant refusal to acknowledge
"the political dimension of criticism", indicates that he

adopted the view of the "middle brow public that has at-
last embraced him for its own".

1314. Donoghue, Denis, "Bellow in Short", Art International, 12
(1969), 59-60, 64.
Examines Mosby's Memoirs and Other Stories in terms of
the thematic concerns and circular structure as
exemplified in Herzog. Maintains that Bellow envisions
a piece of fiction as a circle, "a wheel of feeling",
which explains the disjointed quality of portions of his
works which read like short stories, as well as some of
the weaker stories which appear to be fragments of
incomplete novels, lacking a point of intersection or a
controlling sensibility.

1315. ———"Commitment and the Dangling Man", Studies, 53
(1954), 175-84.
Defines the characterists common to Bellow's
fundamentally passive protagonists. Identifies the
suffering, opposition, alienation, and introspection of
the heroes who appear to be more aware of the symptoms of
the malaise than of the cause. Summarizes the predicament
of the Bellovian hero as an ongoing struggle with societal
pressures and a search for equilibrium, meaning,
salvation, or some form of earthly condition in which the
soul may live.

1316. Drabble, Margaret, "A Myth to Stump the Experts", New
Statesman, 436 (26 March 1971).
A reappraisal of Henderson the Rain King which maintains
that the work is as powerful as it had been at its first
reading a decade before. Notes that the symbolic and
mythical material succeeds on various levels which would
generally be obscure or banal in the hands of most
writers. Decides that Bellow's prose has an extraordinary
capacity for "conveying mental exitement and the most
subtle states of feeling in terms of physical sensation"
which is unexcelled in modern fiction.

1317. Edwards, Duane, "The Quest for Reality in Henderson the
Rain King", Dalhousie Review, 53 (1965), 246-55.
Sresses the excessive amount of Henderson's physical
and emotional energy which negates his desperate attempts
to confront the reality of his existence. Henderson's
gradual transformation is charted through the various
stages of his apprehension of the importance of the role
of "feminine power", through Willatale's wisdom, and his
own adoration of "the old bitch life". Suggests that .
although the hero is instructed to control his emotive
responses in order to grasp the fundamental understanding
of reality, Bellow does not emphasize the limitations of
his character's mind but allows an unusual blending of
fact and illusion.

1318. Eisenger, Charles, "Saul Bellow", in <u>Contemporary Novelists</u>,
       ed. James Vinson, (London, 1973), 111-14.
       A biographical sketch which provides a comprehensive
       coverage of little known details of literary awards,
       teaching assignments, and various accomplishments in
       other fields, along with a survey of familiar information
       about the novelist's literary and familial background.

1319. —————"Saul Bellow: Love and Identity", <u>Accent</u>, 18
       (Summer 1958), 179-203.
       A close examination of the canon reveals the common
       quest of the protagonists for acceptance into the brother-
       hood of man, underlying Bellow's belief that the absence
       of love causes man to be alienated and isolated. Traces the
       Hasidic elements in the novels: the desperate need for
       love and the lyrical joy of existence, both of which
       function without the theism or mysticism of the sect.
       Asserts that Bellow's qualified optimism, while reviving
       the cult of the personality and the primacy of the self,
       has provided a viable solution to the dilemma of the loss
       of community in post-war America.

1320. —————"Saul Bellow: Man Alive, Sustained by Love" in
       <u>Fiction of the Forties</u>, (Chicago, 1963), 341-62.
       A slightly revised version of an earlier article (see
       entry 1318) is collected in an extensive critical
       survey of the literary/historical milieu of the period.
       The updated analysis is presented as the concluding
       statement on the pre- and post-war "search of man
       and America".

1321. Ellmann, Richard, "Search for an Internal Sanctuary",
       <u>Chicago Sun Times Book Review</u>, (27 September 1964), 1.
       Identifies Herzog's adulterous wife as a distinctive
       heroine of our time in her masterful neuroticism and
       "lashing low-down speech". Sees the hero's attempts to
       assimilate Madeleine's inscrutable malevolence into his
       world view and his gradual convelescence from the
       onslaughts of her infinite cruelty as a small but hopeful
       sign for humanity as he retreats to a state of "secular
       blessedness" and equilibrium in his postlapsarian garden.
       Bellow's stylistic and linguistic feats in the blend of
       Yiddish and American dialects are similar to Joyce's
       accomplishments in <u>Ulysses</u> but profoundly American in
       their outspoken buoyancy.

1322. Epstein, Joseph, "Saul Bellow of Chicago", <u>New York Times</u>
       <u>Book Review,</u> (9 May 1971), 4-16.
       Discusses the personal and professional views of the
       "premier American novelist" who as achieved eminence as
       well as anonymity in his hometown. The author comments
       upon current literary scene, his own work, the "gladitorial"
       tendency of modern writers to become "publicity intellectuals",

and the label of the "American Jewish writer" which he finds intellectualy vulgar and unnecessarily parochial-izing. Sammlerian statements about modern society which is likened to "decadent Rome ... with writers chief among the court jesters" are included in one of the most revelatory discussions of Bellow's own work and literature in general.

1323. Fielder, Leslie, <u>Love and the American Novel</u>, (London, 1967), 336-38.
Includes Bellow in the catalogue of American male writers who are congenitally incapable of portraying a convincing heterosexual relationship. The entire canon of Bellow's work is seen to be singularly lacking in vivid female characters; the women presented are either "nympholeptic fantasies" or simply unconvincing. Discusses the recurrence of the "unnatural triangle" in Melville, Hawthorne, and Bellow, underlining the "homo-sexual imperative" in much of Bellow's fiction, illustrated most dramatically in <u>The Victim</u> and <u>Herzog</u>.

1324. ─────<u>No! In Thunder</u>, (London, 1963).
Portions of the book originally appeared in an article of the same name in <u>Esquire</u>, 54 (September 1960); the discussion of Bellow is to be found on 77-79.
Attempts to place Bellow into the schema of negation which dominates modern fiction, emphasizing the tragic implications of the gap between the idealized order in the universe and the actual chaos. Briefly treats Bellow's rendering of the themes of the victimization of man, the mutual torment of the two protagonists who struggle to discover their own humanity, as expressed in <u>The Victim</u>. Dismisses the "unearned euphoria" of <u>Henderson the Rain King</u> which appears forced and empty, although Fielder had earlier regarded Henderson as the most sucessful contemporary hero, a man who has learned that "it is the struggle itself which is his definition". (<u>Esquire</u>, 79).

1325. ─────"Saul Bellow", Prairie Schooner, 31 (Summer 1957), 103-10. Reprinted in I. Malin's <u>Saul Bellow and the Critics</u>, (New York, 1967), 1-9. A revised and abreviated version of the article appeared under the title, "The Breakthrough: The American Jewish Novelist and the fictional Image of the Jew", <u>Midstream</u>, 4 (1957), 15-35. The article was also translated and reprinted in Pierre Dommergues' <u>Saul Bellow</u> (Paris, 1967) under the title, " L'Archetype du Rêve Juif", 92-99.
Sees Bellow as the first Jewish fictionist to enter the American cultural scene, as the inheritor of a tradition of false starts, abject retreats, and grey

inconclusions. Bellow is portrayed as the spokesman for intellectual America, a writer who is capable of transforming its obsessions into myths, and a novelist who has earned his rightful position in the center of American literature. A survey of the canon underlines the predominantly Jewish themes and defines the essential identity of the Bellovian hero as the Jew in perpetual exile, the quintessential Huck Finn.

1326. Finkelstein, Sidney, "The Anti-Hero in Updike, Bellow, and Malamud", American Dialog, 7, 12-14.
    A Marxist art critic discusses the role of the anti-hero as an extension of social consciousness, deciding that American fiction has "hit its lowest point since the end of the anti-fascist war". Accuses Bellow of writing a "bad racist novel which serves the very elements in civilization it pretends to despise under the guise of pseudo-intellectuality in Mr. Sammler's Planet. Updike's Rabbit Redux and Malamud's The Tenants receive similar treatment.

1327. ————"Lost Convictions and Existentialism: Arthur Miller and Saul Bellow" in Existentialism and Alienation in American Literature, (New York, 1965), 252-69.
    A comparative analysis of the two authors from the perspective that the alienated protagonist is inextricably bound to existentialism through the confrontation of the absurdity and nothingness of his existence. Imposes a Marxist ideological solution upon the plights of the heroes in Miller's plays and Bellow's novels who experience the hopelessness of alienation in urbanized America and whose "essence, the consciousness of being" is endangered by external forces which will cause it to "dissolve into death".

1328. Fisch, Harold, "The Hero as Jew: Reflections on Herzog", Judaism, 17 (Winter 1968), 42-54.
    Suggests that the success of Herzog indicates the universality of the Jewish experience within the consciousness of modern man who has become equally exiled and alienated. Identifies the specifically Jewish elements in the novel through an extended comparison with Joyce's Ulysses. Maintains that although the Hebraic tradition comprises an integral portion of Herzog's and Bellow's background, the novel transcends any limitations of the Jewish past or future and makes its own impressive statement.

1329.   Fossum, Robert, "The Devil and Saul Bellow", Comarative
        Literature Studies, 2 (1966), 197-208.
             Underlines the fundamentally religious dimensions of
        the quests of the Bellovian hero who is involved in a
        painful struggle with the overwhelming elements of the
        secular world. The imminent victimization of the protagonist
        is stressed as contemporary society is seen as a force
        which negates man's humanity, reduces him to an object, a
        "thing to be manipulated, thereby preventing him from
        being a person responsible for his own salvation, which
        is his greatness".

1330.   ―――――――"Inflationary Trends in the Criticism of Fiction:
        Four Studies of Saul Bellow", Studies in the Novel, 2 99-
        104.
             Notes that since 1965, a number of critical works have
        been published on Bellow, all of which assert that he is
        the finest living American novelist. Questions whether
        Bellow's fiction warrants the detailed explication given
        by critics such as Tanner, Opdahl, Clayton, and Malin.
        Bemoans the recent tendancy to elevate the role of criticism
        to that of literature itself, resulting in a plethora of
        works which often become tiresome in the art of trivia.

1331.   Frank, Reuben, "Saul Bellow: The Evolution of a Contemporary
        Novelist", Western Review, 18 (Winter 1954), 101-12.
             Traces the stylistic progression from tightness and
        sparsity to a free, diversified form and an attitudinal
        shift from despair to "reserved affirmation" in Bellow's
        three novels. Art and morality are identified as the
        novelist's fundamental concerns, as exemplified in his heroes
        search for definition during the traumatized post-war period
        Names Bellow as the representative voice of the "Silent
        Generation" by his sensitive treatment of current social
        and moral problems which lie "between consciousness and
        action, between tradition and contemporaneity".

1332.   Freedman, Ralph, "Saul Bellow: The Illusion of Environment",
        Wisconsin Studies in Contemporary Literature, 1 (Winter
        1960), 50-65.
             Argues that Bellow's distinctive rendering of the "social
        novel" world has transmogrified the genre into a fiction
        in which the hero and the external world become related to
        one another in a light-hearted dialectic. Bellow's skilful
        use of figurative language, while often raised to a symbolic
        plane, is seen to demonstrate the action of the urban
        environment upon the human consciousness. Considers the
        increasingly abstract terms which are employed to depict
        the contemporary world as an internal, conditioning force
        exerted upon the protagonists, producing both thematic and
        emblematic motifs through the canon.

1333. Friedman, Alan, "The Jews Complaint in Recent American
       Fiction", Southern Review, 8 (1972), 41-59.
          Defines the social and literary role of the Jew as a
       "cultural schizophrenic, a concatenation of past and future
       haunted by a sense of his own uniqueness" and burdened by
       his heritage and vision. Considers Roth's Portnoy, Malamud's
       Fixer, and Bellow's Henderson within the literary/historical
       context, emphasizing a major change of focus in the Fifties
       and Sixties in that the Jews have asserted their rights and
       privileges of writing about themselves.

1334. Frohock, W.M., "Saul Bellow and His Penitent Picaro", South-
       west Review, 52 (Winter 1968), 36-44.
          States that the acute moral awareness of the Jewish
       picaro in Augie March places the hero in a totally different
       moral climate than that of his predecessors. Identifies the
       work as a "confession that adopts the picaresque structure"
       and succeeds by the fortuitous conjunction of the form and
       the uniquely rendered material. The later works appear to
       indicate the novelist's suspicion of a prescribed literary
       form and point to a rejection of any recognizable model.

1335. Fuchs, Daniel, "Saul Bellow and the Modern Tradition",
       Contemporary Literature, 15 (Winter 1974), 67-89.
          Considers Bellow as a writer who has resisted the modern-
       istic trend, eschewing the thesis novel which proceeds from
       an idea, and writing within the tradition of Tolstoi and
       Dostoevsky while creating a distinctive and unique oeuvre.
       Discusses the central thrust of Bellow's fiction which
       rejects absorption into fashionable wave of nihilism,
       "immoralism", and the aesthetic view, preferring the brother-
       hood of man to the aesthete's ironic distance. The author's
       philosophical stance is considered through a close exam-
       ination of his various essays and lectures on the state of
       modern fiction, along with references to unpublished works
       collected in the Bellow Papers (see 14-97 of this book for
       complete details of the collection).

1336. Gallo, Louis, Like You're Nobody: Letters to Saul Bellow
       1961-62, (New York, 1966).
          Sporadic and discursive commentary on Bellow's work in
       a series of unanswered letters to the novelist (see entries
       922 and 926 for details of the correspondence and a carbon
       copy of the draft of the original work entitled The Bellow-
       Gallo Letters which was sent to Bellow for his approval).
       Excerpts from Bellow's single reply in the form of an
       editorial acceptance of Gallo's short story for the journal
       The Noble Savage are included in the collection of
       frustrated, unanswered epistles.

1337. Galloway, David D., "The Absurd Man as Picaro: The Novels of
       Saul Bellow", Texas Studies in Literature and Language, 6
       (Summer 1964), 226-54. An updated, extended version of the

article appeared in Galloway's The Absurd Hero in American
Fiction, (Texas, 1971), 82-139.
Examines the extensive parallels between Bellow's fiction
and the novel of the absurd, with particular attention paid
to Camus's The Stranger. Bellow's rejection of nihilism and
orthodoxy, along with the consistent affirmation of man's
humanity throughout his canon constitute the basis of the
"optimistic" conviction of the absurdist writers. Attempts
to isolate the diversified attitudes of the Bellovian
protagonists which incorporate the "life-enhancing alter-
natives" which he may adopt when confronted by the absurdity
of his quest for identity.

1338. —————"Mr. Sammler's Planet: Bellow's Failure of Nerve",
Modern Fiction Studies, 19 (Spring 1973), 17-28.
Argues that the blatant repetition of thematic concerns
throughout the canon betrays a bankruptcy of Bellow's
novelistic imagination. Commends the comic wit of the work,
the vivid characterization of minor figures and the aged
avuncular hero who offers an authentic voice of the past, the
deft interweaving of motifs, but decides the novel suffers
from a "dissociation of sensibility". The absence of "formal
experimentation" is viewed as the major flow in the novel,
revealing the author's contentment with a narrative formula
which constricts his vision of the modern world and which
causes him to rely upon the force of rhetoric to support the
burden of intellectual meaning ascribed to his characters.

1339. —————"Moses-Bloom-Herzog: Bellow's Everyman", Southern
Review, 2 (Winter 1966), 61-76.
Sees Herzog as a unique blend of Bellow's earlier themes
and devices: the meditative narrative of the impotent
intellectual and the picaresque comedy of the adventurous
rebel. Identifies the source of the name of Moses Herzog in
the Cyclops episode of Joyce's Ulysses and examines the
similarities which exist within the characterization and
actions of Leopold Bloom, and more generally as a "modern
Everyman" who has successfully moved beyond affirmation of
the absurd experience of life to a deeper apprehension of
self in relation to others and the world at large.

1340. Garrett, George, "To Do Right in a Bad World: Saul Bellow's
Herzog", Hollins Critic, 2 (April 1965), 2-12.
Views Bellow's fiction as essentially comic, including
the early works which encompass humorous situations under-
lined by the reactions of minor characters to the super-
ficially serious predicaments of the heroes. Commends the
novelist's imaginative use of "ancient and honorable literar
forms" without a need for flamboyant innovation, as well as
the succesful avoidance of thematic and technical repetition
throughout his work. Herzog is seen as Bellow's supreme
accomplishment, embodying the humanistic response while
demanding logic and perception from all the readers.

1341. Geismar, Maxwell, "The American Short Story Today",
       Studies on the Left, 4 (Spring 1964), 21-27.
            Deplores the short fiction of Salinger, Roth, Updike,
       Malamud, Bellow, and others which exhibits the "increasingly
       narrow range of its visions and content alike" and the
       absence of social, idealogical, metaphisical, or
       emotional horizons. Decries the stress placed upon the
       intricate craftsmanship of the "well-made story" but
       expresses hope in the work of Styron, Algren, Hersey,
       and James Jones.

1342. ———— "The Great Herzog Schande", The Minority of One,
       (December 1964), 29-30.
            Regards the enthusiastic reception of Herzog as the
       "great literary scandal of the year", representing a
       deterioration of Bellow's craft into nihilism, nastiness,
       and spiritual obscenity. The work is seen as representative
       of the mid-sixties mentality of non-involvement which
       dismisses any serious social concerns. Rejects the central
       figure as a "wailing infant excluded from human love and
       human history", a self-indulgent sufferer who pretends to
       entertain a social conscience through a series of letters
       written to political figures. Bemoans the presence of
       "false Jewishness" in the novel which exhibits a sense
       of shame of being a Jew, rather than pride, pleasure and
       joy in the great tradition.

1343. ————"Saul Bellow: Novelist of the Intellectuals" in
       American Moderns: From Rebellion to Conformity, (New
       York, 1958), 210-24. Reprinted in I. Malin's Saul Bellow
       and the Critics, (New York, 1967), 10-24.
            States that Bellow's work represents the prevailing
       standards and values of the intelligentsia, while based
       firmly upon the "social environmental nexus". A brief
       review of the canon reveals a "post-Marxist, nostalgically
       semi-religous" philosophy expressed in Dangling Man and a
       concept of the Jewish hero which verges upon paranoia and
       madness in The Victim, negating any historic sense of the
       Semitic heritage. The entire oeuvre is found lacking
       because of the Judaic force which for Bellow constricts
       and distorts his vision.

1344. Ginden, James, "Saul Bellow", Harvest of a Quiet Eye: The
       Novel of Compassion, (Indiana 1971), 305-36.
            Discusses Bellow's fiction within the context of the
       "tradition of compassion" and the definition of man as
       existential. Joseph in Dangling Man is representative
       of the diminishing American capacity for heroism during
       the 1940's, the first "a-hero" who is alienated from an
       increasingly fragmented world. Considers Herzog to be the
       most distinctive extension of Bellow's themes, a work

139

which far surpasses earlier attempts to "go beyond definition" of contemporary man through the fabulistic or picaresque forms. Believes Bellow to be most successful when he "avoids the fable, the metaphysically directed form, and shapes his material from the dense and complex historical flux".

1345. Glicksberg, Charles I., "The Theme of Alienation in the American Jewish Novel", Reconstructionist, 23 (November 1957), 8-13.
      A brief survey of current Jewish fiction which deals with the alienated existence of the "marginal man" in contemporary society. Focuses upon the introspection and solipsism of Bellow's characters which increase the feelings of enstrangement and isolation. Particular attention is placed on Joseph in Dangling Man and Asa in The Victim.

1346. Gold, Herbert, "Fiction of the Fifties", Hudson Review, 12 (Summer 1959), 192-201. Reprinted in Fiction of the Fifties: A Decade of American Writing, ed. H. Gold, (New York, 1959).
      Names Bellow as an exemplary writer of his generation, a novelist who illustrates the philosophical and religious quest contained within an abiding sense of the transience of existence. The entire canon of his work poses metaphysical questions as Bellow presents the "intensely lyrical and dramatic, onflowing participation in the life of his Chicago, his Africa, his universe". Regards Ellison's Invisible Man as a representative book of the decade in its basic philosophical purpose. Contends that the best writers of the Fifties have both described the disasters of the times and offered tentative notions of order.

1347. Goldfinch, Michael A., "A Journey to the Interior", English Studies, 43 (October 1962), 439-43.
      The American syndrome of youth, materialism, and a sense of exile is said to be exemplified in Henderson's quest for antiquity, spirituality, and rediscovered roots. Traces the mythic patterns of Henderson's venture into the dark "female regions" of Africa and his experiences with the hermaphroditic queen who conveys wisdom and strength. Praises the novel's robust prose, artful characterization, rugged humor, and the mastery of language which resuscitates a myth that in turn "burns up everything merely academic and flares into something living".

1348. Grossman, Edward, "The Bitterness of Saul Bellow",
Midstream, (August/September 1970), 3-15.
   Stresses the weight of the author's "unearned bitterness"
exhibited in Sammler's lengthy cerebrations as he
observes the world of the Sixties with distress and
disgust. Locates the central weakness in the "desperately
bleak and incurious novel" as the stylistic failure to
envoke his character's past and tangible associations,
as Bellow had accomplished so notably in Herzog. Compares
the treatment of perspective and theme in Sammler's
Planet with a similar, yet rarely discussed short story,
"The Old System", which is considered technically perfect
and thematically satisfying.

1349. Guerrard, Albert, "Saul Bellow and the Activists: The
Adventures of Augie March", Southern Review, 3 (July 1967),
582-96.
   Defines Augie's activist stance, not in political
terms, but in the explicit belief in the sheer vitality
of action as a moral good, conveyed by the picaresque hero
who exhibits an authentic observation of life and an
irrepressible will to live. Commends Bellow's stylistic
and linguistic experiment as a courageous attempt which
succeeds in rescuing the novel from pretentious or
impersonal modes of writing. Presents a schematic
description of the problematic mixture of improvisatory
language and syntax of the numerous characters, along with
the ultimate authorial voice which is summoned to dissolve
any discords of style or theme. Points out the lapses
in linguistic control, as well as the successes of the
highly intensifies language and accented prose that
borders on the "sprung rhythm" of Hopkins.

1350. Guttmann, Allen, "Mr. Bellow's America", The Jewish Writer
in America, (New York, 1971), 178-21.
   Sees Bellow as the explorer of "marginality" in
America, of comic and tragic characters in quest of their
uncertain identities. Interprets Joseph's voluntary
surrender of freedom to army regimentation as a defeat,
placed as it is within the emotional economy of Dangling
Man, but reads the subsequent conclusions as affirmations
of life, tentative though they may be.
Stresses the universal "marginal man" in Bellow's fiction,
the American hero whose Jewishness is nominal rather
than religious, and whose efforts are directed towards
a reconciliation between self and society.

1351. ————"Saul Bellow's Mr. Sammler", Contemporary Literature,
14 (2), 157-68.
   Surveys recent criticism of Mr. Sammler's Planet which
dismisses the ironic distance between author and

protagonist and ascribes the hero's "weary humanism"
to Bellow's own misanthropic bitterness. Compares
Sammler's jauniced political and social observations
with the more vehement renunciations of "apocalypticism"
expresses in Herzog. Objects to the tendency to view
Sammler as a mouthpiece for the radical right, as well as
to the inclination to read the novel as a polemic or
political tract which is compatible with Bellow's own
public statements.

1352. Haber, Leo, "Saul Bellow's Discourse", Jewish Frontier, 37
(June 1970), 24-26.
Notes the prevalent biographical reductionism of
critics who are unable to distinguish the cerebrations of
the septagenarian luftmensch from the authorial voice.
Considers whether Saul Bellow is a "Jewish novelist" and
Mr. Sammler's Planet a typically Jewish novel. Decides
the latter is true since the work is saturated with talk,
and since "talk, divine talk, cannot be dissociated from
the Jewish psyche, the Jewish experience, and the Jewish
fate".

1353. Hall, James, "Portrait of the Artist as a Self-Creating,
Self-Vindicating, High-Energy Man", The Lunatic in the
Drawing Room, (Indiana, 1968), 127-80.
Bellow's heroes are depicted as "walking syntheses of
modernism", accidental resolutionists in a crisis-filled
world which threatens to destroy their equilibrium and
self-creation. Notes that external forces and ambiguous
situations in the environment are employed to reveal
aspects of personality of the protagonists. Suggests
that when Bellow avoids alienation in his characterization
he heightens loneliness, and in doing so portrays the
"Irritable Man" whose irascibility is a result of his
attempts to embrace all of life. Names Bellow as the "poet
of self-chosen discomfort".

1354. Handy, William J., "Saul Bellow and the Naturalistic Hero",
Texas Studies of Language and Literature, 5, (1964), 538-
45.
An examination of Bellow's most perfectly constructed
work Seize the Day within the context of the naturalistic
tradition. In a discussion of the characters of Dreiser,
Steinbeck, and Hemingway, Bellow's anti-hero, Tommy Wilhelm,
is seen to be significantly different, more similar to
those of Malamud or Salinger.

1355. Harper, Howard M., Desperate Faith, (Chapel Hill, 1967),
       7-64.
           Defines the dilemma of the Bellow hero in terms
       of an intensive search for meaning and identity in an
       essentially chaotic and meaningless society. Suggests
       that the tentatively affirmative conclusions of the
       quests of the quixotic characters are results of a
       confrontation with reality and subsequent triumph
       over "profound despair".

1356. Harris, James Neil, "One Critical Approach to Mr. Sammler's
       Planet", Twentieth Century Literature, 18 (October 1972),
       235-70.
           Traces the sardonic pattern of parody of theme and
       character, while examining the religious elements of a
       work which is seen to be profoundly concerned with the
       process of acquiring spiritual faith. Stresses Sammler's
       eschatological point of view, reinforced by dicussions of
       Kierkegaard and Meister Eckhardt, along with the aged
       hero's attempts to escape from the temporal prison and
       to enter a realm of sacredness. Emphasizes the use of
       irony which is employed to destroy the dichotomies of
       the human situation, as well as to "reconcile the
       paradoxical nature of religious faith through the paradox
       of the novel's dianoia".

1357. Harwell, Meade, "Picaro from Chicago", Southwest Review,
       39 (Summer 1954), 273-76.
           Sees Augie March as a thematic move from the fiction
       neorosis to an authentic rendering of a vital world of
       common experience. Compares Bellow's picaresque work
       with the fiction of Thomas Wolfe, noting their comparable
       skill in creating vital characters through a dynamic
       image, as well as their common weakness in linguistic
       control. The collection of grotesque characters is viewed
       as an extension of the viciousness and exoticism of the
       American urban jungle. Praises the novel as a revolutionary
       stylistic experiment but questions whether Bellow possesses
       the "greatness of vision, character, and evaluation from
       which a successful revolution can grow".

1358. Hassan, Ihab H., "Five Faces of a Hero", Critique, 3
       (Summer 1960), 28136. An extended version of the article
       appears in Hassan's Radical Innocence: Studies in the
       Contemporary American Novel, (Princeton, 1961), 290-324.
       An extract of Chapter II entitles "Saul Bellow: The Quest
       and Affirmation of Reality" in Radical Innocence has been
       translated and collected in Pierre Dommergues' Saul
       Bellow, (Paris, 1967), under the title "Les Possibilités
       de Augie March", 186-96.
           Suggests that the prime function of Bellow's protagonists
       is to dramatize the assertion that reality is worth the
       neccessary agonies of human existence, despite its
       inherent unintelligibity. Although the heroes continually
       quest for meaning and reason in the universe, the
       predominant mode is seen to be one of lyrical celebration
       of human existence, of pleasure at its mystery. Comments
       upon the essential humility of the protagonists who
       achieve self-knowledge through experience, love an
       "attitude of joyful acceptance" and affirmation of life
       which incorporates an ironic appraisal of its limits and
       transiency.

1359. Heiney, Donald, "Bellow as European", Proceedings of the
       Comparitive Literature Symposium: Modern American Fiction,
       Insights and Foreign Lights, 5 (January 1972), eds.
       W.T. Zyla and Wendell Aycock, 77-88.
           Demonstrates that Henderson the Rain King is an
       anthropological novel in its concern with ritual,
       exorcism, and freedom from "private and collective demons".
       Suggests that the pastoral and Rousseauistic tradition is
       transmuted into Henderson's assault on the African
       setting in his spiritual search amid the primitive
       cultures for a solution to his moral dilemma. Agrues that
       the novel is the culmination of the development of the
       fascination with primitivism and innocence.

1360. Hill, John, "The Letters of Moses Herzog: A Symbolic Mirror",
       Studies in the Humanities, 2 (Summer 1971), 40-45.
           Studies the stylistic device of the letters as an
       innovative solution to the problem of recapitulation of
       events. The thematic quality of the correspondence is
       analysed as an extension of the protagonist's serious
       social and political concerns, as well as an articulation
       of his personal and spiritual dilemmas.

1361. Hobson, Laura, "Trade Winds", Saturday Review of Literature,
       36 (22 August 1953), 6.
       An advance report on Augie March, promoted as the "East
       of Eden for 1953", cites several favorable pronouncements
       by Lionel Trilling, Rober Penn Warren, and others.
       Provides details concerning the novel's gestation, of

Bellow's original intention to publish the work (which
expanded over the years) in two volumes, and of Viking's
suggestion to postpone publication until the monumental
novel of approximately a quarter-million words was
completed.

1362. Hoffman, Frederick J., "The Fool of Experience: Saul
Bellow's Fiction", Contemporary American Novelists, ed.
H.T. Moore (Illinois, 1964), 80-94.
An examination of Bellow's canon underlines the
affirmative impulse of the novelist who rejects super-
ficial and easy optimism but maintains that it is "possible
and neccessary to affirm", Considers Seize the Day to be
Bellow's finest achievement and suggests that the writer
is perhaps better suited to the controled short piece of
fiction.

1363. ————The Modern Novel in America: 1900-1950, (Chicago,
1951), 188-90.
A brief consideration of The Victim as an innovative
extension of naturalism in the significant use of
realistic material from the natural and urban environment
which enforces the psychological and moral concerns of
the victimized protagonist. In a broad historical sketch
of the fiction of the Forties, Bellow's novel is viewed as
an encouraging exercise of the literary advantages made
available to the novelist through several decades of
naturalistic and realistic writings.

1364. Hoffman, Michael J., "From Cohn to Herzog", Yale Review,
58 (Spring 1969), 342-58.
A revisionist view of Hemingway's portrayal of the
archetypal Jew as the peripheral figure in the Wasp
novel isolates the cliche characteristics which reapper
in Bellow's Herzog three decades later. Defines the
Jewish tradition which elevates the self in communion
with others, as well as the tendency to verbalize all
feelings and subjects: "Judaism erects the word into a
magical totem". Distinguishes Bellow's comic rendition of
the absurd plight of his suffering hero from Hemingway's
humorless and horrific vision of life. Both Herzog and
Cohn are seen as "naifs in the American tradition of the
radical innocent".

1365. Hopkinson, Tom, "The Adventures of Augie March by Saul Bellow",
London Magazine, (June 1954), 82-86.
Proposes that the rambling exultations over the
mysteries of modern existence be seen as a work of
revelation in the eighteenth-century sense, in which "the
existence and essential goodness of God can be deduced
from the complexity and multifariousness of his handiwork".

145

Generally praises the flood of fresh minor characters which enliven the prose, but finds the women characters lacking in verve and depth. Reflects the favourable British reception of the work in the contention that the novel offers a double appeal to the reader's sense of enjoyment and perception.

1366. Howe, Irving, "Introduction to Seize the Day", Classics of Modern Fiction, ed. I. Howe, (New York, 1968), 457-66.
       A review of the basic plot structure and characterization of Bellow's most technically perfect work. Emphasizes the thematic concerns of the work and discusses the deliberately ambiguous conclusion in which the protagonist's grief releases him from the external societal and familial pressures and enables him to recognize his own humanity.

1367. ————"Mass Society and Post-Modern Fiction", Partisan Review, 26 (Summer 1959), 420-36.
       A discussion of recent fiction by Ellison, Gold, Morris, Salinger, Malamud, Algren, and Bellow which underlines the societal pressures of an urbanized existence. Sees Augie March as a "paean to the idea of personal freedom in hostile circumstances" with its central character moving magically beyond the barriers of American society. Henderson the Rain King is considered an extravagantly wild tale which ultimately refers to America "where many spirits sleep".

1368. ————"Odysseus, Flat on His Back", New Republic, 151 (19 September 1964), 21-26.
       Considers Herzog to be Bellow's finest work, establishing him as "a virtuoso of fictional technique and language". Notes weakness in several minor characters, notably the women, which are drawn without psychological insight or nuance and appear as caricatures. Commends the ingenious device of the letters which skilfully solves the problem of flashbacks and creates the illusion of simultaneity while the narrator's consciousness randomly explores events on all time scales. Bellow's "serious intentions" is traced throughout his canon as a consistent concern with the Self in modern society and the belief in the brotherhood of man. Although Herzog is viewed as "a novel driven by an idea", the ramifications of the central concerns are found lacking in depth, conviction, and articulation.

1369. Hughes, D.J., "Reality and the Hero: Lolita and Henderson the Rain King", Modern Fiction Studies, 6 (Winter 1960-61), 345-64. Reprinted in I. Malin's Saul Bellow and the Critics (New York, 1967), 69-91.
       Compares the two works in terms of the importance placed

on theme, structure, contemporaneity, reality, and
the much-heralded crisis in the novel. Both writers
present a version of reality which is parodic and farcical,
yet tempered by the rendering of the anguish and self-
discovery of the protagonists who do not suffer from
satiric reduction. Suggests that Lolita is to Humbert
what the dark continent is to Henderson in that desirable
realities exist outside the immediate realm of existence
for both heroes. Through the familiar rituals of quest
and initiation, Henderson is seen from an unfamiliar
parodic perspective which reveals his suffering psyche,
wish-engendered fantasies, and a modern form of madness.

1370. Hull, Byron D., "Henderson the Rain King and William
James", Criticism, (13), 402-14.
A detailed comparison of James's Principles of
Psychology and Henderson's bizarre rehabilitation program
as designed by the Wariri King. Notes the similarities
between the Jamesian somatic psychology and Dahfu's
directed therapy which is applied to the "ills of the
self". Compares the explicit instructions which are
purported to remove inhibitions which obstruct Henderson's
mental channels with extensive quotations from Jamesian
theories of psychotherapy.

1371. Hutchens, John K., "On an Author", New York Herald Tribune
Book Review, (4 October 1953), 2.
A brief biographical sketch which includes familiar
details from various sources, along with little-known
facts about the genesis of Augie March. Reports that
Bellow had prepared himself for the picaresque style and
form by writing monologues in the persona of the "half-
bums" who congregated about Newberry Library in Chicago.
Bellow describes them as "eccentric men, frequently
learned in a lopsided way, who had theories about every-
thing". The novelist's own life in the academic world is
regarded as a compromise, an asylum which, in his own
words, "offers the intellectual stimulation of civilized
people" in an urban setting; he prefers to be "near
metropolitan life but to have one leg outside".

1372. Hux, Samuel, "Character and Form in Bellow", Forum (12)
(1974), 34-38.
Stresses Bellow's strengths as a master of organization,
an expert craftsman of novelistic structure, pointing to
the anarchic quality of the longer works in which the
form is "cultivatedly anti-literary". Views the structural
looseness as a major achievement, a consciously
sophisticated literary project. In an attempt to define
Bellow's attitude toward form and characterization, the
author's essays and lectures are closely examined, along

with a survey of recent critical commentary on his work.
Aristotelian definitions of plot and character identity
are also applied.

1373. Jones, David R., "The Disappointment of Maturity: Bellow's
        The Adventures of Augie March", The Fifties: Fiction,
        Poetry, and Drama, ed. Warren French, (Florida, 1970),
        83-92.
            Studies the problems of focus and language in Bellow's
        picaresque bildungsroman which tend to blur the dual
        identity of Augie as narrator and "actor". States that
        Bellow's prose is either "daringly successful or very
        aggravating", and questions whether the style of the hero's
        high-pitched reminiscences is justifiable. Maintains
        that the Whitmanesque catalogues, the learned anologies,
        the Biblical and mythological parallels, used so skilfully
        by Joyce, appear in Bellow's novel to be devices which are
        "undirected, superficial, and warying". Augie and the
        city of Chicago are viewed as the book's main characters
        which unfortunately have become overwhelmed by the flood
        of details and characters.

1374. Josipivici, Gabriel, "Bellow and Herzog", Encounter, 37
        (November 1971), 49-55.
            An early version of the extended study of Herzog (see
        entry 1375) in which a series of meaningless external
        events provide a sense of turmoil which is symptomatic
        of the ceaseless cerebral activity which plagues the hero.

1375. ————"Herzog: Freedom and Wit", The World and the Book,
        (Stanford, California, 1971), 221-35.
            Presents a schematic description of the intellectual
        and emotional alignments in Herzog in which "a rejection
        of two false extremes" is seen as the novels thematic
        and structural center. Identifies the dichotomies of
        Herzog's existence as the philosophical approach of
        "crisis ethics" and the emotional indulgence in "potato
        love". Herzog's increasing self-awareness and assimilation
        of the verities of his situation are illustrated
        diagrammatically as a triadic movement towards inner peace:
        "dissolution of the self in universal truth; acceptance
        of responsibility for oneself; dissolution of the self
        in universal love".

1376. ————"Introduction", The Portable Saul Bellow, (New York,
        1974), vii-xxxiv.
            The tenor of Bellow's fiction is described as "a tone
        of voice that combines the utmost formality with the
        utmost desperation". A review of the canon reveals that
        each Bellovian protagonist is a "dangler", a confused
        member of our increasingly urbanized and oppressive society
        who voluntarily withdraws or remains aloof from the world
        in an attempt to gain a clearer perspective of his life.
        Considers the thematic concerns central to all of the

works: death, responsibility, self, truth, love, meaning,
imagination. Praises the novelist's ability "to speak
the truth, to convey the pleasurable ease of the imagination
while refusing the delusion that the imagination and the
world are one".

1377.   Kalb, Bernard, "The Author", <u>Saturday Review of Literature</u>,
        36 (19 September 1953), 13.
            A brief coverage of biographical details, along with
        interesting authorial anecdotes about the writing of <u>The</u>
        <u>Adventures of Augie March</u>. Bellow refers to the novel as
        a "fantasy holiday" which commenced after having written
        one hundred thousand words of a grim novel entitled <u>The</u>
        <u>Crab and the Butterfly</u>. Considers the creation of the
        picaresque work to be one of his greatest pleasures as
        "ideas were taken away from him by the characters".

1378.   Kaplan, Harold, "The Second Fall of Man", <u>Salmagundi</u>, 30
        (Summer 1975), 66-89.
            Interprets <u>Herzog</u> as a comic rendering of the Emersonian
        theme of the inherent possibilities of an intellectual
        and spiritual community of mankind. A fundamental
        reconciliation of the complex needs and desires of the
        Bellovian hero is dramatically portrayed throughout the
        canon as the questing hero achieves self-knowledge and
        identity as a member of the brotherhood of man. Traces
        the Emersonian concept of "transcendent humanity" through
        Herzog's and Sammler's lengthy cerebrations on existence
        and death.

1379.   Kazin, Alfred, "Bellow's Purgatory", <u>New York Review of</u>
        <u>Books</u>, (28 March 1969), 32-36. Reprinted in a slightly
        revised version as the introduction to the Fawcett
        edition of <u>Seize the Day</u> (Conneticut, 1968), v-xviii.
            Surveys the modern trend of avante-garde writers towards
        pedantic, experimental excesses which are designed to
        outwit the common reader. Commends Bellow's apparent
        "counter-efforts" as a creator of fiction which supports
        his vision of the truth of experience and conveys that
        truth without artifice. Focuses upon the novella <u>Seize</u>
        <u>the Day</u> which is seen as a "masterpiece in urban American
        fiction" in that it infuses the environment of the
        turbulent American megalopolis with meaning as it becomes
        an extension of the character of Bellow's "representative
        Jew". Notes a consistent pattern of constraint and
        expansion, release and retreat, hope and despair at work
        throughout the canon.

1380.   ————Bright Book of Life, (London, 1974), 25-38.
            Explores the novelists's evolution from the Jewish ghetto
        experience into the secular urban life of America. Traces
        the evolution of the acrid style of Bellow's post-war

writing with its "hallucinated clarity of details"
to the vital rendering of the vertiginous clamour of
New York in the Sixties. Considers the whole of the
Bellow's fiction to be a comprehensive "book of wisdom"
composed by introspective Jewish personae during various
times of crisis.

1381.   ————"Midtown and the Village", Harper's, 242 (January 1971)
         82-89.
              Reminiscenses of the atmosphere and events surounding
         the publication of the journal The New Republic during the
         war years, including impressions of literati, such as
         Van Wyck Brooks, Edmund Wilson, Isaac Rosenfeld, and Saul
         Bellow. Recalls a palpable sense of destiny which
         emanated from the young writer who had emerged from the
         Mid-west with a confidence, an intellectual directness, and
         a keen sense of inner freedom.

1382.   ————"My Friend Saul Bellow", Atlantic Monthly, 215
         (January 1965), 51-54. Also translated and reprinted
         under the title, "Mon Ami Saul Bellow" in Pierre
         Dommergues' Saul Bellow, (Paris, 1967), 71-83.
              Identifies Bellow's image of life as a continual
         confrontation of opposites, "a marriage of unlikely
         possibilities", a battle which is enacted in his novels
         of personal struggle. Informally portrays the writer as
         an unpretentious person, without the slightest verbal
         inflation, an intellectual, a scholar, a storyteller who
         creates "new myths out of himself and everyone he had
         ever known, fought, loved, and hated", a man in whom
         "anguish and wit have always been natural companions".

1383.   Kermode, Frank, "Herzog", New Statesman, (5 February 1965),
         200-01.
              A survey of Bellow's oeuvre underlines the speculative
         quests of the heroes who attempt to grasp the complexities
         of human destiny by understanding their own, resulting in
         a sequence of extravagantly comic or pathetic gestures.
         Sees Herzog as a departure in the methodology of conveying
         farcial exitements of thinking as distinct from acting.
         Praises the technical trick of the letters which not only
         bear the freight of speculation in the novel and
         demonstrate an intellectual's behavior in the modern world,
         but become a delightful vehicle of comedy in themselves.
         Views Herzog's world as a slightly caricatured universe
         inhabited by women as unreal as Smollett's, accompanied by
         men who are equally comic, grotesque, and distorted; all
         of which are rendered with great powers of invention,
         intellect, and comic energy.

1384.   Klein, Marcus, "A Discipline of Nobility: Saul Bellow's
         Fiction", Kenyon Review, 24 (Spring 1962), 203-26. Reprinted
         in Joseph J. Waldemeir's (ed.) Recent American Fiction:

Some Critical Views (New York, 1963), 121-38; also in
Marcus Klein's After Alienation (Cleveland, 1964), 33-
70; also in I. Malin's (ed.) Saul Bellow and the Critics
(New York, 1967), 92-113. An extract of the article was
translated and reprinted under the title, "Ainsi parlait
Henderson", in Pierre Dommergues' Saul Bellow (Paris,
1967), 197-202.
   Reduces the thematic concerns of Bellow's canon to a
single problem: "to meet with a strong sense of self
the sacrifices of the self demanded by the social
circumstance", thus focusing upon the historical/social
dialogue between alienation and accommodation. The five
novels exemplify the struggle of the soul to freedom,
from isolation to affirmation in Nietzschen terms. Traces
the Zarathustrian parallels as Henderson steadily moves
towards harmony within the natural laws. Radical self-
assertion and existence of personality for its own sake
are seen as virtues derived from necessity inherent in
the tradition of Yiddish literature and constitute an
important step in the heroes' progress towards the
salvation of the self, through the inherent bestiality
of human nature into a coalescence of selflessness and
selfhood which for Bellow is a sense of nobility.

1385. Knipp, Thomas R., "The Cost of Henderson's Quest", Ball
       State University Forum, 10 (Spring 1969), 37-39.
          Recounts the details of the plot, underlining the
       failures and evaded responsibilities of "the heavy-handed
       neo-colonialist" who leaves desolation and destruction
       in his wake. Totals the inordinately high costs of
       resurrection and regeneration imposed upon the Arnewi and
       Wariri tribes by the egocentric quester who is identified
       as an allegorical representation of American foreign
       policy.

1386. Krupnick, Mark, "He Never Learned to Swim", New Review, (22),
       33-39.
          A backward glance at the circumstances surrounding
       the premature demise of Philip Rahv's literary journal
       Modern Occasions (1970-72). The culturally conservative
       disposition of the editor and his magazine attracted
       writers who contributed angrily eloquent essays in defense
       of classical modernism, an older humanism, and a sense of
       the past. Bellow's polemic on the rise of "publicity
       intellectuals", who behave not as literary men but as gurus
       for the bohemianised masses, appeared in the second issue
       (see entry 48) and set the tone for the subsequent
       publications. The Sammlerian jeremiad, praised as a
       "contemporary Dunciod", illuminates the writer's
       conservative politics and his exasperation with the modern
       literary scene.

1387.   Kuehn, Robert E., "Fiction Chronicle", Contemporary
        Literature, (1964), 132-39.
            Considers Herzog's letter an effective literary device
        which dramatically illustrates the complexity of modern
        life and thought, while providing a therepeutic means by
        which the protagonist is able to remain sane in an insane
        world. Argues that although the struggle of the hero is
        a paradigm for the universal dilemma of the sensitive
        everyman, the split which exists between the letters and
        the commentary on existences reduces the lasting impact
        of Herzog's private anguish. Points to a basic lack of
        design, an absence of a coherent significant story which
        causes the work to waver and sprawl, lapsing into lengthy
        philosophical digressions which tend to bore the reader.

1388.   Kunitz, Satnley, "Saul Bellow", Twentieth Century Authors,
        (New York, 1955), 72-73.
            A brief biographical sketch in which familiar details
        are recounted, along with the author's recollections of
        his student days at the University of Chicago which was
        seen as a "terrifying place", where wisdom and culture
        were immense and he "hopelessly small". Charts his
        subsequent move to Northwestern, the unsuitability of
        graduate school, and finally his decision, in "his
        innocence" to become a writer. Includes a survey of
        Bellow's works to date, a sampling of critical commentary
        on Augie March, a listing of literary awards and teaching
        commitments.

1389.   Lamont, Rosette C., "Bellow Observed: A Serial Portrait",
        Mosaic, 8:1, 247-57.
            An informal portrait which provides heretofore
        undisclosed details of the writer's public and private lives
        circumstances surrounding the writing of various novels,
        authorial comments on specific novels and characters which
        have not been recorded elsewhere. Humorous anecdotes
        on a variety of subjects are recounted, about women whose
        "fig leaves have turned to price tags", on today's hippie
        communes whish are described as an "Arcadia with rats
        instead of sheep", to facetious remarks about this "art-
        polluted world".

1390.   Leach, Elsie, "From Ritual to Romance Again", Western
        Humanities Review, 14 (Spring 1960), 223-24.
            A brief consideration of the similarities in plot
        and structure of Henderson's mythic journey to Africa
        with its fertility rites and initiation experiences and
        those delineated by J.L. Weston in his books on the subject,
        From Ritual to Romance, published in 1920. Stresses the
        importance of ritual, quests, mythology, and symbols of
        the Grail legend in Henderson the Rain King as fundamental
        to a complete understanding of the work.

1391. Lehan, Richard, "Existentialism in Recent American Fiction:
       The Demonic Quest", Texas Studies in Literature and
       Language, 1 (Summer 1959), 181-200.
           Attempts to demonstrate the profound influence the
       French novel has exerted upon recent American novelists
       through a discussion of Sartre and Camus. The recent
       novels of Bowles, Wright, Ellison, and Bellow are explored
       as examples of works which employ "an existential hero in
       search of existential values". Compares Joseph of Dangling
       Man to Camus' Meursault and Sartre's Roquentin in his
       growth from philosophical innocence to an enlightened
       confrontation of the absurd, in his completely autonomous
       and self-enclosed existence.

1392. Levenson, J.C., "Bellow's Dangling Men", Critique, 3 (Summer
       1960), 3-14. Reprinted in I. Malin's Saul Bellow and the
       Critics, (New York, 1967), 39-50.
           Identifies the classic American pattern of
       individualism and uniformity, of rootlessness and detachment
       as exemplified in the Bellovian hero. A distinctive comic
       voice emerges through the interanimation of American and
       Jewish strains in a dramatic rendering of gesture, language,
       and conception of character. Bellow's humanism is seen as
       a synthesis of American and European traditions, while
       echoing Emersonian and Whitmanesque admonishments to live
       fully in the brotherhood of mankind.

1393. Levine, Paul, "Saul Bellow: The Affirmation of the
       Philosophical Fool", Perspective, 10 (Winter 1959), 163-
       76.
           Sees Bellow's protagonists as generally uncommitted
       individuals, while Salinger's heroes are said to be
       devoted to innocence, Capote's to narcissism, and McCuller's
       to a form of Christian love. A discussion of Bellow's
       works accentuates his European and Russian affinities and
       places him outside the tradition of indigenous American
       writing. Identifies him as a "socially conscious writer"
       who creates an open world which offers unlimited
       possibilities to his heroes as part of a fundamental
       reconciliation with society.

1394. Ludwig, Jack, Recent American Novelists, (Minnesota, 1962),
       7-19. Reprinted in On Contemporary Literature, ed. Richard
       Kostelanetz, (New York, 1966).
           Places Bellow in the mainstream of young American
       writers who have attempted to break with the "Beat" literary
       fashion. Analyses the dramatic shift in focus and tone
       of Bellow's pre- and post-war writings to the comic mode of
       novels such as Augie March, Henderson the Rain King, and
       Herzog, revealing the author's Talmudic wit, Yiddish humor,
       and belletristic tendencies. Suggests that the theme of
       the victim is central to the understanding of all Bellovian
       protagonists.

1395. Majdiak, Daniel, "The Romantic Self and <u>Henderson the Rain King</u>", <u>Bucknell Review</u>, 19, (Autumn 1971), 125-46.
Argues that the theme of the decline and fall of Romanticism in modern life provides the most comprehensive rationale behind Bellow's opposition to the nihilistic trend in modern literature. A survey of his critical essays clarifies the writer's view of the individual in conflict with a society which attempts to negate the Romantic concept of selfhood, the spiritual, ennobling aspect of man. Discusses the allusions to Blake, Coleridge, Wordsworth present in <u>Henderson the Rain King</u> which constitute the basis of the romantic mode and key metaphors of the work. Notes the recurring humorous parodies of Romantic literature, including the Wordsworthian metaphor of the "cloud of glory" with which the novel concludes.

1396. Malin, Irving, <u>Contemporary American - Jewish Literature: Critical Essays</u>, (Indiana, 1973).
Imposes a theological framework upon the critical collection, stressing the fact that Jewish writers celebrate traditional religious moments of exile, covenant, transcendency, and redemption, dramatizing a heritage from which they cannot escape. Peripheral remarks about Bellow's fiction are included in several of the essays, along with one full-length study of <u>Mr. Sammler's Planet</u>.

1397. ————<u>Jews and Americans</u>, (Illinois, 1965).
Bellow comprises an important part of a discussion of seven writers who artistically and consciously have expressed their Jewish tradition and mentality. Maintains that Bellow has obliquely acknowledged his heritage through the distinctly Hasidic flavor of his ebullient characters. Interprets the quests of the protagonists as a dramatization of the tension between the search for the Promised Land and the resistance to the temptation of <u>Galuth</u> or Exile.

1398. ————"Saul Bellow: Reputations XIV", <u>London Magazine</u>, 10 (January 1965), 43-54.
Traces the theme of the "madness" of contemporary society through the Bellow canon, underlining the key components of the distractions of the central characters which are identified as "narcissism, abstractionism, and compulsion". Examines the rituals of inhuman cruelty in <u>Dangling Man</u> with hypnosis emerging as "the objective correlative of all the preceding madness". Suggests that Bellow's "prophetic" style in subsequent works is designed to capture the extravagant behavior of his comic heroes.

1399.   ─────Saul Bellow and the Critics, (New York, 1967).
         Presents a representative group of essays (all
         previously published) which cover the current critical
         assessment of Bellow's fiction. Philosophical, thematic,
         and stylistic studies are collected, along with a critical
         essay by Bellow, entitled "Where Do We Go From Here: The
         Future of Fiction" (for details see entry 97).

1400.   Maloney, Stephen R., "Half-way to Byzantium: Mr. Sammler's
         Planet and the Modern Tradition", South Carolina Review,
         6 (November 1973), 31-40.
         Compares Sammler's ascetic detachment and disinterest
         to the attitudes expressed by Yeats's aged spokesman in
         "Sailing and Byzantium". In their mutual desire to
         escape the sensual world of physical supremacy, both
         characters are seen to search for a "Byzantium-like
         wholeness". Structurally, the novel is likened to The
         Wasteland, continuing in the "Eliot line of sensibility".
         Direct allusions to Yeats and Eliot present in the work
         suggest Bellow's affinities to the poets who portray the
         spiritual and intellectual dessication of contemporary
         man, thus placing the novelist firmly in the modern
         literary tradition.

1401.   Markos, Donald, "Life against Death in Henderson the Rain
         King", Modern Fiction Studies, 17 (1971), 193-205.
         Considers Henderson to be a powerfully imagined
         alternative to the modernist "wasteland outlook" with its
         hallmarks of alienation, despair, and isolation. Proposes
         that the hero be viewed as a middle-aged American Adam
         who encompasses both the life-denying symptons of
         alienation and the vitality of regeneration and renewal,
         the latter assuming prominence as a source of motivation,
         symbolism, and imagery in the novel. Stresses the tension
         between the opposing forces of Henderson's temperament
         as defined by N.O. Brown as a means of understanding the
         protagonist's progress towards the "ultimate harmonization
         of human forces", as advocated and epitomized by Dahfu
         and Willatale.

1402.   Mathis, James C., "The Theme of Seize the Day", Critique,
         7 (1965), 43-45. Collected in the Bellow Papers, see
         entry 647.
         Discusses the significance of the title of the novella
         in terms of the carpe diem theme as an integral part of
         the narrative development. Wilhelm's fundamentally
         romantic nature is apparently revealed through his
         recollections of the opening lines of "Lycidas" and
         Shakespeare's seventy-third sonnet. Maintains that Tamkin's
         "fiscal philosophy" of the "here and now" allows Wilhelm's
         true soul to find expression in love and compassion for
         others.

1403. McSweeney, Kerry, "Saul Bellow and the Life to Come",
      Critical Quarterly, 18 (Spring 1976), 67-72.
          A discussion of _Humboldt's Gift_ advocacy of
      transcendental postulates and the central character's
      belief in the life hereafter. Bellow's eighth novel is
      seen as a recapitulation of familiar themes and strategies,
      with Citrine as the "incarnation of the perennial Bellow
      protagonist", a fraternal twin of Herzog. Enumerates the
      weaknesses in the work: the zany inventiveness, bold-faced
      coincidence, lack of ironic distance between Citrine and
      the reader, a plethora of superfluous detail. Suggests
      that the works principal thematic concern of Citrine's
      spiritual growth remains unrealized and unconvincing
      because of Bellow's "inability to incorporate satisfactorily
      in fictional form his new-found interest in the life to
      come".

1404. Mallard, James, "_Dangling Man_: Saul Bellow's Lyrical
      Experiment", _Ball State University Forum_, 15:2 (1970),
      67-74.
          Examines the lyrical expressive form of the journal
      which allows the protagonists to record objectively his
      cerebrations, working through an essentially religious
      and intellectual crisis and achieving a tentative
      resolution. Defines the "contours" of the lyric novel
      which are not drawn by temporal or spatial limits but
      by the hero's point of view, thus accounting for
      difficulties in discontinuity within the dangerously
      solipsistic work.

1405. Morrow, Patrick, "Threat and Accommodation: The Novels
      of Saul Bellow", Midwest Quarterly, 8 (1967), 389-411.
          Traces the Bellovian belief that man's participation
      in society is preferable to self-imposed alienation as
      expressed in a variety of concessions illustrated through-
      out his canon. Discusses the myriad threats exerted by
      the hostile urban environment upon the individual and the
      ways in which the hero succeeds or fails to accomodate
      the exigencies of life. Commends the author's dramatic
      portrayal of "romantic suffering" and his ability to
      reconcile "tragic roles within a comic perspective".

1406. Mosher, Harold, "The Synthesis of Past and Present in Saul
      Bellow's _Herzog_", _Wascana Review_, 6 (1970), 28-38.
          Stresses Herzog's profession as historian in an analysis
      of the hero's understanding of himself and the
      contemporary world which is based upon a realistic acceptanc
      of past and present. Explores the work as a philosophical
      dialogue between the hero's appraisal of his past
      professional and marital failures and those of western
      man, as seen in relation to the history of civilization.
      Sees Herzog's impulsive bursts of travelling as an objectiv
      correlative for his escape from himself, likened to the
      vague questing of the Cervantes hero.

1407. Moss, Judith, "The Body as Symbol in Saul Bellow's
      Henderson the Rain King", Literature and Psychology, 20
      (1973), 51-61.
          In the light of Freudian conversion symptomology,
      Henderson's body is identified as the central dramatic
      symbol which shapes the narrative and "metaphorically
      generates the themes of regeneration and recovery". Suggests
      that the hero's somatic ills exacerbate his egocentrism
      and appear to emerge in response to constant emotional
      conflicts, thus illustrating a classic case of Freudian
      "conversion hysteria". Traces the archetypal return motif
      through the pattern of birth imagery which underlines the
      dramatic function of the body on a metaphorical level.

1408. Mudrick, Marvin, "Who Killed Herzog? Or, Three American
      Novelists", University of Denver Quarterly, 1 (Spring
      1966), 61-97.
          Compares the differing Jewish milieu and background
      of writers, such as Bellow, Malamud, and Roth, who have
      undertaken the task of creating the contemporary fictional
      Jew. Points to Bellow's abortive early attempts to
      convert current themes into allegory and literature,
      maintaining that he stakes everything on the unimpaired
      survival of the topical, "as if newspapers were history".
      A discussion of the works of the three novelists underlines
      the opinions that they are in desperate need of new subject
      matter since the American Jew as hero has disappeared in
      the morass of their novels, obliterated by the featureless
      and solopsistic landscapes of contemporary America.

1409. Nault, Marianne, "Saul Bellow's Humboldt The First",
      American Notes and Queries, (Winter 1976).
          A survey of the critical speculation about the possible
      source of Bellow's most recent protagonist reveals that
      the tormented, self-destructive character is a thinly
      disguised portrait of the avant-garde writer of the Thirties,
      Delmore Schwartz, with touches of John Berryman and Randall
      Jarrell. Cites Bellow's own words on the subjects of
      the origins of the character, as recorded in various
      British interviews. Presents evidence from the Bellow
      Papers to show that several of the major scenes between
      Humboldt and his wife appear in the early manuscripts
      of Herzog, indicating that Bellow had attempted to write
      his "composite picture" of Schwartz prior to the poet's
      death in 1966. (For further details of manuscripts, see
      entries

1410. Noble, David, The Eternal Adam and the New World Garden,
      (New York, 1968), 216-26.
          An historical view of Bellow's fiction in which the
      ideological "conflict between the Eternal and American
      Adams" is explored, revealing the bankruptcy of the myth.

Traces Bellow's diagnoses of the sickness of American
society through the metaphysical quests for an alternative
set of values to replace the traditional faith. Suggests
that Herzog's movement out of the promised land of the
chosen people into the realm of the "sinful brotherhood
of mankind" may symbolize a major shift in American
cultural history.

1411. O'Connell, Shaun, "Bellow: Logic's Limits", Massachusetts
Review, X (Winter 1969), 182-87.
Portrays Bellow's fictional world as a realm of the
mind, in which the characters struggle beneath the burden
of truth and identity, unable to function normally since
they are passionate prisoners of their own perceptions.
A study of the short stories in Mosby's Memoirs reveals a
number of unhibited characters, "Augie Marches without
chutspah", who are plunged into the turbulent elements
of modern existence, incapable of controlling the course
of events with ideas or escaping from life through
ratiocination.

1412. Opdahl, Keith M., The Novels of Saul Bellow, (Pennsylvania,
1967).
Stresses the Bellow protagonists' desire for involvement in communal action which in turn threatens to absorb
the self. Identifies the thematic core of the oeuvre as
a conflict between love and will, faith and skepticism,
manifested in a recognition of evil which is portrayed as
a metaphysical component of the human will. Considers
the heroes to be essentially religious men who achieve a
sense of self through acts of love, behavior which is
infused with Hasidic principles, "the Jewish movement
which feels the presence of the divine within the factual
world".

1413. Overbeck, Pat T., "The Women in Augie March", Texas Studies
in Language and Literature, 10 (Winter 1969), 471-84.
Suggests that the women characters serve as an emotional
fulcrum around which Augie and the action of the fiction
circle in a recurring pattern, thus providing structural an
thematic support to the novel. The females appear to fall
into two distinct categories, the virago and the victim,
as they provide a source of spiralling adventures which
threaten to overwhelm the hero who assumes the role of a
devoted celebrant of the love rite.

1414. Pearce, Richard, "Harlequin: The Character of the Clown in
Saul Bellow's Henderson the Rain King and John Hawke's
Second Skin", Stages of the Clown: Perspectives on Modern
Fiction from Dostoevsky to Beckett, (Illinois, 1970),
102-16.
Presents the archetypal figure of the harlequin in
literature which functions as a rebellious spirit, thriving

in chaos, yet striving to build rather than to destroy.
Henderson is seen as a modern manifestation of the
harlequin's situation, nature, and role in an absurd
world, a variation of the braggart soldier of classical
comedy. Argues that Bellow's hero achieves a degree of
understanding of self and human destiny through an
ironic elevation of status from clown to king, a reversal
of the Lear descent.

1415. Pearson, Carol, "Bellow's Henderson: The Myth of the King,
       Fool, and Hero", Notes on Contemporary Literature, 5
       (November 1975), 8-11.
            Explores the various changes the archetypal myth has
       undergone in order to assimilate the conditions of the
       contemporary world. Henderson's attainment of "heroic
       wholeness" through his role of Rain King is seen as a
       reversal of the mythic pattern of the rise of the fool to
       the ranks of royalty. The barren setting of the concluding
       scene suggests that Henderson, unlike the traditional hero,
       is unable to restore fertility to the modern world.

1416. Pinsker, Sanford, "Moses Herzog and the Modern Wasteland",
       Reconstructionist, 34 (December 1968), 20-27.
            Compares Herzog's movement from despair at the apparent
       meaninglessness of contemporary society to a qualified
       affirmation that the values of humane civilization may
       prevail with T.S. Eliot's depiction of the void in The
       Wasteland. Structural and thematic similarities and
       differences between the two works are discussed.

1417. ————"Moses Herzog's Fall into the Quotidian", Studies
       in the Twentieth Century, 14 (Fall 1974), 105-16.
            Discusses Herzog's focetious querie concerning Heidegger's
       polysyllabic phrase as to the exact time the fall occurres.
       Stresses the Biblical implications of the "fall" of Herzog,
       his loss of innocence, his bitter knowledge gained through
       experience, his penchant for suffering which reveals a
       distinctive blend of the schlimiel-like acceptance of
       cuckoldry with Job-like moral sensitivity. Additional
       allusions underline the hero's "self-styled role as an
       avatar of the Biblical Moses", creating a new code of behavior
       in opposition to the prevailing anarchy of modern times.

1418. ————"Saul Bellow in the Classroom", College English,
       34 (April 1973), 975-82.
            Reports on a lecture delivered by Bellow at Franklin
       and Marshall College (see entry 98 for details of the
       unpublished manuscript) and the discussion which followed.
       Specific questions about characters, themes, and style
       are answered by the novelist in a candid manner, explications
       which cannot be found elsewhere.

1419.   ————The Schlimiel as Metaphor, (Illinois, 1971), 125-
         57.
              Emphasizes Bellow's Yiddish background as a major
         contributory factor to his success as a novelist who
         has integrated the Jewish anecdotal repertoire into the
         fabric of the American literary experience. Re-examines
         Bellow's canon from a primarily Jewish perspective,
         defining the victimized protagonists as schlimiels and
         schlimazzels with Herzog portrayed as a mensch or
         suffering fool, epitomizing the charm of the Yiddish
         archetypal character which possesses tha ability to absorb
         defeat with equal measures of humorous acceptance and
         bitter disappointment.

1420.   Podhoretz, Norman, "The Adventures of Saul Bellow", Doings
         and Undoings, (London, 1965), 205-27.
              Names Bellow as the "leading American novelist of the
         post-war period", a writer who is primarily concerned
         with ideas without being pedantic or Alexandrian. Sees
         his prescient first novel as a challenge to the tradition
         that rebellion is the only form of heroism in modern
         society. Stresses the abstract metaphysical questions
         which arise naturally and powerfully from the plot of
         The Victim, a work characteristic of the post-war ethos
         in its "oppressively pessimistic tone". Augie March is
         viewed as the exemplification of the exuberant impulse
         of the Fifties to celebrate the American spirit, pointing
         to the resultant problems in style and language. Challenge
         Bellow's ability in his later works to locate the source
         of modern malaise with the ambiguities and forced
         affirmations which tend to weaken his fiction to date.

1421.   ————Making It, (New York, 1967).
              Provides interesting anecdotes surrounding the critic's
         unfavorable review of The Adventures of Augie March for
         Commentary, (see entry 1031). A discursive, informal
         portrait of the "family" of the journal's staff, of
         which Bellow is depicted as an elder member and a spokes-
         man for the Jew's right to play more than a marginal role
         in American literary culture. Notes Bellow's turn away
         from alienation towards a heavy-handed affirmation of the
         Jew as American, which is seen as part of the aesthetic
         and stylistic failure of Augie March. Suggests Bellow's
         search for a solution to the problem of "literary pluralism"
         has become an obsessive concern in his attempts to cross
         the literary language boundaries with the dramatic
         rendering of the American-Jewish idiom.

1422.   ————"The New Nihilism and the Novel", Partisan Review,
         25 (Autumn 1958), 578-90.
              Examines the striking trend in the literature of the
         Fifties which reveals a preoccupation with the modernist

theme of loss of values and a revulsion against ideology, which in turn is transformed into a positive virtue, the liberation from rigid systems of belief. Contends that Bellow lacked the conviction whcih stood behind the progressive mood of Augie March, and as a result preceeded to explore the agonized gloom of modern man Seize the Day. The novella is considered Bellow's best work to date.

1423. Porter, M. Gilbert, "Herzog: A Transcedental Solution to an Existential Problem", Forum, 7 (Spring 1969), 32-36.
Describes Herzog as a romanticist in an existential world who attempts to relieve himself of an essentially neoclassicist's burden. Diagnoses the hero's dilemma as psychological instability stemming from a constant conflict which exists between his intellect and his sensibilities. Through a recapitulation of the themes and action of the novel in existential terms, Herzog's final resolution is seen as an inevitable result of an arduous journey which begins with an essentially Romantic perspective, moving through the alienation and absurdity of existentialism, and on to the tentative, transcedental return to Nature.

1424. ————"Whence the Power? The Artistry and Humanity of Saul Bellow", (Missouri, 1974).
Assumes a formalist stance as the studies of Bellow's fiction are based upon the assumptions of the New Criticism, delineated by Cleanth Brooks. Defines the critical approach as "a close analysis of intrareferential relations" of themes and forms, structure and texture. Discussions of individual works explore the conflict between realistic and symbolic levels of presentation, dramatic scenes are equated with poetic images, the prominence of archetypal themes and patterns of imagery which relate each scene to the "organic central metaphor" of the novel. Explores the intellectual resolution of onflicts by a move from existentialism to transcendentalism (an expanded treatment of an earlier study, see entry 1423) and the tension between Bellovian themes and "fictional concretions".

1425. Pritchett, V.S., "In That Time and That Wilderness", New Statesman, (28 September 1962), 405-06.
A survey of the strengths and weaknesses of the post-Faulknerian "freeway novelists" who capitalize upon the "garrulousness which has been formative in American literature". Suggests that Bellow's Henderson is provided with a "rich and outrageous dream life, far fuller than any Walter Mitty stuff", a character who is worthy of uproarious success and ludicrous disaster.

1426. ————"Augie March", New Statesman, (19 June 1954), 301.
Commends the author for his notable gift of image, fantasy, incident, and character as illustrated in a festively inventive American version of the picaresque

novel. Objects to the style of portions of the work which is seen as affected, monotonous, coagulated, and self-intoxicating. Bellow's comic treatment of the brothel scene is lauded as "an advance on the terrible sentimental compulsion which exposes the imaturity of most American realists when they write about sex". The overwhelming sense of the distinctively American phenomena gives the novelist a fervor and dramatic advantage which is found lacking in English novelists.

1427.   Quinton, Anthony, "The Adventures of Saul Bellow", London Magazine,6 (December 1959), 55-59.
         A survey of Bellow's canon reveals a bewildering variety of forms and charcters involved in the defiant yet metaphysical quest for truth which is viewed as a condition for salvation. Henderson the Rain King is described as a protracted fantasy, stripped of any vestiges of naturalistic fiction, but a brilliant variation on a humanistic theme which is explored throughout the oeuvre.

1428.   Rans, Geoffrey, "The Novels of Saul Bellow", Review of English Literature, 4 (October 1963), 18-30.
         Objects to the critical tendency to interprey Bellow's novels as stages in his spiritual autobiography and to regard the difficulties in style or the problems of the heroes as Bellow's own. Argues that confusion arises in the depiction of the characters' "eternal naivete" which is reflected in the tone and language of the works. Praises the novelist's mimetic virtuosity which enables the reader to experience fully the wide range of conflicts vividly depicted through the eyes of his characters.

1429.   Read, Forest, "Herzog: A Review", Epoch 14 (Fall 1964), 81-96. Reprinted in I. Malin's Saul Bellow and the Critics (New York, 1967), 184-206.
         Regards Herzog as an extraordinary comic novel which elucidates "the biggest chunk of reality since Jocye got his into Ulysses", exhibiting a vital interchange between the artist and his character which is more compelling than that between Joyce and Bllom. A Shakespearean sense of variety is realized in an intense, complulsive, encyclopedic rendering of character, scene, and meditation as Herzog registers and records the vivid and relevant events, individuals, cerebrations of his world, as his metaphysical odyssey unfolds.

1430.   Richardson, Jack, "Chasing Reality", New York Review of Books, (13 March 1969), 12-14.
         A brief survey of Bellow's major works underlines a consistent notion of fate which is that "good men are destined to misconceive life again and again". Explores the presence of the encircling sense of mortality in Seize

the Day, and the stories in Mosby's Memoirs. Considers "Leaving the Yellow House" and "Mosby's Memoirs" excellent illustrations of the "comic indomitability of the human will" and prime examples of Bellow's far-reaching creative range and capabilities.

431. Richmond, Lee J., "The Maladroit, the Medico, and the Magician: Saul Bellow's Seize the Day", Twentieth Century Literature, 19 (1961), 15-26.
      Discusses the personal manipulation of Wilhelm, the pathetic suffering hero, by his supercilious father and a calculating charlatan. The successful man of medicine is viewed as an ironic exemplification of the doctor's inability to heal himself of his ailing offspring. Suggests that Dr. Tamkin, a "fakir" or "shaman" in modern dress, constitutes the thematic nexus of the work, emphasizing the magician's indispensability in Wilhelm's progress towards truth, awareness, and regeneration.

1432. Rodrigues, Eusebio L., "Bellow's Africa", American Literature, 43 (1971), 242-56.
      Presents evidence to indicate Bellow's firm foundation in anthropological research, particularly African ethnography, thus accounting for accurate details which lend an air of verisimilitude to Henderson's "Africa of the mind". Traces the author's incorporation and transmogrification of abstract cultural facts into memorable scenes and characters. Argues that the creation of the Wariri King was inspired by the historical figure King Gelele and cites various sources of marked similarities between the two kings.

1433. _____"Bellow's Confidence Man", Notes on Contemporary Literature,3 (1972), 6-8
      Stresses the importance of the role of the charlatan Dr. Tamkin in Bellow's Seize the Day as Wilhelm's surrogate father.

1434. _____"Koholeth in Chicago: The Quest for the Real in 'Looking for Mr. Green'", Studies in Short Fiction, 11 (1974), 387-93.
      Considers Bellow's "most complete and compact short story" to be a simple Dreiserian piece which has been transformed into a metaphysical parable by the author'd remarkable "lifting power". The hero is viewed as a modern Koheleth (Hebrew for preacher) in a modern dramatization of Ecclesiastes.

1435. _____"Reichianism in Henderson the Rain King", Criticism, 15 (1972), 212-33.
      Cites Wilhelm Reich and his theories of character analysis and "orgonomy" as an important influence on Bellow throughout the Fifties and early Sixties. Traces

the comic extravagances of Reichman behavior in Henderson's adventures in Africa, emphasizing the serious dimension of the therapeutic methodology behind the frivolity. A structural analysis of the work reveals a tri-part division which mirrors the three Reichian stages of treatment.

1436. ————"Saul Bellow's Henderson as America", Centennial Review, 20 (Spring 1976), 189-95.
    Explores the character, actions, and complexities of Henderson as a personification of America, endowed with huge physical dimensions, an amalgam of contradictory forces. Maintains that Henderson illustrates the shaping spirit of the American past, as well as the despair of the terrible technological present. Suggests that the healing prophetic knowledge which Henderson achieves in communion with others dramatizes the regenerative hope in his harried American soul and allows him to return home in a lyric celebration of the "twin sources of America's strength Machinery and Transcendentalism".

1437. Ross, Theodore J., "Notes on Saul Bellow", Chicago Jewish Forum, 18 (1959), 21-27.
    Objects to Bellow's fictional attempts to Christianize "the uniquely Jewish experience and spirit" in order to appeal to a wider audience. Rejects the "decidedly un-Jewish endeavor" and the solipsistic stance of the first Bellovian protagonist whose ambivalent feelings about war are interpreted as an unjustifiable lack of authorial response to the widespread butchery of the Jews. Criticizes the treatment of the anti-semitic theme in The Victim as weak in its failure to dramatize the realities of the social and emotional experience of the Jews, as well as neglecting the tragic truths of history.

1438. Rovit, Earl, "Bellow in Occupancy", American Scholar, 34 (Spring 1965), 292-98. Reprinted in I. Malin's Saul Bellow and the Critics, (New York, 1967), 177-83.
    Suggests that Herzog may provide a crystallization of contemporary confusions as Dos Passos' USA accomplished in its day. The device of the muliple point of view is seen to increase the intimate identification of the reader with characters. Locates weaknesses in the unbalanced ironic perspectives, scenes which "smack too rawly of emotion untempered by art", unconvincing erotic scenes, and a monotonous texture of the novel in which episodes, cerebrations, and characterizations merge together

1439. ————Saul Bellow, University of Minnesota Pamphlets on American Writers, 65, (Minnesota, 1974).
    Sees Bellow as "the most significant American to come to maturity since World War II" who has developed a style of "grotesque realism" modulated by a sense of irony. The protagonists are depicted as lonely, suffering men of

integrity who refuse to acquiesce to a meaningless
existence. Stresses the comic strain throughout the
canon, a "a double-or triple-voice response to the
mortal enigma of consciousness", the hero who mocks
himself and finds salvation in laughter.

440. ————Saul Bellow: A Collection of Critical Essays,
      (New Jersey, 1975).
         Features a number of articles from a wide range of
      critical perspectives, methodologies, and thematic
      interests, many of which have been published previously,
      but have been recently revised for inclusion in the
      collection. Includes five essays which are presented
      for the first time, along with an analysis of Bellow's
      full-length drama The Last Analysis.

441. Rubenstein, Richard, "The Philosophy of Saul Bellow",
      Reconstructionist, 30 (22 January 1965), 7-12.
         Considers Herzog to be "the best novel by a Jew about
      contemporary Jews", a story of the emotional catharsis
      which enables the hero to "affirm himself as a man and
      as a Jew". Commends the author's avoidance of maudlin
      sentimentality which often accompanies the affirmative
      note in literature. Diagnoses Madeleine's paranoia,
      conversion, adultery, and discontent as symptomatic of a
      "primordial inability" of a Jewish female intellectual
      to be content with "simply being a wholesome woman".
      Suggests that Herzog's ironic meditations about the
      role of the Jew in the twentieth century have accomplished
      more to demolish the "pseudo-historicism" of Toynbee
      and Spengler than professional scholars have done throughout
      the years.

1442. Rupp, Richard, "Saul Bellow: Belonging to the World in
      General", Celebration in Post-war American Fiction,
      (Florida, 1970), 189-208.
         Underlines the false festivity with which Bellow's
      early heroes celebrate reality as their empty affirmations
      are revealed as "bravura rhetoric". A reversal of forms
      is evidenced in Augie March in which the individual
      experience is enlarged to mythic dimensions in a hero
      who becomes the apotheosis of the Thirties. Stresses
      the protagonist's indomitable spirit and unswerving
      belief in the future which are viewed as the essential
      constituents of celebration. Defines true freedom in the
      Bellovian sense as the "active participation in the real",
      the ideal interaction of the individual and society,
      expressed largely in secular celebrations.

1443. Russell, Mariann, "White Man's Black Man: Three Views",
      College Association Journal, 17, 93-100.
         Examines the roles of the Northern urban black
      characters in Updike's Rabbit Redux, Malamud's The

Tenants, and Bellow's Mr. Sammler's Planet. Maintains
that the black man becomes a convenient mataphor in
the novels for the anarchic elements in white society,
as well as a mirror image of the prevailing white culture.
Describes the black thief in Bellow's work as "a new
barbarian", splendidly dressed, sexually aggressive, in
short, a stereotype of the black as primitive. Suggests
that the character remains an image in the work, an image
which manipulates a set of preordained responses in the
reader, despite his fascinating exterior.

1444. Russevelt, Karyl, "Saul Bellow", People's Weekly, (8
       September 1975), 60-63.
            An informal biographical sketch which includes
       interesting humorous and anecdotal details of Bellow's
       public and private lives. The auther discusses his most
       recent novel Humboldt's Gift which he regards as his "best
       and funniest book". Refers to the "special kind of
       satisfaction when you've been able to give the best of
       what you've got", and that, he suggests, is to be found
       in Humboldt.

1445. Salter, D.P.M., "Optimism and Reaction in Saul Bellow's
       Recent Work", Critical Quarterly, 14 (Spring 1972),
       57-66.
            Identifies Bellow as a writer with a moral function
       who approaches his life and fiction with a qualified
       optimism. Attempts to avoid the danger of the intentional
       fallacy of seeing Sammler as a mouthpiece for Bellow's
       views by focusing upon the weaknesses of characterization
       and in the basic structure of the novel. Presents evidence
       to show similarities in attitudes, bias, and smugness in
       Sammler and his creator which are considered to be
       "common to Jewish mandarin intellectuals". Considers
       Bellow's illustrations of contemporary events and attitudes,
       as provided in Sammler's Planet, to be unconvincing,
       incomplete, and perhaps "unmodified by reality".

1446. Samuel, Maurice, "My Friend, The Late Moses Herzog",
       Midstream, (April 1966), 3-25.
            A tour de force in which conversations with Herzog are
       fabricated as a means of discussing Bellow's "transposed
       terms" of actual events and relationships without a sense
       of falsification. Presents an extended comparison of
       Herzog and Leopold Bloom, underlining their attempts to
       deal with their Jewishness and their adulterous wives.
       Diagnoses Herzog's dilemma as the natural result of the
       negation of "his Jewish feelings which were too powerful
       for the minimal practical role he assigned to them".

1447. Scheer-Schäzler, Brigitte, Saul Bellow, (New York, 1967).
       A survey of the major works includes analyses of
       rarely-discussed short fiction and essays, as well as
       an informative biographical sketch. Sees Bellow as a
       "compassionate author" who becomes totally absorbed in
       his characters. Locates the complete identification as
       a major shortcoming in that it eliminates the portrayal
       of "a convincing, dramatic, effective chain of action".
       Finds the resolutions of the novels sadly lacking for the
       novelist never clearly demonstrates the process by which
       the questing protagonists achieve balance, harmony, and
       a state of equilibrium.

1448. Schneider, Harold W., "Two Bibliographies: Saul Bellow
       and William Styron", Critique, 3 (1960), 71-91.
       A partially annotated checklist of Bellow's major
       works, short fiction, essays, and miscellaneous which
       attempts to be comprehensive but omits several works
       by the author. An incomplete but helpful listing of
       secondary criticism includes several foreign items,
       as well as British and American critical commentary on
       Bellow's and Styron's works.

1449. Schueler, Mary D., "The Figure of Madeleine in Herzog",
       Notes on Contemporary Literature, (1 March 1971),
       5-7.
       A brief exploration of the origins of characterization
       which are located in the mainstreams of two literary
       traditions: the Bible and the French novel. Stresses
       the Magdalene aspects of character in Madeleine's fallen
       state and her search for a savior. Cites Proust's use
       of the image of "the little crumb of Madeleine" in
       A la recherche du temps perdu as a possible source.

1450. Schultz, Max F., "Saul Bellow and the Burden of Selfhood",
       Radical Sophistication: Studies in Contemporary Jewish-
       American Novelists, (Ohio, 1969), 110-53.
       Attempts to define the distinctively Jewish "tenuous
       equipoise of irreconcilables" in the existence of the
       marginal man in an urban contemporary society. Argues
       that the increasingly cerebral tendency in modern man is
       both dangerous and ennobling. Suggests that Bellow's
       fictional treatment of the current problem reveals his
       own distrust of the intellectual stance as a viable
       solution. Points to illuminating Blakean analogies and
       underlines the exhortative tradition in Bellow's novels.

1451. Scott, Nathan, "Bellow's Vision of the 'Axial Lines' ",
       Three American Moralists, (Indiana, 1973), 99-150.
       A revised and considerably expanded version of the
       essay published in Craters of the Spirit (see entry
       1452). Includes a discussion of Mr. Sammler's Planet

with a decidedly theological emphasis on the "deeply
felt requiem" with which the novel concludes. Argues
that Bellow's conviction, as expressed by Sammler, that
"the way into blessedness and felicity" is possible
through Gelassenheit, Heidegger's term for man's
acquiescent submission to the multifarious mystery of
existence.

1452.　————"Sola Gratia:　The Principles of Bellow's Fiction"
Craters of the Spirit, (Washington D.C., 1968), 233-66.
Reprinted in Adversity and Grace, ed. N. Scott, (Indiana,
1968), 27-57.
Considers Bellow's later fiction as dramatizations
of the "adventure of atonement" as opposed to the
stiflingly solipsistic mode of the early works. Identifies
the presence of Martin Luther's formula of "sola gratia"
throughout the canon as an illustration of the influences
of the Hasidic strain of Jewish spirituality on the
author. Sees Herzog as a story of spiritual salvation
and a modern treatment of Paradise Regained. While
acknowledging the fact that Bellow's fiction does not
embrace a dogmatic tradition, the novel is viewed as
"one of the most profoundly religious renderings of
experience in the literature of our time".

1453.　Schulman, Robert, "The Style of Bellow's Comedy", Publications
of the Modern Language Association, 83 (March 1968),
109-17.
·Suggests that Bellow has reanimated the expansive
style of ideological, comic prose fiction by successful
experimentation in his three "open form" novels. Places
the novelist firmly in the baroque tradition of writers
who have created "encyclopedic comedies of knowledge",
most notably Rabelais, Sterne, Melville, and Joyce. The
heroes of Bellow's high comedy are said to re-enact mythic
patterns which incorporate the picaresque, philosophical,
essayistic, and confessional modes of the past.

1454.　Sloss, Henry, "Europe's Last Gasp", Shenandoah, 22 (Fall
1970), 82-86.
Identifies Sammler as the possessor of a mind and
soul of a European castaway in the midst of an urban
American jungle in the Sixties. The cerebral
septugenarian's inability to love or communicate with
others is seen as a flaw in characterization and
novelistic technique in that an unbearable plenitude of
Sammlerian meditations replaces interaction and dialogue
in the work. Defines Sammler's wisdom as a European
sagacity which interprets, analyzes, and attempts to
perceive and understand all, thus posing a threat to all
he encounters.

1455. Steig, Michael, "Bellow's Henderson and the Limits of
      Freudian Criticism", Paunch, 36 (1973), 39-46.
           In part a reply to J. Moss's article (see entry 1407)
      which is seen as a drastic oversimplification and
      distortion of Henderson's physical and spiritual illnesses.
      Argues that the character's apparent psychosomatic
      symptoms should not be seen as symbols, nor as indications
      of "conversion hysteria" or any other psychic conflict.
      Discards the Freudian approach in favor of a Reichian
      interpretation of character and action, stating that
      Bellow's "loose and shaggy African novel will continue to
      elude any critic who would confine it within a Freudian
      framework".

1456. Stern, Richard, "Henderson's Bellow", Kenyon Review, 21
      (Autumn 1959), 655-61.
           Explores the imaginative topography of Henderson's
      Africa which is considered neither conscientiously
      symbolic or artificial, but objectifies and nourishes
      the novel's bizarre themes. Professes a knowledge of
      Bellow's interest in the somatic psychology of Wilhelm
      Reich which is based upon personal communication with
      the author during the early stages of the writing of
      Henderson.

1457. Stock, Irwin, "The Novels of Saul Bellow", Southern Review,
      3 (January 1967), 13-42.
           Stresses the essentially romantic nature of Bellow's
      fiction as the protagonists are depicted as Christ-like
      figures who voluntarily assume the suffering of others.
      Explores the role of the carpe deum philosophy as a
      viable method.of living, with "feelings open". Compares
      English Romanticism with the closely-knit familial
      circle in Jewish homes, emphasizing the primacy of
      feelings, the brotherhood of man, and the revered
      innocence and beauty of a child, a zisse neshumeleh.

1458. Tanner, Tony, "The American Novelist Saul Bellow",
      Listener, 81 (23 January 1969), 113-14.
           Speculates about a desirable future trend in Bellow's
      fiction which would depict a character moving beyond a
      static cerebral existence into the world of action. Sees
      the perspectives and themes of the short stories in
      Mosby's Memoirs as an indication that Bellow is becoming
      increasingly absorbed in the ambiguities of the American-
      Jewish experience. A survey of the ironically-distanced
      narrators underlines the author's attempt to curb the
      enthusiasm of affirmation which is central to each
      novel and which sometimes approaches sentimentality.
      Depicts Bellow as a writer who abhors both programmatic
      nihilists and facile optimists in life and literature.

1459.   ———City of Words, (London, 1971), 64-73.
            Emphasizes the process of fictional recall in Bellow's
        craft of fiction, the shaping and recording of the
        structure and tone of his intensely experienced
        recollections. Locates Henderson and Augie in a tenuous
        position between society and the void, somewhat fixed
        in the "desperate expansiveness" of the exuberant rhetoric.
        Argues that Augie's particular "mode of motion" is a
        series of involvements with "versions, visions, fabrications'
        of reality but rarely reality itself. Suggests that Augie,
        like many other American protagonists, believes that
        "social life is based on certain kinds of dissembling",
        and therefore adjusts his own behavior accordingly.

1460.   ———Saul Bellow, (Edinburgh, 1965). Portions of Chapter
        2 have been translated and appear in Pierre Dommergues'
        Saul Bellow, (Paris, 1967), under the title "L'homme de
        Buridan", 163-71. (The work is also collected in the
        Bellow Papers, see entry 720).
            The first critical study of Bellow's fiction stresses
        the "coalescence" of Russian, Jewish, and American
        traditions which animate the entire oeuvre. Express the
        distinctive use of language which juxtaposes the sublime
        and the ridiculous, the elevated and the mundane, the
        literary and the demotic. Points to weaknesses in the
        fiction's lack of plot and of "dramatic necessity".
        Underlines Bellow's awareness of the "thousand negatives"
        present in the contemporary world, as well as his
        unswerving belief in Americans desire to discover the
        "sacred affirmative".

1461.   ———"Saul Bellow: An Introductory Note", Salmagundi,
        30 (Summer 1975), 3-5.
            A brief essay which stresses Bellow's critical
        assimilation of the exigencies of contemporary existence,
        while reflecting upon the forces at work in the "present
        historical moment". Focuses upon the problematic nature
        of the novelist's recent work which is seen as
        conservative and perhaps reactionary. Suggests that the
        trend is a possible result of the production of a "fixed
        version of reality" caused by an overwhelming amount of
        crisis chatter, deluge of print, and intolerable noise
        level present in modern times. Maintains that Bellow's
        qualified optimism lies in the "successful nonintimidation
        by doom".

1462.   ———"Saul Bellow: The Flight from Monologue", Encounter,
        24 (February 1965), 58-70.
            Argues that Bellow's canon consists of a "series of
        monologists whose most vital conversation is with
        themselves". A survey of the major works underlines the
        basic rhythm which develops into the characters' approach
        towards others and eventual retreat, a search for identity
        and fear of definition. Suggests that Bellow's comedies
        of self-concern explore the dangers of the over-valuation

of the self but present no dramatic dialectic between
man and environment, merely "lonely flights of
metaphysics".

1463. Toth, Susan A., "Henderson the Rain King, Eliot, and
Browning", Notes on Contemporary Literature, (1 May 1971),
6-8.
    Compares Bellow's use of the avidity and sterility of
the African topography to Eliot's Wasteland, along with
similar images of stone and shadow employed as "illusory
relief" in both works. Henderson's spiritual quest is
likened to Browning's Childe Roland's search amid the
barren lands populated by malevolent creatures. Considers
the masterful use of literary allusions to be an effective
additive to the emotional power behind the humor of Bellow's
work.

1464. Trachtenberg, Stanley, "Saul Bellow's Luftmenschen: The
Compromise with Reality", Critique, 9 (Summer 1967),
62-73.
    Identifies the Yiddish characteristics of the
luftmensch as the character's influence in a fluid social
environment imposes a pattern of motion on the various
quests. A survey of the canon underlines the eccentric
figures (e.g. Alf Steidler in Dangling Man, Allbee in
The Victim, Mintouchian in Augie March, Tamkin in Seize
the Day, Dahfu in Henderson, Gersbach in Herzog) who
enable the speculative heroes to distinguish the palpable
reality of the luftmensch from the philosophical realm
into which they are tempted to retreat.

1465. Trowbridge, Clinton W., "Water Imagery in Seize the Day",
Critique, 9 (March 1967), 37-61.
    A detailed analysis of the imagistic patterns which
emphasizes the Romantic aspect of the novella in the
Wordsworthian affirmation present in Wilhelm's "rebirth".
Traces the closely related images which link the plight
of the suffering hero to that of a drowning man, enforced
with lyric reverberations from Milton's Lycidas. The oft-
disputed conclusion is interpreted as an unequivocally
redemptive scene in which Wilhelm has survived a meta-
phorical watery death and is "buoyed up by the greater
life into which he has finally entered".

1466. Uphaus, Suzanne H., "From Innocence to Experience: A
Study of Herzog", Dalhousie Review, 46 (Spring 1966),
65-79.
    Defines the plot as a movement from a state of innocence
to experience which involves a dramatic alteration of the
protagonist's mental state. Enumerates the various threats
to Herzog's stability, viewing sex as a dangerous
enslaving force, a solipsistic perspective which distorts
reality, and a tendency towards "primitive self-attachment".

Speculates that the writing of Herzog has been a
compulsive activity for the novelist, just as letter
writing had been for Herzog.

1467. Vogel, Dan, "Saul Bellow's Vision beyond Absurdity:
       Jewishness in Herzog", Tradition, 9 (Spring 1968),
       65-79. Reprinted under the same title in Judaism, 17
       (1968), 42-54.
            Discusses the themes and characterization from a
       Jewish perspective, pointing to the Hasidic tradition
       implicit in the work. Argues that the author's Jewish
       background has enabled him, and his characters, to look
       beyond the apparent meaninglessness and absurdity of
       contemporary existence to a well-defined humanism.

1468. Way, Brian, "Character and Society in The Adventures of
       Augie March, Bulletin of the British Association for
       American Studies, 8 (June 1964), 36-44.
            Explores the "dual aspect of time" in the novel which
       provides a sense of the immediate present as history in
       Bellow's dramatic depiction os a specific historical and
       social situation. Despite the "complete breakdown" in
       structure and language which is said to occur in the
       work, character and society are fused in a vision which
       transcends the social realities conveyed in past
       American novels of urban life.

1469. Weber, Ronald, "Bellow's Thinkers", Western Humanities
       Review, 22 (1968), 305-13.
            Stresses the parodoxial nature of the Bellovian
       hero's perilous journey through the intellectual realm
       in search of truth and identity. Focuses primarily on
       Herzog and The Last Analysis in a discussion of the
       inherent threats of isolationism and voluntary escape
       into the chaotic privacy of one's mind. Suggests that
       Bellow depicts the activity of the minds of his charcaters
       in a manner which reveals it to be as "dangerous and
       deceptive" as it is "ennobling".

1470. Weinberg, Helen, The New Novel in America: The Kafkan
       Mode in Contemporary Fiction, (New York, 1970), 29-
       107.
            Illustrates the metaphysical and spiritual affinities
       Bellow shares with Kafka. Compares the importance of "lyric
       interludes" in Augie March and The Castle, emphasizing
       the emergence of the hopeful hero which becomes part of
       the "exploration to the varietal form of self". The
       two writers are linked in their basic distrust of
       ideology and their creation of striving activist characters
       who refuse to "take an eternal no for an answer".

1471. Weiss, Daniel, "Caliban on Prospero: A Psychanalytic
       Study on the Novel, Seize the Day", American Imago,
       19 (Autumn 1962). Reprinted in Psychoanalysis and
       American Fiction, ed. I. Malin, (New York, 1965),
       279-307. Also reprinted in I. Malin's Saul Bellow
       and the Critics, (New York, 1967), 114-41. An extract
       of the essay has been translated and appears under
       the title "un fils, au jour le jour" in Pierre
       Dommergues' Saul Bellow, (Paris, 1967), 176-85.
            Identifies Wilhelm as a moral masochist who is
       involved in the ambivalent clash of generations,
       a situation which is exacerbated by oral and anal
       fixations and a neurotic sensibility. The surrogate
       father, Dr. Tamkin, introduces "a sadistic homo-
       sexual" element to the relationship he offers to
       the suffering hero, along with discussions of the
       "guilt aggresion cycle" which is likened to
       Menninger's essay on charcater derivatives.
       Interprets the conclusion as the symbolic fulfillment
       of the death-wish which Wilhelm has entertained
       during the traumatic day of reckoning. The final
       regeneration through tears is seen as part of the
       "phylogenetic process by which he is reconciled
       to his living father".

1472. West, Anthony, "A Crash of Symbols", New Yorker, (26
       September 1953), 128-33.
            Identifies Bellow as a disciple of the New
       Cricitism as the characters and events in Augie
       March appear as archetypal symbols and "loose
       politico-sociological allegories". Equates Augie's
       brother Simon with the practise of simony, the
       eagle with male pride, and Augie with the
       corrupted will of man. Thea is seen as a malevolent
       facet of the American female, "the White Whale
       of the book". (Bellow's warning to symbol-
       hunters, "Deep Readers of the World, Beware!",
       entry 49, was partially in response to this particular
       article, and generally to this type of analysis.
       Collected in the Bellow Papers is a letter to the
       New Yorker from Bellow, dated 25 September 1953,
       concerning West's review. For details see entry
       104.)

1473. Widmer, Kingsley, "Poetic Naturalism in the Contemporary
       Novel", Partisan Review, 26 (Summer 1959), 467-72.
            Attributes the increasing degeneration of naturalism
       to the traditional American desire for "a mythic
       depth of awareness", as illustrated in works by
       Fitzgerald, Anderson, Saroyan, Malamud, and Bellow.
       A brief survey of Bellow's fiction reveals that the early

works reflect a "social-realist tradition" while
Augie March indicates a shift whereby "sociology has
been submerged in symbolism". Despite the picaresque
mode and ebullience of character, the novel is viewed
as another version of "Bellow's obsessive concern with
the urban phenomena of the social-and-self-alienated
marginal man".

1474. Wisse, Ruth, "The Schlemiel as Liberal Humanist", The
Schlemiel as Modern Hero, (Chicago, 1971), 92-107.
Reprinted in Saul Bellow: A Collection of Critical Essays,
ed. Earl Rovit, (New Jersey, 1975), 90-100.
Considers Herzog to be the most Jewish protagonist in
Bellow's fiction, his "most typical schlemiel" and the
most entertaining variation of the Yiddish fool. Notes
that Herzog's intelligence and his self-consciousness
distinguish him from the verbose, suffering characters
in Jewish literature. Stresses the family relationship
which has constituted "the basic psychodynamics of
Jewish humor", details of which create a "sensuous back-
ground" for Bellow's character which was absent in earlier
portraits of the Gimpel-like hero.

1475. Young, James Dean, "Bellow's View of the Heart", Critique
7 (Spring 1965), 5-17.
Conducts a "prismaticP study of Herzog in which time
shifts, point of view, character, and theme are linked
through the effective letter-writing device. Suggests
that Madeleine is the generating force of the novel
in that the search for the truth about her nefarious
deeds leads Herzog to the truth about himself. Considers
Herzog to be Bellow's finest work, a masterpiece which
establishes its creator as America's "greatest living
novelist".

1476. Anonymous, "A Vocal Group: The Jewish Part in American
Letters", Times Literary Supplement, (6 November 1959),
35.
A brief survey of the current works of the Jewish-
American writers and their role in the American literary
tradition. Bellow is praised as the most notable of the
modern school of Jewish writers who have made a substantial
contribution to contemporary letters.

Foreign Criticism

1477. Arnavon, Cyrille, "Histoire littéraire des Etats Unis", (Hachette, Paris, 1953).

1478. ————"Le roman africain de Saul Bellow, Henderson the Rain King", Etudes Anglaises, (January 1961), XIV, 25-35.

1479. Bakker, J., "In Search of Reality: Two American Heroes Compared", Dutch Quarterly Review of Anglo-American Letters, 4, 145-61.

1480. Balotă, Nicola, "Saul Bellow si romanul inadăptarii", ("Saul Bellow and the novel of misfitting"), Romania Literara, (July 1972), 13.

1481. Bašić, Sonja, "Portret pisca: Saul Bellow", ("The Author's Portrait: Saul Bellow"), Književna smotra (Zagreb, Yugoslavia), (4), 48-73.

1482. ———— "Prikaz od Hercog", Telegram, Zagreb, 10 March 1967, VIII.

1483. ———— "Saul Bellow: Johanez Tolhuzen antiapolinijski tip ruskog simbolisma" - Književna smotra, Novi Sad, 1973, IV.

1484. Berger, Yves, "Saul Bellow's Herzog", L'Express, 22 June 1961, 523.

1485. Binni, Francesco, "Percorso Narrativo di Saul Bellow", Ponte, (1966), XXII, 831-42.

1486. Bloch-Michel, Jean, "A Review of Saul Bellow's Herzog", Nouvel Observateur, (9 December 1966).

1487. Braem, Helmut M., "Der Weg Saul Bellows", Neue Rundschau, (4), 1971, 742-52.

1488. Brezianu, Andrei, "Epistolarul lui Herzog sau Labirintul spre Adamville", (Herzog's epistolary or the Labyrinth to Adamville"), Secolul 20, (9), 104-9.

1489. Brodin, Pierre, Présences Contemporaines: Ecrivains Américains d'aujourd'hui, (Nouvelles Editions Debresse, 1964).

1490. Brown, John, Panorama de la Littérature Contemporaine aux Etats Unis, (Gallimard, Paris, 1954).

1491. Buitenhuis, Peter, "A Corresponding Fabric: The Urban World of Saul Bellow", Costerus, (Amsterdam), 8, 13-36.

1492. Cabau, Jaques, "La Prairie Perdue", (Le Seuil, Paris, 1966).

1493.   _____ "Herzog", L'Express, (20 November 1966).

1494.   Cambon, Giauco, "Il nuovo romanzo di Saul Bellow",
        Aut Aut, (Milan), 53 (September 1959), 318-20.

1495.   Chametsky, Jules, "Notes on the Assimilation of the
        American Jewish Writer: Abraham Cahan to Saul Bellow,
        Jahrbuch für Amerikastudien, 9 (1964), 172-80.

1496.   Cixous, Hélène, "Herzog de Saul Bellow", Lettres
        Nouvelles", January-February 1967.

1497.   _____ "Situation de Saul Bellow", Lettres Nouvelles,
        no. 58, (March 1967), 130-45.

1498.   Cordesse, Gerard, "L'unité de Herzog", Caliban, (7),
        99-113.

1499.   Cornis-Pop, Marcel, "Alienarea si necesitatea reinteg-
        rarii in societate". ("Alienation and the Necessity
        of Reinstallment in Society") Orizont, (22 May 1971),
        51-57.

1500.   Dittmar, Kurt, "Analyse dieser Welt, Saul Bellow's
        Mr. Sammler's Planet", Frankfurter Hefte 27, (1972),
        525-26.

1501.   Djankov, Krastan, "Planetat na Belou", (Mr. Bellow's
        Planet"), Ne izpuskaj denja, (Introduction to Bulgarian
        translation of Seize the Day), Sofia: Narodna Kultura,
        1973, 5-8.

1502.   Dommergues, Pierre, Les Ecrivains Américains d'aujourd'-
        hui, (Que-sais je ? - P.U.F. 1965).

1503.   _____ Les USA - à la récherche de leur identité,
        (Grasset, Paris, 1967).

1504.   _____ "Herzog de Saul Bellow", Le Monde, (30 October
        1966).

1505.   _____ "Herzog", Magazine Littéraire (28 November 1966).

1506.   _____ "Herzog", Preuves (January 1967).

1507.   _____ Saul Bellow, (Grasset, Paris, 1967).

1508.   Drndić, Daša, "Saul Bellow: Planeta gospodina Semlera",
        Književne Novine, Beograd, 22 (25 April 1970), 363.

1509.   Duesberg, Jacques C., "Un jeune romancier américain:
        Saul Bellow", Synthesis, 10 (May-June 1955), 149-50.

1510.   Eror, Gvozden, "Košmarna farsa o žrtvi Sola Beloua", Knji, (57), 99-108.

1511.   Erval, François, "Herzog", Information et Documents, (September 1965).

1512.   Estang, Luc, "Henderson de Saul Bellow", Le Figaro Littéraire, (8 July 1961).

1513.   Farmer, A.J., "Bellow's Victim", Education Nationale, (10 June 1965).

1514.   Flamm, Dudley, "Herzog - Victim and Hero", Zeitschrift für Anglistik un Amerikanistik, (East Berlin), (17), 174-88.

1515.   Franck, Jaques, "Saul Bellow: Herzog", Revue Generale Belge (Brussels), (February 1967), 113-20.

1516.   Gabánizza, Clara, "La Vittima di Saul Bellow", Italia che scrive, (50), 52 (April 1967).

1517.   Gluščević, Zoran, "Prikaz od Henderson, Kralj Kiše", Kultura-umetnost, 1962, (VI), 285.

1518.   Hadari, Amnon, "Ha-professor Eino Me'uban; Cohav Ha'likhet Shel Mar Sammler Me'et Saul Bellow", Shdemot, (44), 102-13.

1519.   Hasenclever, Walter, "Grosse Menschen und Kleine Wirklichkeit", Monat, 13 (February 1961), 71-75.

1520.   Honma, Nagayo, "Saul Bellow no Gendai Bunka Ron", Eigo Seinen, (Tokyo), (118), 260-1.

1521.   Iwamoto, Iwao, "Judea-kei Sakka no Miryoku - Bellow to Malamud, Eigo Seinen, (118), 257-60.

1522.   Iwayama, Tajiro, "Marginal Man no ikiru Joken - Saul Bellow no Herzog to Mr. Sammler's Planet", ("Marginal Man's Condition to Live"), Eigo Seinen, (118), 133-35.

1523.   Jotterand, Franck, "Herzog", La Quinzaine, (15-30 November 1966).

1524.   Jurak, Mirko, "Mesto in Vloga junakov Saula Bellowa v sodobni družbi", ("Place and Role of Saul Bellow's Heroes in Contemporary Society"), Dialogi, Ljubljana, 1969, V.

1525.   Katan, N., "Saul Bellow ou L'Amérique Redécouverte" Revue de L'Université Laval, 17 (December 1962), 316-34.

1526.   Komnenić, Milan, "Prikaz od Hercog", Borba, (Yugoslavia), (20 April 1967).

1527.   Kuna, F.M, "The European Culture Game: Mr. Bellow's Planet", English Studies (Amsterdam), (53), 531-34.

1528.   Kyria, Pierre, "Saul Bellow's The Victim", Revue de Paris, (January 1965).

1529.   Lamont, Rosette, "The Confessions of Moses Herzog", Langues Modernes, (September-October 1966), 116-20.

1530.   Las Vergnas, Raymond, "Saul Bellow's Herzog", Les Nouvelles Littéraires, (29 December 1966).

1531.   Löfroth, Erik, "Herzog's Predicament: Saul Bellow's View of Modern Man". Studia Neophilologica, (44), 315-25.

1532.   Lombardo, Agostino, "L'arte di Saul Bellow" in Realismo e Simbolismo: Saggi di Letteratura Americana Contemporanea, (Biblioteca di Studi Americani, No. 3), (Rome, 1968), 245-54.

1533.   ————"La Narrativa di Saul Bellow", Studi Americani: 2 (1965), 309 - 44.

1534.   Lucko, Peter, "Herzog - Modell de acceptance: Eine Erwiderung", Zeitschrift für Anglistik und Amerikanistik, (17), 189-95.

1535.   Maksimović, Miodrag, "Prikaz od Henderson, Krajl Kiše", Ilustrovana Politika, 1962, V.

1536.   ———— "Prikaz od Ne propusti dan", (Review of Seize the Day), Ilustrovana Politika, 1963, VI, 263.

1537.   Mandel, Arnold, "Herzog de Saul Bellow", Information Juive, (January 1967).

1538.   Manske, Eva, "Das Menschenbild im Prosachaffen Saul Bellows: Anspruch und Wirklichkeit", Zeitschrift für Anglistik und Amerikanistik (East Berlin), (21), 270-88, 360-83.

1539.   Marienstras, Richard, "Saul Bellow's Herzog", Les Nouveaux Cahiers, No. 8.

1540.   Mathy, Francis, "Zetsubo no kanata ni", ("The Humanism of Saul Bellow and John Updike") Sophia: Studies in Western Civilization and the Cultural Interaction of East and West (Tokyo), 19 (1970), 356-77.

1541.   Maurocordato, Alexandre, "Les quatre dimensions du Herzog",Archives des Lettres Modernes, 1969 (6), no. 102. Also in Archives Anglo-Américaines, No. 14.

1542.   Megret, Christian, "Saul Bellow's Henderson", Carrefour, 882, (9 August 1961).

1543.   Miloradović, Mirko, "Prikaz od Hercog", Nedeljne Informative Novine, Beograd, 26 February 1967, XVII.

1544.   Milošević, Dragan, "Prikaz od Henderson, Kralj Kiše" Borba, 26 August 1962, XXVII.

1545.   Mohrt, Michel, Le Nouveau Roman Americain, (Gallimard, Paris, 1955).

1546.   ─────"Saul Bellow", Figaro littéraire, (31 March 1962).

1547.   ─────"Les Romans de Saul Bellow", Le Monde,(8 May 1965).

1548.   ─────"Saul Bellow's Herzog", Figaro littéraire, (19 January 1967).

1549.   Moro, Kochi, "Monolog and Dialog: The Distance between J. Joyce and S. Bellow", (1973), Studies in the Humanities, Sukado, Iruma-Gun, Suitama, Japan.

1550.   Mukherji, N. "The Bellow Hero", Indian Journal of English Studies, IX, 74-86.

1551.   Nathan, Monique, "Saul Bellow", Esprit, 34 (September 1966), 363-70.

1552.   Nevius, Blake, "Saul Bellow and the Theater of the Soul", Neuphilologische Mitteilungen, (73), 248-60.

1553.   Normand, J., "L'homme mystifié: Les heros de Bellow, Albee, Styron, et Mailer", Etudes Anglaises, XXII, 370-85.

1554.   Parot, Jeanine "Review of Henderson the Rain King". Lettres Françaises, 881, (22-28 June 1961).

1555.   Petillon, P.Y., "Les héros de roman américain à pris de l'age", Critique, (January 1967), 159-76.

1556.   Popescu, Petru, "Omul oscilant: Debutul lui Saul Bellow", Luceafărul, (Bucharest), (19 March 1966), 1.

1557.   Praz, Mario, "Impressioni italiane di ámericani dell ottocento", Studi Americani, 4 (1958), 85-108.

179

1558. Puvačić, Dušan, "Prikaz od Ne propusti dan", (Seize the Day), Život, Sarajevo, 1964. XIII, 6.

1559. Rabi, R, "A Review of Saul Bellow's Henderson the Rain King", Terre Retrouvée, (18 February 1962).

1560. Racković, Miodrag, "Prikaz od Hercog", Književost, Beograd, 1967, XXIII, 4.

1561. Radeljković, Zvonimir, "Prikaz od Hercog", Izraz, Zagreb, 1967, XI.

1562. Raes, Hugo, "Amerikaanse Literatuur: Saul Bellow", Vlaamse Gids, 42 (December 1958), 283-84.

1563. Rao, R., "Chaos of the Self; An Approach to Saul Bellow's Dangling Man" Osmania Journal of English Studies, 8, (1971), 89-103.

1564. Ribnikar, Jara, O "Hendersonu, kralju kise" Knjževnost, Beograd, 1961, XVI, Knj. XXXII, 2.

1565. Rosenthal, Jean, "Saul Bellow", Club du Livre Américain, No. 2, (December 1961 - January 1962.)

1566. Rosenthal, Jean, Review of Herzog, Réforme, (29 April 1967).

1567. Rosu, Anca,. "Picaresque Technique in Saul Bellow's Adventures of Augie March", (Analele Universitatii Bucuresti-Limbi Germanice), (22), (1973), 191-97.

1568. Rothermal, Wolfgang P., "Saul Bellow", Amerikanische Literatur der Gegenwart, Stuttgart, 1968, 69-104.

1569. Sabljak, Tomislav, "Prikaz od Ne propusti dan", (Seize the Day), Telegram, Zagreb, 13 March 1964, V, 203.

1570. ————"Prikaz od Doživljaji Augie Marcha", Telegram, Zagreb, 11 March 1966, VII.

1571. Sanavio, Piero, "Il romanzo di Saul Bellow", Studi Americani, 1956, II, 261-83.

1572. Santyanarayana, M.R., "The Reality Teacher as Hero: A Study of Saul Bellow's Mr. Sammler's Planet", Osmania Journal of English Studies, 8, (1971) 55-68.

1573. Saporta, Marco, "Saul Bellow's Herzog", Preuves, (November 1965), 66-73.

1574. Sastri, P.S., "Bellow's Henderson the Rain King: A Quest for Being" Panjab University Research Bulletin for the Arts, (3), 9-18.

1575.   Scheer-Schäzler, Brigitte, "A Taste for Metaphors:
        Die Bildersprach als Interpretationsgrundlage des
        modernen Romans, dargestellt au Saul Bellows Herzog"
        Moderne Sprachen: Litteratur, un Padagogik, 2, Vienna.

1576.   _____"Die Farbe als dichterisches Gestaltungsmittel in
        den Romanen Saul Bellows", Die Sprachkunst (2), 243-64.

1577.   Shastri, N.R. "Self and Society in Saul Bellow's The
        Victim", Osmania Journal of English Studies, 1971, 105-
        12.

1578.   Shibuya, Yusaburo, "Saul Bellow Ron--Moralist to shite
        no Sokumen wo Chushin", ("Study of Saul Bellow--
        Discussion of his moralistic aspect"), Eigo Seinen,
        (118), 254-56.

1579.   Soosaar, E., Afterword to Estonian translation of Herzog,
        Tallin: Eesti raamat, 1968.

1580.   Sremec, D., "Prikaz od Henderson, Kralj Kiše", Bilten
        Saveza ustanova i organizacija za širenje knjige NRH,
        1962, I, 5-6.

1581.   Stefanović, Aleksander, "Prikaz od Hercog", Kultura-umetnost
        XI, 533.

1582.   Suško, Mario, "Nada i apsurd u djelu Saul Bellowa - o
        romanima Dozivljaji Augie Marcha i Hercog", ("Hope and
        Absurdity in the Works of Saul Bellow The Adventures of
        Augie March and Herzog"), Izraz, Zagreb, 1966, X, 6.

1583.   _____"Prikaz od Ne propusti dan", ("Review of Seize
        the Day"), Književne Novine, Beograd, 3 April 1964, (25),
        220.

1584.   Suvin, Darko, "Prikaz od Henderson, Kralj Kiše", ("Review
        of Henderson the Rain King") Republika, 1962, 18, 9.

1585.   Teodorescu, Anda, "Introduction" to Hungarian trans-
        lation of Seize the Day, Traieste-ti clipa, Bucuresti:
        University, 5-11.

1586.   Tijeras, Eduardo, "Saul Bellow", Cuardernos
        Hispanoamericanos, Madrid (274), 182-86.

1587.   Ustvedt, Yngvar, "Saul Bellow - en amerikansk natods-
        dikter", ("Saul Bellow - a contemporary American
        writer") Samtiden (80), 273-82.

1588.   Van Egmont, Peter, "Herzog's Quotation of Walt
        Whitman", Voprosy Literatury, 1967, I, 215-17.

1589.   Vidan, Ivo, "Roman američkog intelektualca - o
        romanu Sola Belowa Hercog", Forum, 1965, IV,
        (3), 494-510.

1590.   Villelaur, Anne, "Saul Bellow's Seize the Day",
        Lettres Françaises, 941 (30 August - 5th September 1962).

1591.   Vojvodić, Rade, "Prikaz od Henderson, Kralj Kiše",
        Duga, 1962, XVIII.

1592.   Vučković, Radovan, "Prikaz radiodrame 'Soufflé od
        naranči", (Review of the radio play, "The Orange Soufflé")
        Telegram, Zagreb, 26 September 1969, X.

1593.   Walker, Marshall, "Herzog: The Professor as Drop-out?",
        English Studies in Africa, (15),39-51.

1594.   Weinstein, Norman, "Herzog, Order and Entropy",
        English Studies, (Amsterdam), (54), 336-46.

1595.   Zietlow, E.R., "Saul Bellow: The Theater of the Soul",
        Ariel (4), 44-59.

1596.   Anonymous, "Planeta lui Saul Bellow si mutatiile
        Extremului Occident", ("Mr. Sammler's Planet and the
        Shiftings in the Far West"), Romania Literara, (Bucharest),
        (September 1970), 20.

1597.   Anonymous, "Prikaz od Henderson, Kralj Kiše", Politika,
        30 September 1962, LIX, 17595.

1598.   "L'anatomie de Herzog" in Saul Bellow, ed. Pierre
        Dommergues (Paris, 1967), 203-31. A round-table discussion
        of the work by a group of international critics and writers:
        Cyrille Arnavon, Yves Berger, Francois Bondy, Jean Bloch-
        Michel, Hélène Cixous, Pierre Dommergues, Eric Kahane,
        Robert Merle, Mary McCarthy, Michel Mohrt, and Jean
        Rosenthal. Extracts from unidentified sources by Norman
        Mailer and Saul Bellow precede the discussion, along with
        excerpts from several critical articles and reviews
        published in America and Britian (e.g. Elliott, Rahv,
        Maynahen, Richler, Howe, Bradbury, Hyman, Trevor, Kermode,
        Steiner, etc).

Doctoral Dissertations

1599.   Allen Mary Lee, "The Flower and the Chalk: The Comic
         Sense of Saul Bellow", (Stanford University, 1968, 3997A).

1600.   Atkins, George, "Freedom, Fate, Myth, and Other
         Theological Issues in Some Contemporary Literature",
         (Emory University, 1971 DA (32) 6529A).

1601.   Blanch, Mable, "Variations on a Picaresque Theme: A
         Study of Two Twentieth-Century Treatments of Picaresque
         Form", (University of Colorado, 1966, DA, (28) 1427A)

1602.   Buckton, Rosalind, "The Novels of Saul Bellow",
         (University of Leicester, 1975).

1603.   Clayton, John Jacob, "Saul Bellow: In Defense of Human
         Dignity", (Indiana University, 1966, DA (27), 2147A).

1604.   Cohen, Sarah Blacher, "The Comic Elements in the Novels
         of Saul Bellow", (Northwestern University, 1969, DA (30),
         3000A-1A).

1605.   Craig, Harry Edward "The affirmation of the Heroes
         the Novels of Saul Bellow", (University of Pittsburgh,
         1967 (27), 5012A).

1606.   Dickstein, Felice W., "The Role of the City on the Works
         of Theodore Dreiser, Thomas Wolfe, James Farrell, and
         Saul Bellow", (City University of New York, 1972 (33),
         6350A-51A).

1607.   Durham, Joyce Roberta, "The City in Recent Women's Lib:
         Black on White. A Study of Selected Writings on Bellow,
         Mailer, Ellison, Baldwin, and Writers of the Black
         Aesthetic", (University of Maryland, 1974, DA 75-18,
         752).

1608.   Dutton, Robert Roy, "The Subangelic Vision of Saul
         Bellow: A Study of His First Six Novels, 1944-65",
         (University of the Pacific, DA, (27), 1363A).

1609.   Galloway, David Darryl, "The Absurd Hero in Contemporary
         American Fiction: The Works of John Updike, William
         Styron, Saul Bellow and J.D. Salinger", (University of
         Buffalo, 1962, DA (23) 4356-7).

1610.   Golden, Daniel, "Shapes and Strategies: Forms of Modern
         American Fiction in the Novels of Robert Penn Warren,
         Saul Bellow, and John Barth", (Indiana University,
         1972, DA (33), 2933A-4A).

1611.   Golden, Susan Landan, "The Novels of Saul Bellow:
         A Study in Development", (Duke University, 1975, DA
         75-29, 501.

1612.   Greenberg, A.D., "The Novel of Disintegration: A
         Study of a World View in Contemporary Fiction",
         (University of Washington, 1965 DA (25) 5278).

1613.   Hartman, Hugh Callow, "Character Themes and Tradition
         in the Novels of Saul Bellow", (University of Washington,
         in DA (29), 898A-9A).

1614.   Hux, Samuel Holland, "American Myth and Existential
         Vision: The Indigenous Existentialism of Mailer, Bellow,
         Styron, and Ellison", (University of Conneticut, 1965,
         DA (26), 5437).

1615.   Kar, Prafulla C. "Saul Bellow: A Defense of the Self",
         (University of Utah, 1973 DA, (34), 778A).

1616.   Kuggelmass, Harold, "The Search for Identity: The
         Development of the Protean Model of Self in Contemporary
         American Fiction" (University of Oregon, 1973 (34),
         1285A-86A).

1617.   Leese, David Allen, "Laughter in the Ghetto: A Study
         of Form in Saul Bellow's Comedy". (Brandeis University
         1975, DA 75-15, 112).

1618.   Lewin, Lois Symons, "The Theme of Suffering in the
         Work of Bernard Malamud and Saul Bellow",
         (University of Pittsburg, 1967, DA (28), 5021A-2A).

1619.   Marin, Daniel B., "Voice in Structure in Saul Bellow's
         Novels", (University of Iowa, 1974, DA (35), 6920A-21A).

1620.   Markos, Donald William, "The Humanism of Saul Bellow",
         (University of Illinios, 1966, DA (27), 3875A).

1621.   Massey, J. "The Treatment of Isolation and Disassociation
         in the Novels of Saul Bellow", (University of London,
         External, 1970).

1622.   Merkowitz, David Robert, "Bellow's Early Phase: Self
         and Society in Dangling Man, The Victim and The
         Adventures of Augie March", (University of Michigan, 1971,
         DA (32), 6439A-40A).

1623.   Michael, Bessie, "What's the Best Way to Live: A Study
         of the Novels of Saul Bellow", (Lehigh University,
         1960, DA (30), 5451A-2A).

1624.   Morag, Gilead, "Ideas as a Thematic Element in Saul
         Bellow's Victim Novels", (University of Wisconsin, 1973,
         DA (34), 6599A-600A).

1625.   Noble, A.J., "Saul Bellow and the Tradition of the Novel",
        (University of Sussex, 1969).

1626.   Opdahl, Keith Michael, "The Crab and The Butterfly":
        The Themes of Saul Bellow", (University of Illinios,
        1961,DA (22), 3670-1).

1627.   Porter, Marvin Gilbert, "The Novels of Saul Bellow:
        A Formalist Reading", (University of Oregon, 1969,
        DA (31), 1287A).

1628.   Riehl, Betty Ann Jones, "Narrative Structures in Saul
        Bellow's Novels", (The University of Texas at Austin,
        1975, DA-75-24, 945).

1629.   Rodrigues, Eusebio L., "Quest for the Human: Theme and
        Structure in the Novels of Saul Bellow", (University of
        Pennsylvania, 1970, (31), 2936A-37A).

1630.   Rosenthal, Melvyn, "The American Writer and His Society:
        The Response to Estrangment in the Works of Nathanael West,
        Randolph Bourne, Edmund Wilson, Norman Mailer and Saul
        Bellow", (University of Conneticut, 1969, DA (29).
        3108A).

1631.   Sheres, Ita G., "Prophetic and Mystical Manifestations
        of Exile and Redemption in the Novels of Henry Roth,
        Bernard Malamud, and Saul Bellow", (University of
        Wisconsin, 1972, (33) 6375A).

1632.   Tajuddin , Mohammad, "The Tragicomic Novel: Camus,
        Malamud, Hawkes, Bellow", (University of Indiana 1967,
        DA (28), 2698A-9A).

1633.   Wallach, Judith Dana Lowenthal, "The Quest for Selfhood
        in Saul Bellow's Novels: A Jungian Interpretation",
        (University of Victoria,(Canada), 1975. (To obtain
        microfiche copy, order directly from the National Library
        of Canada at Ottawa).

1634.   Warner, Stephen Douglas, "Representative Studies in the
        American Picaresque: Investigation of Modern Chivalry,
        Adventures of Huckleberry Finn and The Adventures of
        Augie March, (Indiana University, 1971, DA (32), 4528A).

1635.   Wieting, Molly S., "A Quest for Order: The Novels of
        Saul Bellow", (University of Texas, Austin, 1960,
        DA (30), 3030A-31A).

1636.   Williams, Patricia W., "Saul Bellow's Fiction: A
        Critical Question", (Texas A & M, DA, (33), 6379A-80A).

Index

Aaron, Daniel 1215
Aldridge, John 1260, 1261
Alexander, Edward 1262
Allen, Bruce 1216
Allen, Mary Lee 1599
Allen, Walter 1046
Alpert, Hollis 1047
Alter, Robert 1264, 1265, 1266
Amis, Kingsley 1017
Arnavon, Cyrille 1477, 1478
Atchity, Kenneth 1267
Atkins, Anselm 1268
Atkins, George 1600
Axthelm, Peter 1210, 1269

Bailey, Jennifer 1270
Baim, Joseph 1271
Baker, Carlos 1078
Baker, Sheridan 1272
Bakker, J. 1479
Balota, Nicola 1480
Barrett, William 1113
Baruch, Franklin R. 1273
Bašić, Sonja 1481, 1482, 1483
Battaglia, Frank 1114
Baumbach, Jonathan 1274
Bayley, John 1049, 1163, 1275
Belitt, Ben 1276
Berger, Yves 1484
Bergler, Edmund 1277
Bezanker, Abraham 1278
Binni, Francesco 1485
Blanch, Mable 1601
Bloch-Michel, Jean 1486
Bolling, Douglass 1279
Boroff, David 1280
Bošnjak, Branko 950
Boulger, James D. 1281
Bowen, Robert 1050
Boyers, Robert 1239, 1282, 1283
Bradbury, Malcolm 1115, 1217, 1284, 1285, 1286, 1287, 1288
Braem, Helmut M. 1487
Braine, John 1164
Bragg, Melvin 1240
Brandon, Henry 1242

Breit, Harvey 1241, 1289
Brezianu, Andrei 1488
Brodin, Pierre 1489
Brown, John 1490
Broyard, Anatole 1165, 1218
Brustein, Robert 1292
Buckton, Rosalind 1602
Buitenhuis, Peter 1491
Bujas, Željka 970
Burgess, Anthony 1290
Burns, R.K. 1291
Burns, Robert 1116

Cabau, Jacques 1492, 1493
Cambon, Giauco 1494
Campbell, Jeff 1294
Capon, Robert F. 1117, 1293
Cassidy, T.E. 1018
Casty, A. 1118
Cecil, L. Moffitt 1295
Chamberlain, John 986
Chametsky, Jules 1495
Chapman, Abraham 1296
Chapman, Sara S. 1297
Chase, Richard 1298
Chevigny, Bell Gale 1119
Ciancio, Ralph 1299
Cixous, Helene 1496, 1497
Clayton, John J. 1300, 1603
Clurman, Harold 1301
Cohen, Sarah Blacher 1303, 1304, 1604
Cohn, Ruby 1305
Connole, John 1019
Cook, Bruce 1306
Coonley, Donald 1307
Cordesse, Gerard 1498
Coren, A. 1080, 1120
Cornis-Pop, Marcel 1499
Corrigan, R.W. 1188
Cowley, Malcolm 1302
Craig, Harry E. 1605
Crane, Milton 1020, 1051
Cretkovski, V. 985
Cromie, Robert 1243
Crozier, Robert D. 1308
Cruttwell, Patrick 1081
Curley, T.F. 1082, 1121

Davenport, Guy 1122

Davis, Robert Gorham   1021,
   1309
Demarest, David   1310
De Mott, Benjamin   1166
Detweiler, Robert   721, 1311,
   1312
De Vries, Peter   987
Dickstein, Felice W.   1606
Dickstein, Morris   1313
Dittmar, Kurt   1500
Djankov, Krastan   1501
Dommergues Pierre   1244, 1502
   1503, 1504, 1505, 1506,
   1507, 1598
Donoghue, Denis   1314, 1315
Downer, Alan S.   1002
Drabble, Margaret   1316
Drndić, Daša   1508
Duesberg, Jacques C.   1509
Durham, Joyce R.   1607
Dutton, R.   1608

Edelman, L.   1123
Edwards, Duane   1317
Eisenger, Chester   1318,
   1319, 1320
Ellmann, Richard   1321
Elliott, George P.   1124
Enck, John   1245
Epstein, Joseph   1167
Eror, Gvozden   1510
Erval, Francois   1511
Estang, Luc   1512

Farmer, A.J.   1513
Farrelly, John   1003
Fearing, Kenneth   988
Fenton, Charles A.   1052
Fiedler, Leslie   1004, 1053,
   1323, 1324, 1325
Finklestein, Sidney   1326, 1327
Finn, James   1022
Fisch, Harold   1328
Flamm, Dudley   1514
Fletcher, Janet   1168
Flint, R.W.   1054
Fossum, Robert   1329, 1330
Frajd, Marta   951
Franck, Jacques   1515
Frank, Reuben   1331
Freedman, Ralph   1332

Friedman, Alan   1333
Frohock, W.M.   1334
Froncek, Tom   1125
Fuchs, Daniel   1335

Gabanizza, Clara   1516
Gallo, Louis   1336
Galloway, David   1246, 1337
   1338, 1339, 1609
Garrett, George   1340
Gavris, K.   1247
Geismar, Maxwell   1023, 1341,
   1342, 1343
Gibbs, Wolcott   1005
Gilbert, Felix   1083
Gill, Brendan   1055, 1126
Gilman, Richard   1056, 1219
Ginden, James   1344
Glicksberg, Charles   1345
Gluščević, Zoran   1517
Gold, Herbert   1057, 1084,
   1346
Golden, Daniel   1610
Golden, Susan L.   1611
Goldfinch, Michael   1347
Goldreich, G.   1127
Goran, L.   1128
Gornick, Vivian   1220
Gray, P.E.   1169
Greenberg, A.D.   1612
Greenberg, Martin   1006
Gross, Beverly   1129, 1170
Gross, J.   1130
Grossman, Edward   1348
Guerard, Albert J.   1349
Guttmann, Allen   1350, 1351
Gutwillig, Robert   1248

Haber, Leo   1352
Hadari, Ammon   1518
Hale, Lionel   989, 1007
Hall, James   1353
Handy, William   1354
Hansenclever, Walter   1519
Hardwick, Elizabeth   1085
Harper, Gordon L.   1249
Harper, Howard   1355
Harper, Hugh C.   1613
Harris, James Neil   1356
Harwell, Meade   1024, 1357
Hassan, Ihab H.   1358

Maurocordato, Alexandre   1541
Mayberry, George   993
Mayne, Richard   1224
McSweeney, Kerry   1403
Megret, Christian   1542
Mellard, James   1404
Merkowitz, David R.   1622
Michael, Bessie   1623
Mihaljević, Mignon   955
Mihelićeva, Mira   969
Miller, Karl   1095
Miloradović, Mirko   1543
Milošević, Dragan   1544
Mizener, Arthur   1028
Mohrt, Michel   1545, 1546,
   1547, 1548
Morag, Gilead   1624
Moro, Kochi   1546
Morrow, Patrick   1405
Mosher, Harold   1406
Moss, Judith   1407
Moynahan, Julian   1137
Mudrick, Marvin   1408
Muggeridge, M.   1138
Mukherji, N.   1550

Nash, Jay   1255
Nathan, Monique   1551
Nault, Marianne   1225, 1409
Nevius, Blake   1552
Newman, Charles   1226
Noble, A.J.   1625
Noble, David   1410
Nordell, Roderick   1228
Norman, J.   1553

Oates, Joyce Carol   1178
O'Brien, Kate   994
O'Connell, Shaun   1411
Offen, Ron   1255
Opdahl, Keith   1179, 1412,
   1626
Overbeck, Pat T.   1413

Parot, Jeanine   1554
Pearce, Richard   1414
Pearson, Carol   1415
Pearson, Gabriel   1229
Perrott, Ray   1096
Pešin, R.   1247

Petillon, P.Y.   1555
Pickrel, Paul   1030, 1065,
   1097, 1140
Pinsker, Sanford   1416, 1417,
   1418, 1419
Planel, Danielle   984
Podhoretz, Norman   1031, 1098,
   1420, 1421, 1422
Poirier, R.   1141
Poore, Charles   1010
Popescu, Petru   1556
Popkin, Henry   1032
Porter, Gilbert M.   1423, 1424,
   1627
Praz, Mario   1557
Prescott, Orville   1033, 1099
Price, Martin   1100
Priestly, J.B.   1034
Pritchett, V.S.   945, 1142,
   1425, 1426
Pryce-Jones, David   1256
Puvačić, Dušan   1558

Quinton, Anthony   1427

Rabi, R.   1559
Racković, Miodrag   1560
Radeljković, Zvonimir   1561
Raes, Hugo   1562
Rahv, Philip   1143
Raider, Ruth   1144
Rans, Geoffrey   1428
Rao, R.   1563
Raphael, Frederick   1230
Read, Forest   1429
Rhodes, Richard   1231
Ribnikar, Jara   956, 960, 1564
Richardson, J.   1213, 1430
Richler, Mordecai   1196, 1145
Richmond, Lee J.   1431
Riehl, Betty A.J.   1628
Robinson, Robert   1257
Rodrigues, Eusebio L. 1432, 1433,
   1434, 1435, 1436, 1629
Rogoff, Milton   1067
Rolo, Charles   1035, 1066, 1101
Rosenberg, Dorothy   1036
Rosenthal, Jean   972, 1565,
   1566
Rosenthal, Melvyn   1630
Rosenthal, T.G.   1197

189